F R A M E W O R K S

Public Relations

Fifth Edition

Frank Jefkins

Revised and edited by

Daniel Yadin
MA, MCIM

FINANCIAL TIMES

Prentice Hall

An imprint of **Pearson Education**

Harlow, England · London · New York · Reading, Massachusetts · San Francisco
Toronto · Don Mills, Ontario · Sydney · Tokyo · Singapore · Hong Kong · Seoul
Taipei · Cape Town · Madrid · Mexico City · Amsterdam · Munich · Paris · Milan

Pearson Education Limited
Edinburgh Gate, Harlow
Essex GM20 2JE, England
and Associated Companies throughout the world

Visit us on the World Wide Web at:
http://www.pearsoneduc.com

First published in Great Britain 1980
Fifth edition published 1998

The right of Frank Jefkins and Daniel Yadin to be identified as
authors of this work has been asserted by them in accordance with
the Copyright, Designs and Patents Act 1988.

© Pearson Professional Limited 1998

ISBN 0 273 63432 1

British Library Cataloguing in Publication Data
A CIP catalogue record for this book can be obtained from the British Library.

10 9 8 7 6 5 4 3
04 03 02 01 00

Printed and bound in Great Britain by Bell and Bain Ltd, Glasgow

The Publishers' policy is to use paper manufactured from sustainable forests.

CONTENTS

PREFACE

Public Relations has now reached its fifth edition. Why has it remained such a popular standard book since it first appeared? Partly because each edition has been thoughtfully updated, in the light of the latest developments in PR techniques and communications technology. Certainly because it explains the tools and techniques of the profession in a frank and uncomplicated way. Most of all because it continues to help readers to understand the true purpose of PR; to help them give ever-improving service to management and clients; to get the best both from in-house PR departments and external consultants. And, of course, to pass examinations.

PR seems more misunderstood than practically any other business. For example, many believe that PR can create favourable images for an organisation. Or that it can polish a tarnished image. The text of this book explains the reality of these misconceptions. How can you avoid overspending on PR? The book shows how to control your budget. Can public relations influence, and possibly improve, management–employee relationships? The answer is inside. Do PR practitioners have morals? You will find an insight into the ethics of PR here. And much more besides.

This new edition reflects the ever-changing nature of public relations and its environment. There are more illustrations than in previous editions. The various codes of practice have been updated, and the text of the current CAM and LCCI syllabuses included. There are some excellent new cases in the chapter on corporate identity, and a wealth of new information on today's leading-edge printing processes.

One thing this book proposes beyond any doubt: we realise that the more we learn about the practice of professional PR, the more there is to learn. I hope this new edition will help you succeed in meeting the challenge. And give you a good read too.

Daniel Yadin

1

HISTORY OF PUBLIC RELATIONS

1. How new is PR?

It is sometimes said that public relations is new, as if it had been invented during the last few years or since the Second World War; or just this century. In countries which have gained their independence during the last thirty years, public relations may well seem new.

Among those who associate public relations with the older industrialised world, it is sometimes claimed that public relations is an American invention.

How new is public relations? Is it an American invention?

Public relations existed long before America. The Americans may have invented Mickey Mouse, Coca-Cola and Hollywood. But they did not invent public relations.

2. What is PR?

It depends what you mean by public relations. If you mean trying to create a favourable image or a favourable climate of opinion, or trying to polish a tarnished image ... these are false concepts. They owe more to the misunderstandings of the advertising and marketing worlds than to public relations. Largely, they are false because an image can only be what is in people's minds. In real life not everything is favourable, and we sometimes have to explain the unfavourable.

For example, it is difficult for anyone – workers, employers, passengers or government – to find anything favourable to say about a railway strike, or the people and organisations involved in it. It is a disaster for all concerned. In public relations we are constantly having to explain such disasters. Crisis management has become a major area of PR activity.

So before we consider how new or old it is, let us be clear about the meaning of public relations. There are many definitions of our profession. Essentially, public relations is about creating understanding through knowledge, and this often involves effecting change.

Public relations is therefore a form of communication. It applies to every sort of organisation, commercial or non-commercial, in the public or private sector. It is far bigger than marketing or advertising, and existed long before they did.

3. Early forms of communication

Mankind has always tried to communicate and make itself understood. Before there were alphabets, characters and numerals, there were pictograms (of which Chinese characters still provide examples). In the caves of primitive peoples, thousands of years ago, there were wall paintings. Ancient buildings such as the pyramids, early temples, and the cave paintings of Zimbabwe, bear pictorial messages. People also wrote on tablets of stone; and on leather, parchment and papyrus, as with the Dead Sea Scrolls.

It could also be said that the holy books of the world's religions contain a form of public relations, in that ancient scribes were seeking to create an understanding of their faiths. This type of communication is even older than the early relics of Greek and Roman advertisements, such as those announcing the sale of slaves, and events at the Coliseum.

Public relations techniques have been applied down the centuries. Today, at airports, we are able to recognise airlines by their livery and logos; and by the uniforms of cabin and other staff. The identity of each airline is clearly defined. We call it 'corporate identity' or 'branding'. It involves such elements as logo, colour scheme and typography. This is excellent communication, because it enables us to see and to recognise.

But the idea is so old that we would need to take a time machine back through thousands of years to discover where it began. Public relations is as new as civilisation.

4. Origins of corporate identity

When the Phoenicians and Vikings set sail to explore and conquer, their sails were decorated with birds or animals which identified them. When an army went into battle centuries ago, it would be led by its king whose shield bore his distinctive emblem. This was rather dangerous if you happened to be a king. Army uniforms were devised so that all the men on each side could be readily identified. By that time kings were able to stay at home, as political leaders do today.

Uniforms or livery were taken up by all forms of transport, from sailing ships to steamers; from stage-coaches to trams, buses, trains, delivery vehicles and airliners. Corporate identity is to be seen everywhere in the world of transport. Sixty years ago London was full of buses painted in the different colours of the various operators. This lasted until they were all taken over by London Transport, whose corporate colour was red. Thus the red London bus became synonymous with London; unlike the trams of Hong Kong, which display the colour of the advertiser who monopolises each tram. Now in London, since the deregulation of London Transport, and private bus operators have been encouraged to take over bus routes, we again have buses of many colours.

Today, the video has become a popular PR medium; but the magic lantern and the slide were being used for PR purposes more than a hundred years ago. The documentary film claims, as one of its most famous examples, Shell's film, made some sixty years ago.This shows an Imperial Airways Heracles airliner being refuelled at Croydon, London's airport in the 1930s.

5. History of house journals

If we go back only 150 years, we find the house journal one of our oldest forms of created public relations. In his book *American Notes*, published in London in 1842, Charles Dickens records the *Lowell Offering*, edited by the women working in a cotton mill in New England. When I.M. Singer began selling sewing machines in America in 1855, he published his *Gazette* to teach his customers how to use a sewing machine.

The Lever brothers, who made soap from the fat of cattle imported from America to Liverpool, published an employee journal a hundred years ago. They also built the garden city of Port Sunlight for their workers. About the same time the Manchester Co-Operative Society published one of the first house journals.

6. Some origins of modern PR

As in many developing countries where the government has had to take the initiative in effecting social change, public relations techniques were applied by governments in Europe and America.

In 1809, the British Treasury appointed a press spokesman. In 1854 the Post Office, in its first annual report, declared the necessity of explaining its services to the public. One of the first uses of PR tactics by the British government came in 1912. Lloyd George, Chancellor of the Exchequer, organised a team of lecturers to explain the first old-age pension scheme.

After the First World War, the government used PR techniques to explain its health and housing schemes. Between 1926 and 1933, one of the biggest PR efforts in Britain was that of Sir Stephen Tallents on behalf of the Empire Marketing Board. It spent £1m on making fruits and other Empire products better known to the British public, using films, posters and exhibitions. In 1948, Tallents became the first President of the Institute of Public Relations. Today there is a Sir Stephen Tallents medal, awarded annually by the current President of the IPR.

It is significant that 1948 was an historic year both in British and American public relations. In that year the Institute of Public Relations in Britain and the Public Relations Society of America were founded.

7. Development of PR consultancies

It would be unfair not to pay tribute to the development of the PR consultancy in America. One of the first was set up by a journalist, Ivy Ledbetter Lee, who handled PR for the anthracite coal industry and the Pennsylvania Railroad. In 1914, he became adviser to oil tycoon John D. Rockefeller.

There was nothing favourable about his PR work, for he had to try to get a fair press during coal-mine and railway disasters. He did this by creating better relations between the employers and the press. He went further and established basic principles for press relations work. These were contained in his famous statement to the press of 1906, which promised unequivocally that he would 'supply prompt and accurate information concerning subjects which it is of interest and value to the public to know about.'

While governmental PR began nearly 200 years ago in Britain, it is true that consultancy business began later in Britain than in the USA. This was largely because of the Second World War, when trade was almost negligible in Britain and essential goods were rationed. But after the war, in the late 1940s, many of the advertising men who had been engaged in propaganda work for the Ministries turned to PR consultancy work.

8. Need for PR between the two world wars

Even so, during the 1920s and 1930s between the wars, the business and commercial world was involved in in-house PR. Some of it was called 'advertorial'. New products such as cars and radios were becoming popular, and won a great deal of editorial interest. Created media such as house journals, slide presentations, documentary films and travelling lecturers were well-used PR techniques.

9. Development of communication media

In parallel with the rise of public relations over the past 200 years has been the development of the means of communication. Before the advent of newer techniques such as television, videos and satellite broadcasting, a vital part was played by press, radio and cinema. Associated with all these media has been the development of education and literacy.

Perhaps the reason why there is a mistaken idea that public relations is something new, is because in recent years we have enjoyed so many new ways of communicating. It has become both easier and more necessary to explain and create understanding about so many topics.

But the new communications techniques have their disadvantages as well as advantages. They are bringers of bad tidings as well as good ones. As we have seen, international television news services such as Cable News Network can tell us the worst as it actually happens. If this concerns a company or a government, the public relations officer has to work very fast to counteract any misinformation, or to present the true facts about a disaster. There is no time for favourable images if your chemical works blows up, your aircraft crashes or your hotel burns down.

Today more than ever, public relations has to deal with the facts as they are – good, bad or indifferent. In that sense public relations has to be as new as the world in which it operates.

Progress test 1

1. Why is it a fallacy to use the expression 'favourable'?

2. How did corporate identity originate?

3. What is meant by livery?

4. Who wrote about the *Lowell Offering?*

5. Why did I.M. Singer publish a house journal?

6. What was one of the first uses of PR by the British government?

7. Who was Sir Stephen Tallents and what is his significance in British PR?

8. Who was Ivy Ledbetter Lee and what was his promise about the content of his news releases?

9. Why was there a need for PR in the 1920s and 1930s?

10. What problems are created by instant international TV news?

2

PUBLIC RELATIONS DEFINED AND DISTINGUISHED

DEFINITIONS OF PUBLIC RELATIONS

1. Introduction

Public relations concerns any organisation, commercial or non-commercial. It exists whether we like it or not – you cannot decide to have or not have public relations. Public relations consists of all communications with all the people with whom an organisation has contact. An individual also experiences public relations, unless he or she is utterly isolated and beyond human contact.

So misunderstood is public relations that the last place to look for a satisfactory definition is a dictionary. Let us examine three internationally respected definitions which are familiar to PR professionals.

2. Definition of the (British) Institute of Public Relations (IPR)

'Public relations is the planned and sustained effort to establish and maintain goodwill and mutual understanding between an organisation and its publics.'

Analysis

(a) It is *'the planned and sustained effort'* – meaning that PR activity is organised as a campaign or programme and is a continuous activity, it is not haphazard.

(b) Its purpose is *'to establish and maintain mutual understanding'* – that is, to ensure that the organisation is understood by others. This mutual understanding is thus between an organisation and its *publics*, since many groups of people are involved.

3. The author's (FJ) own definition

'Public relations consists of all forms of planned communication, outwards and inwards, between an organisation and its publics for the purpose of achieving specific objectives concerning mutual understanding.' (*See* 1:2.)

Analysis

(a) The first part of this definition tidies up the IPR version and specifies that the purpose is not merely mutual understanding but achievement of specific objectives. These objectives often involve solving communications problems, e.g. converting negative attitudes into positive attitudes, that is effecting change.

(b) The management by objectives method is applied to PR. When there are objectives, results can be measured against them, making PR a tangible activity. This challenges the false idea that PR is intangible. If a PR programme is mounted to achieve a declared objective, the result can be observed or measured. If necessary, marketing research techniques can be used to test the degree of success or failure of a PR campaign.

4. The Mexican Statement

Following the World Assembly of Public Relations Associates in Mexico City in August 1978, this statement was agreed: 'Public relations practice is the art and social science of analyzing trends, predicting their consequences, counselling organisation leaders, and implementing planned programmes of action which will serve both the organisation's and the public interest.'

Analysis

The special significance of this international definition lies in the beginning and the end.

(a) The Mexican Statement speaks of 'analysing trends', which implies the application of research techniques (*see* Chapter 20) before planning a PR programme.

(b) The definition embraces the public affairs and social science aspects of an organisation, that is its responsibility to the public interest. An organisation is judged by its behaviour. Public relations is about goodwill and reputation.

PR DISTINGUISHED FROM ADVERTISING

5. Definition of advertising

The definition of the (British) Institute of Practitioners in Advertising (IPA) is as follows: 'Advertising presents the most persuasive possible selling message to the right prospects for the product or service at the lowest possible cost.'

7

Analysis

(a) *'Advertising presents the most persuasive possible selling message'* through the creative skills of copywriting, illustration, layout, typography, scriptwriting and video-making based on a theme or 'copy platform'. The emphasis is on *selling*, which differs from the PR role of *informing*, *educating* and *creating understanding through knowledge*. A major relationship between advertising and PR is that advertising is more likely to succeed when prior PR activity has created knowledge and understanding of the product or service being promoted.

This is sometimes better known as market education and is a practical example of how PR can help the marketing strategy. It is practical and more sensible than relying solely on advertising to break into a new market or to introduce a new and unknown product or service. A number of new products have failed to sell simply because there was no build-up of market education, and the advertising spend was a waste of money.

(b) By the use of marketing research to discover who is most likely to buy the product or service, which advertising appeal will provoke the best response and which media will reach most prospects most economically, the advertising can be made most effective.

(c) Following on from **(b)**, the choice and use of media to achieve maximum results at minimum cost will make the advertising cost-effective. A good advertising agency uses creative, research and media-buying skills to produce economically-productive advertising. The cost of some campaigns may seem huge, but this investment is related to the size of the market, production capacity and the volume of sales (often repeat sales) which are sought.

6. How does public relations differ from advertising?

Let us consider some of the major differences between these two forms of communication. These distinctions are based on the fact that PR is *not* a form of advertising and is, in fact, a much bigger activity than advertising. This is because PR relates to all the communications of the total organisation, whereas advertising – although it may cost more than PR – is mainly limited to the marketing function, with minor exceptions such as recruitment or financial advertising. Not until this is fully understood will the student have a clear idea or image of PR.

Public relations is neither 'free advertising' nor 'unpaid-for advertising'. There is nothing 'free' about PR: it is time-consuming and time costs money. This money may be represented by either staff salaries or consultancy fees. If a story appears in the news column or bulletin, its value cannot be reckoned by advertisement rates for space or time because editorial space and radio or television programme time is priceless.

Advertising may not be used by an organisation, but every organisation is involved in public relations. For example, a fire brigade does not advertise for fires or even advertise its services, but it does have relations with many publics.

Public relations embraces everyone and everything, whereas advertising is limited to special selling and buying tasks such as promoting goods and services, buying supplies, recruiting staff or announcing trading results. Public relations has to do with the total communications of an organisation: it is, therefore, more extensive and comprehensive than advertising. On occasions, PR may use advertising which is why PR is neither a form of advertising nor a part of advertising.

7. Financial differentiation of PR and advertising

Yet another difference lies in the finances of the two. There are several ways in which advertising agencies receive their income, but basically the commission system is universal, agencies receiving commission from the media on the space or air time which they buy. The PR consultancy can sell only its time and expertise, and fees are charged according to the volume of service performed. Moreover, in advertising most of the budget is spent on media and production costs whereas in PR most of the money goes on time, whether this is represented by staff salaries or by consultancy fees.

PR DISTINGUISHED FROM MARKETING

8. Definition of marketing

The definition of the (British) Chartered Institute of Marketing (CIM) is as follows: 'Marketing is the management process responsible for identifying, anticipating and satisfying customer requirements profitably.'

Analysis

(a) Emphasis is placed on the *management* aspect of marketing – that is, the responsibility of top management to market professionally, not sell goods or services haphazardly.

(b) Professional marketing management makes itself responsible for finding out precisely what the market needs (and this may be the absence of some product or service which people would buy if it was supplied) and for satisfying this need if it can be done at a profit.

(c) This is a challenge to business management, some of which may be content to go on making and selling the same things without applying any modern marketing techniques at all. Marketing calls for imaginative enterprise, but it also needs the responsibility of PR-mindedness, for goodwill will be squandered if the pursuit of maximum profits is at the expense of the customers. As communicators, marketers and PR practitioners have a lot in common.

PRODUCT	PLACE	PROMOTION

Product research
Marketing research
Product design
Product range
Packaging
Branding
Warranties
After-sales care
New product planning
	Channels:
	  Retailers
	  Wholesalers
	  Multiples
	  Direct sales
	  Overseas distributors
	  Direct export
	  Sales to governments
	  Sales to multinationals
	  Sales to trading blocs
		Advertising
		PUBLIC RELATIONS
		Branding
		Positioning
		Sales promotion
		Competitions
		Premiums
		Pack offers
		Direct marketing
		Merchandising
		Sales force effort

PRICE	Physical distribution:
	  Supplies
	  Stock
	  Handling
	  Storage
	  Transportation
	  Warehousing
		Sales force support
		Telesales
		Sales literature
		Mailers and flyers
		Educational literature
		Tech spec literature

Pricing policy Regional differentials Discounts Commissions Retail mark-up Wholesale mark-up Impact of VAT Test marketing Impact of offers Impact of discounts		

Fig 2.1   PR's role in the marketing mix

9. Marketing in relation to PR and advertising

In the commercial world, or private sector of the economy, PR and advertising will be associated with marketing. While marketing is only one function of a business and PR also has to do with the financial and production functions too, PR can be applied to every part of the marketing mix, of which advertising is but one ingredient. The *marketing mix* consists of every element in the marketing strategy – to mention only a few: naming, packaging, research, pricing, selling, distribution and after-sales services. All of these bear some degree of communication and goodwill. Market education can be a vital PR contribution, on which the success of advertising may well depend.

PR DISTINGUISHED FROM SALES PROMOTION

10. Definition of sales promotion

Sales promotion consists of short-term schemes, usually at the point-of-sale but also in direct response marketing, to launch products or to revive or increase sales.

Analysis

(a) Sales promotion consists of 'below-the-line' efforts (that is, the use of media other than traditional mass media) to help move goods out of the stores.

(b) Sales promotion may push sales by means of (i) long-term schemes such as regular product demonstrations, as with sewing machine demonstrations in stores, or (ii) short-term promotional schemes such as money-off offers using flash packs, competitions, free gifts, premium offers of goods at low prices in return for tokens from packs plus cash, and cash refunds if packs are sent in.

(c) Sales promotion is often used as an alternative to media advertising. For instance, a gift, price cuts or special offer is a promotional cost, just like advertising.

11. Sales promotion in relation to PR

Public relations is sometimes confused with sales promotion. This may be because sales promotion does bring the producer closer to the customer. It is a more personal form of marketing communication than traditional media advertising. While it does have PR aspects – it is foolish for a sales promotion offer to cause disappointment, e.g. when delivery of a premium offer is delayed – sales promotion is not PR as the definition above should make clear.

PR DISTINGUISHED FROM PROPAGANDA

12. Definition of propaganda

Propaganda is the means of gaining support for an opinion, creed or belief.

Analysis

(a) Propaganda is distinguished by its concentration on matters of the heart and mind. These are emotional, intellectual or spiritual topics such as causes, politics or religion, with which people may not agree.

Propaganda has a long history. It was used by the ancient Greeks when an orator announced the state's political policy. In 1662 a committee of cardinals in Rome sent missions abroad to propagate the Gospels.

(b) For the recipient of propaganda, there is often little tangible gain, perhaps only some inner satisfaction. The position may be different from the point of view of the propagandist: for example, Hitler's investment of time, effort and money in propaganda resulted in gain of power, and religious propaganda may result in expansion of church membership through

Fig 2.2 Public relations, advertising or propaganda? A 1997 election poster which could be all three. The lines of distinction are sometimes too fine to distinguish.

conversions. Another interesting case was that of Roosevelt's radio talks in the late 1930s: he won popular support for his New Deal and the American public enjoyed a psychological uplift even if the New Deal actually failed to produce the economic recovery promised. From this it may be seen that there is no straightforward exchange situation – no goods for money – involved in propaganda, at least as far as the recipients are concerned.

(c) Propaganda may be used for good, bad, indifferent (and some very strange) causes. Thus propaganda, like advertising, is prejudiced in favour of its topic: good PR, on the other hand, should be factual, unbiased and free of self-praise. A news release which is otherwise will be rejected by editors because it will be a 'puff', the editorial word for disguised, or even intentional, advertising or propaganda. Sometimes, advertising to wholesalers and retailers is called 'trade propaganda', but this misuse of terms should be avoided.

13. Propaganda in relation to PR

This is yet another form of communication which is often quite wrongly regarded as PR. The two could not be more different, if only because to be successful PR must be credible, whereas propaganda is liable to invite suspicion or, at least, disagreement. The problem is sometimes to distinguish between the propaganda and the PR elements in information issued by, for instance, government departments. Propaganda would be aimed at keeping the government in power but PR would be aimed at getting its services understood and used properly.

PR DISTINGUISHED FROM PUBLICITY

14. Publicity defined

A simple definition is as follows: publicity results from information being made known.

Analysis

(a) Publicity is a *result*.

(b) This result may be uncontrollable and it may be good or bad for the subject concerned. Some personalities receive both good and bad publicity. A pop star may gain good publicity from a concert or record, but bad publicity if accused of taking drugs. Behaviour has a great bearing on whether publicity is good or bad and PR is very much about the behaviour of individuals, organisations, products and services. However, the word is used loosely, and especially in America is confused with PR.

Publicity yields an image and, subject to adequate information, the image of any subject can only be what it truly is. The problem is obtaining information that is complete, accurate and unbiased and ascertaining by some means that it is so; hence it is possible for a personality, for example, to be presented by different images in different newspapers.

15. Publicity and advertising

In the advertising world the word publicity is used very loosely, e.g. 'publicity manager' as a superior title for an advertising manager. Publicity and advertising are not the same thing: publicity may be sought and, as in the definition above, gained as a result of information being published or announced.

IMAGES

There are several kinds of image and we will now consider five kinds: the mirror, current, wish, corporate and multiple image.

16. The mirror image

This image is the one people in an organisation, especially its leaders, believe to be the impression outsiders have of the organisation. This could be an illusion bred on wishful thinking because knowledge and understanding of outside opinion is lacking. It is a common situation, often based on 'everybody loves us' fantasies. An opinion or image study could reveal that a very different and perhaps unexpected and disconcerting perceived image exists.

17. The current image

This is the one held by people outside the organisation, and it may be based on experience or on poor information and understanding. Public relations deals with a world of hostility, prejudice, apathy and ignorance which could result in an unfair current image. The current image depends on how little or how much people know and in a busy world their knowledge will be less perfect than that of those people within the organisation. For example, those living in a particular country know more about their own country than do foreigners living hundreds or thousands of kilometres away. This is the great communication problem of the Third World: the current images of most developing countries are poor in the West, due to apathy and ignorance. This is not helped when countries change their names!

Not surprisingly, therefore the mirror and the current image can be very different, and this variance may not be appreciated by management. One of the jobs of the public relations officer (PRO) may be to interpret the attitudes of outsiders *to management*, who may well have false ideas about outside opinion. These outsiders could be important publics: they could be potential staff, customers, shopkeepers, politicians, journalists, TV and radio presenters – all kinds of people whose comprehension of the organisations is important. It is not just their good opinion that is necessary – it is also necessary that their impression, their mental picture, of the organisation or its people, products or services is correct – not *favourable*, but correct. A PR image results from a correct impression. A prison is not likely to win a *favourable* impression but at least it can be correctly represented – whether it is a men's or women's, what sort of offender is imprisoned there, whether it is an 'open' or top security jail, how many convicts share a cell and so on.

18. The wish image

This is the desired image, the one management wishes to achieve. Again, it is not so much a favourable or preferred image as a true one. For instance, when Gordon Selfridge opened his department store in Oxford Street, London, many years ago, he wanted people to think of his store as a place where they could enjoy shopping as a day's outing, full of colour and pleasure, instead of the usual drudgery. The wish image mostly applies to something new when outsiders are as yet completely uninformed.

19. The corporate image

Here we have the image of the organisation itself rather than of the products or services. The corporate image may be made up of many things such as the company history, financial success and stability, quality of production, export success, industrial relations and reputation as an employer, social responsibility and research record. Marks and Spencer plc has an excellent corporate image which has been established internationally. A corporate image is important in financial PR, the success of a new share issue often depending on the corporate image.

20. The multiple image

A number of individuals, branches or other representations can each create a particular image which does not conform to a uniform image for the total organisation. There can be as many images as there are, say, sales staff. The problem may be overcome by the use of uniforms, vehicle liveries (decoration), symbols, badges, staff training and in the case of shops by the use of identical shop design, name displays, interior layout and display material, as seen with chain-stores. An airline is a good example of many devices to produce a recognisable *corporate identity*. The liveries of aircraft – such as distinctive tail fin designs – and the dress of air crews all contribute to this standard identity.

21. Good and bad images

In **14** above mention was made of the good or bad publicity enjoyed or endured by public figures, resulting in good or bad current images. It has been argued above that the ideal PR image should only be a true impression based on experience and knowledge and understanding of the facts. It follows that an image cannot be 'polished' (since it would distort it). A better image has to be *earned* by putting right the causes of the bad image – whether they be faulty behaviour or faulty information. To attempt to falsify an image is an abuse of PR. There are many erroneous ideas in management and marketing circles – among the people who buy and abuse PR and so help to give it a bad name – that falsifying images is a legitimate task. This is not the case. If PR is to be credible it must avoid false image making. The importance of this stand lies in the fact that the media are prejudiced about PR to the extent of expecting false image polishing. It is not helped when advertising agents, who are so often ignorant about PR, claim that they aim to polish the image of this or that client. PR practitioners make no such claims.

WHAT MAKES A GOOD PR PRACTITIONER?

22. Necessary qualities

The demands on PR consultants or PR managers are very great. They are often regarded as oracles and expected to perform miracles. Yet, no matter how great their intelligence, training and experience, they can never be experts in everything. It may have been noticed from the comparisons with advertising that the advertising world has a division of labour that is almost non-existent in PR. Consequently, the PR man or woman has to be sufficiently humble and adaptable to be able to accept that in PR one never stops learning. The ability and the willingness to find out is critical. The following seven attributes sum up the good PR practitioner, no matter what his or her background may be:

(a) Ability to get on with all kinds of people: this means understanding, sometimes tolerating, people, not flattering them.

(b) Ability to communicate: that is, explain by means of spoken or written word or by visual device such as photography.

(c) Ability to organise: that calls for patient planning.

(d) Personal integrity in both professional and private life.

(e) Imagination: that is a creative sense, as when designing a house journal, writing a script for a film or videotape, planning campaigns and seeking solutions to problems.

(f) Ability to find out: that is to have ready access to information. The PRO is often expected to be an oracle.

(g) Ability to research and evaluate the results of a PR campaign, and learn from these findings.

Progress test 2

1. What is the IPR definition of public relations?

2. What is especially important about the Mexican Statement?

3. Give three reasons why PR is neither advertising nor a part of advertising.

4. What is the IPA definition of advertising?

5. What is the CIM definition of marketing?

6. How does sales promotion assist advertising and selling?

7. What in particular distinguishes propaganda from public relations?

8. What have propaganda and advertising in common?

9. Why are publicity and advertising not the same thing?

10. Give some examples of good and bad publicity which have resulted from good or bad behaviour.

11. What is the mirror image?

12. What is the current image?

13. What is the wish image?

14. What is the corporate image?

15. What is the multiple image?

16. Why is it impossible to polish an image?

17. What seven qualities are required of a PR practitioner?

3

PUBLIC RELATIONS DEPARTMENTS

DEPARTMENT OR CONSULTANCY

1. Need for an internal department

Another difference between advertising and public relations is that when a company is beginning to spend a lot of money on advertising it becomes sensible to appoint an advertising agency, but the opposite is true with PR. The clients share the specialist services of the advertising agency staff instead of having to employ full-time staff of their own to plan and buy media, write and design advertisements and produce them for the press, television and radio. With certain exceptions, e.g. large department stores and big travel agents, the advertiser would not need this expensive specialist staff all the year round.

But when a company is engaging in a lot of PR work it may be preferable to handle it through an internal PR department. The consultancy is useful when it does not pay to set up an in-house PR department or as a means of augmenting the internal PR staff when special skills are wanted, i.e. financial PR or simply outside professional advice.

In saying this it is not suggested that the PR department is better than a PR consultancy or vice versa. They are different and a large organisation will probably use both. But there is another interesting difference. The advertising agency is usually employed for two reasons: its skills in planning and buying space and broadcasting time efficiently and economically, and its creative skill in devising original, compelling and sales-promoting advertisements.

The PR practitioner is more of an all-rounder, a communicator, adviser and campaign planner. But while a product or service can be given to an agency to advertise, the PR practitioner's source of information, creativity and production is the company itself. The more the PRO knows about the organisation the better, for he or she speaks on its behalf. The PRO is concerned with staff, dealers, consumers and all kinds of relations. If he or she is to know and represent the organisation thoroughly he or she has to be at the heart of things and in touch with all the organisation's people. This intimacy is not so essential to the advertising agency and lack of it can handicap the outside PR consultancy.

2. Size of PR departments

Internal or in-house PR departments may be large or small according to:

(a) The size of the organisation

(b) The company's need for effective PR and the value placed on PR by management

(c) The special PR requirements of the organisation.

Taking (c) a stage further, a mass consumer product manufacturer may spend much on advertising and little on PR, whilst a technical or industrial company may spend little on advertising and rely strongly on PR activities to do with market education. No two organisations are alike. The important thing is that management should use PR because it needs to communicate with identified publics. The PR impulse must start at the top.

3. PR staff

Thus a PR department may consist of no more than a PR manager and a secretary, while others will contain specialist assistants, such as press officers, a house journal editor, a print designer, a photographer and so on. There will also be organisations which do not employ a full-time PR specialist but the responsibility (perhaps in liaison with a consultancy) is handled by a marketing, sales or advertising manager. In some organisations – voluntary bodies, for instance – PR may be included in the duties of the director, appeals officer or membership secretary. In some local authorities, PR is handled by the mayor's secretary, although most British local authorities now have full-time PR staff.

From these remarks it will be seen that most PR work is conducted outside the consultancy world – the opposite to advertising where agency personnel predominate – and that PR departments and staff will be found in numerous non-commercial organisations which never or hardly ever advertise (maybe only for recruitment purposes). In fact, according to a recent survey conducted by Cranfield School of Management, 63 per cent of PR practitioners in Britain are employed in-house. During the recession in 1991, when consultancies were losing clients and shedding staff, an increasing amount of PR was being handled in-house.

The chart in Figure 3.1 shows the possible staffing of a PR department in a large manufacturing company.

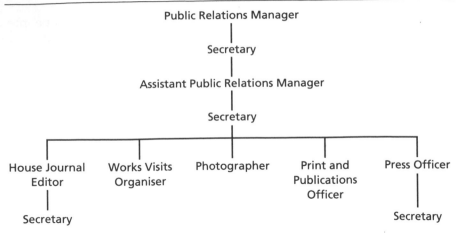

Fig 3.1   Possible staffing of a PR department in a large manufacturing company

THE PR MANAGER

4. Title of the PR manager

The head of the department may be given any one of many titles that have been invented. They range from 'director of public affairs' to 'communications manager'; some attempt to mix two distinct jobs, e.g. 'advertising and public relations officer'. Dislike for the government title of 'public relations officer' (PRO) has led to some of these variations and fancy titles. Attempts to separate corporate PR and the social conscience of business from the day-to-day task of producing staff newspapers and product publicity news have led to either superior or commonplace titles. However, the division between public affairs and public relations – an American idea – is artificial.

Sometimes, PR is seen as part of another job, which is a pity because it tends to play down the PR role. In the Third World, PR is sometimes the responsibility of the personnel manager. This may be all right for internal relations, but hardly satisfies the needs of external relations.

Again, we have the all-embracing title of marketing services manager in which PR is sometimes ignominiously submerged.

In the end, what we are talking about is an executive who manages the company's PR, so we will call this person the *public relations manager*. If such a manager sits on the board, the title will be *public relations director*. The wider expression *public relations practitioner* will refer to any professional PR person, whether they work in-house or in a consultancy. Other titles will be ignored, with the exceptions of the *press officer*, who is a specialist in media relations (and is not to be confused with the public relations manager), and the *public relations consultant*, whose title is self-explanatory.

5. Responsibilities of the PR manager

These may be defined as:

(a) To set targets or define objectives for PR operations

(b) To estimate the working hours and other resources that need to be costed

(c) To decide priorities that will control the choice of publics, media to reach them, timing of operations, and best use of manpower and other resources such as equipment

(d) To decide the feasibility of carrying out the declared objectives in the light of available funds, existing staff and equipment.

6. The fourfold specialist task of the PR manager

The task of the PR manager can be seen as fourfold:

(a) To establish and maintain a correct image of the organisation and of its policies, products, services and personnel

(b) To monitor outside opinion and convey this intelligence to management

(c) To advise management on communication problems, solutions and techniques

(d) To inform publics about policies, activities, products, services and personnel so that maximum knowledge and understanding is won.

7. How the PR manager and management can cooperate

Cooperation should be effected on the following lines:

(a) The PR manager should be a competent professional practitioner so that he or she is respected by management as an expert in that particular field.

(b) The PR manager should set up internal lines of communication – know everyone and be known by everyone – and invite the confidence of everyone, so that information can be obtained at all times from all sections of the organisation.

(c) Similarly, the PR manager should create external lines of communication, so that he or she is regarded as a reliable source of material. Outside sources of information may also be needed, often in order to achieve feedback.

(d) The PR manager must keep top management well briefed for interviews, speeches, public occasions.

(e) Management must be able and willing to communicate, and the PR manager may have to arrange rehearsals before press receptions, and television familiarisation sessions before TV appearances.

(f) Management must keep the PR manager fully informed – preferably in advance and by direct contact – which means that the PR manager must have access to management.

To cooperate effectively, the PR manager needs to be positioned so that he or she is responsible to top management and serves all departments of the organisation. Ideally, the PR manager should have board director status, as happens in the world's most successful companies. This is demonstrated in Figure 3.2.

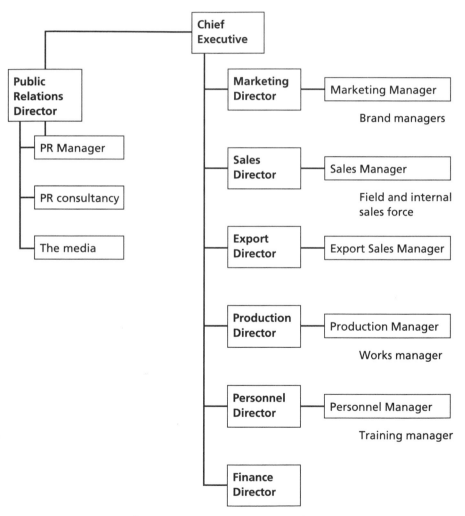

Fig 3.2   Positioning of a PR manager so that he or she reports direct to top management and services all functional divisions of the company

THE PR DEPARTMENT'S ACTIVITIES

8. A to Z of work undertaken

The kind of work carried out by a PR manager and staff will obviously differ from one organisation to another and is capable of many variables. The year's work may consist of any or all of the following:

(a) Writing and distributing news releases, photographs and feature articles to the press, compiling press lists.

(b) Organising press conferences, receptions and facility visits.

(c) Maintaining a media information service.

(d) Arranging press, radio and television interviews for management.

(e) Briefing photographers and maintaining a picture library.

(f) Editing and producing staff magazines or newspapers, and organising other forms of internal communication such as videotapes, slide presentations, wall newspapers, etc.

(g) Editing and producing external journals aimed at distributors, users, customers, etc.

(h) Writing and producing print such as educational literature, company histories, annual reports, induction literature for new staff, educational posters for schools, etc.

(i) Commissioning audio-visuals such as synchronised slide presentations and videotapes together with their distribution, cataloguing, showing and maintenance.

(j) Commissioning and organising PR exhibitions and displays, including provision of vehicles.

(k) Commissioning and maintaining forms of corporate identity and house styling such as logos, colour schemes, print house style and typography, livery of vehicles, distinctive clothing, etc.

(l) Handling PR sponsorships

(m) Organising works or similar visits, e.g. facility flights, sailings, site tours, etc.

(n) Attendance at appropriate meetings of the board and meetings of production, marketing, sales and other executives.

(o) Attendance at sales and dealer conferences.

(p) Representation of the company at trade association meetings.

(q) Liaison with PR consultancy if one is employed.

(r) Training PR staff.

(s) Commissioning opinion surveys (or other research).

(t) Supervising advertising – liaison with advertising agency – if this comes within the PR department.

(u) Liaison with politicians and civil servants.

(v) Official openings of new premises – arrangements for VIPs, guests and press.

(w) Arranging visits by royalty, MPs, VIPs, foreign visitors.

(x) Celebrating centenaries, Queen's Award for Industry, etc.

(y) Organising feedback of press cuttings, radio and television transcripts and monitorings and other reports from outside.

(z) Analysis of feedback and evaluation of the results of efforts in relation to the declared objectives.

All such varied activities have to be fitted into a planned PR programme for the year and be conducted within the agreed budget, as will be explained in Chapters 5 and 11. This A to Z list also highlights the kaleidoscopic nature of PR work and the high risk of failure if too little effort is expended on too many projects. It also emphasises the need for training and professional qualifications such as the CAM Diploma.

ADVANTAGES AND DISADVANTAGES OF A PR MANAGER AND DEPARTMENT

9. Five advantages

Generally, it can be said that irrespective of whether or not a PR consultancy is retained, the advantages of having an in-house PR unit run by a PR manager are as follows:

(a) The PR manager is familiar with his or her own organisation.

(b) The PR manager may also have specialist knowledge or experience of the trade, industry or subject with which the organisation is concerned.

(c) The PR manager can easily establish lines of communication inside the organisation and so get reliable information quickly.

(d) The PR manager is on the spot and can act swiftly, or get quick decisions in an emergency.

(e) The PR manager is in a strong position to give management day-to-day advice.

10. Five disadvantages

While it is advisable for any organisation to have a qualified PR manager, there can be pitfalls such as the following:

(a) The PR manager could be so close to the organisation, or so enthusiastic about it, as to be biased. This could be reflected in his or her writing, to the disadvantage of the organisation. The media are very cynical about this sort of thing. Similarly, if the mistake is made of mixing PR with other activities, such as advertising, marketing or sales, the media will be very suspicious of material coming from, for instance, a 'publicity manager' or a 'publicity department'. Advertising, marketing and sales people are so used to buying space from the advertisement departments of the media that they rarely understand that PR material has to be supplied to the editorial departments, which speak a totally different language, want news, do not want 'puffs' and generally get 'puffs' from non-PR sources, although sometimes from company PR managers.

(b) If he or she is not properly trained and qualified, the PR manager could be a liability.

(c) The PR manager may lack sufficient executive status to enjoy the respect of management and of the media.

(d) The PR manager may be simply given the title of PRO by management which sees this as a good way of promoting a senior person 'sideways' and so he or she will dabble in a profession about which little is known.

(e) Management may not have agreed a job specification which enables the PR manager to take on the responsibilities set out in 5 above or do the work outlined in the A to Z list (*see* 8).

Progress test 3

1. Why do companies appoint advertising agencies when they are spending a lot of money on advertising, but set up internal PR department when they are spending a lot of money on PR?

2. Why are most advertising personnel employed in advertising agencies but most PR people are employed in various commercial and non-commercial organisations?

3. What staff would you expect to find in a large PR department?

4. What are the principal responsibilities of the PR manager?

5. What are the PR manager's four specialist tasks?

6. List some of the activities which the PR manager of an insurance company might engage in.

7. What are the advantages of having an in-house PR manager and department?

8. List any possible disadvantages in having a staff PR manager.

9. What is likely to be the reaction of an editor who receives a news release from the 'publicity manager' or the 'publicity department?

4

PUBLIC RELATIONS CONSULTANTS

INTRODUCTORY DEFINITION OF TERMS

1. Definition of a PR consultancy

'Public relations consultancy practice is the provision of specified technical and creative services by an individual or a group of individuals, qualified to do so by reason of experience and training, and having a legal corporate identity registered for the purpose of business in the United Kingdom. The whole or principal income of the corporate body so formed will be by way of professional fees paid for its services by clients under contract to the consultancy' (Public Relations Consultants Association).

The ambiguous expression 'PR agency' is sometimes misused for PR consultancy, but it is an abuse of language since it is physically, legally and financially impossible for a PR consultancy to be an agency. It does not act like an estate agent, art agent, employment agency or advertising agency. There is confusion here with 'advertising agency' which, strictly speaking, is the agent of the media for whom it receives its remuneration by way of commission on media purchases. A PR consultancy is no one's agent, and is paid commission by no one, least of all by the media. Unfortunately, the trade press tends to perpetuate this misnomer, largely because it is more familiar with advertising agencies.

PR consultancies tend to be the more glamorous side of PR, and new aspirants to the profession are often unaware that consultancies employ only 37 per cent of those working in PR, according to the Cranfield survey (*see* 3:3). This survey also estimated that there were 19,500 PR professionals with 15,000 support staff.

Analysis

(a) The 'specified technical and creative services' are dealt with in a subsequent definition (*see* 4 below), but normally these services do not include advertising (except when used for PR purposes) which rightly belongs to advertising agencies. However, this point becomes a little confused because some organisations offer all kinds of marketing communication services, while there are advertising agencies which have either PR departments or PR subsidiaries. An 'independent' PR consultant is one who has no connection with an advertising agency.

(b) The method of remuneration is the fee, and methods of arriving at fees will be discussed later in this chapter. This is one other reason why consultants do not usually produce advertising, since advertising agencies are mostly remunerated under the commission system.

2. Consultancies in the UK

There are more than 1,200 PR consultancies in the UK and most of them are listed in *Advertisers Annual* and the *Hollis Press and Public Relations Annual*, the latter also listing consultancies in some 60 other countries. Inevitably, the majority of these firms are small, but since they do not have the division of specialist labour to be found in advertising agencies even a one-person PR consultancy can be thoroughly efficient. Small may be beautiful in PR, less so in advertising, which is yet another difference between the two. Moreover, many consultancies concentrate on a special branch of PR or in a particular industry or interest such as fashion or parliamentary liaison.

The Public Relations Consultants Association (PRCA) has more than 100 members of various size representing more than 1,000 clients, plus some overseas associate members. Its *Public Relations Yearbook* lists members, clients, directors and partners, MPs and holders of public office employed or retained by member firms, detailed information about members and their business structure, and the PRCA Code of Consultancy Practice.

3. Definition of a client

'A client is an organisation, corporate body, individual or group of individuals which retains the professional services of a public relations consultancy for an agreed programme (or project) of advice or activity, for a specific period on terms previously agreed between the consultancy and the client and binding on both.' (PRCA)

Analysis

(a) Be careful of the word 'retains'. A 'retainer' is usually a token fee paid to an adviser so that he or she is ready to serve a particular client at any time, thus guaranteeing exclusivity. Retainers are seldom used in PR, fees being calculated to cover actual work.

(b) A 'project' would be a short-term *ad hoc* job such as handling PR for an exhibitor at an exhibition.

(c) The 'period' is usually one year, with an agreed period of advance notice of cancellation, say three months.

4. Definition of services

'The services provided by a public relations consultancy may comprise, in all or in part, the following:

'Establishing channels of communication with the client's public or publics, management communications, marketing and sales promotion related activity, advice or services relating to political, governmental or public affairs, financial public relations, personnel and industrial relations, recruitment training and higher and technical education (this list is not intended to be exhaustive).

'Not all public relations consultancies will claim competence in every area; some will confine their practice to certain industries or interests, while others may offer consultative but not executive services. However, all members of the Association who do not offer a full range of services to clients but specialise in certain areas must be competent to recommend to their clients a full range of services from other members, if required by the client to do so.' (PRCA)

Analysis

(a) Students should note that an ideal definition is limited to one concise sentence, and the above is more of a useful description than a definition.

(b) It does show that a PR consultancy can offer numerous services and that they are not limited to press relations. The full range may be as extensive as the A to Z or PR department services specified in 3:8.

(c) The point is made that some consultancies tend to specialise. This makes them very useful to organisations with their own PR departments which may find it convenient, efficient and economical to employ an outside PR unit for either occasional or particular work; this is demonstrated by Figure 4.1. For example, a house journal may be edited internally, but designed externally.

(d) 'Consultative' rather than 'executive' services, better described as 'counselling', means advisory services. The consultant – or counsellor – will study a communication problem and make recommendations but not carry out the proposed work. The actual work may be done by the PR manager, or by an executive PR consultant.

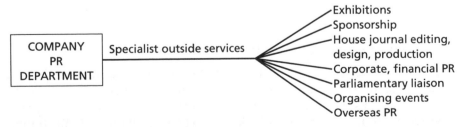

Fig 4.1   In-house PR department use of specialist outside PR consultancy

CHARGING AND BUDGETING FEES

5. Consultancy fees

Calculation of fees takes into account the following:

(a) There are many ways by which consultancies arrive at their fees but the recommended method is to charge on the basis of time (working hours), plus the cost of materials (stationery, postage, photographs, etc.), plus the cost of expenses (hospitality, travel, etc.).

(b) The time is calculated on the number of hours estimated for carrying out the PR programme.

(c) An hourly rate is calculated and charged so that it recovers the cost of salaries, administration expenses, office overheads and allows a profit. Sometimes a daily rate may be charged.

(d) Sometimes the hourly rate is based on the salary of the account executive and a secretary (and as a rough guide if this combined salary figure is trebled it will recover all the other costs which comprise the hourly rate and show a profit).

(e) Other consultancies calculate the workload of everyone associated with the programme, and charge their time on the basis of salary plus a percentage on-cost.

6. Profit-making

To make a profit, and stay in business, the PR consultant has to be good at business. He or she is selling time and expertise, and salaries (including his or her own) are the major expense. The only people who will pay the costs are clients and consequently any money that is not recoverable has to come out of the PR consultant's gross profit.

Nor can the PR consultant afford to undercharge in order to gain new business, hoping to be able to increase the fee later on. The result of this unbusinesslike practice is that either the PR consultant will lose money, or other clients will have to subsidise those low fees – to the disadvantage of those clients. The old saying 'You get what you pay for' must apply to fees. As we shall see presently, budgeting is vital to both business success as a client, and to good client relations.

7. Only part of consultancy time is saleable

The consultant does not sell 100 per cent of his or her working time. In fact, such are the duties of running a business that the consultant will be lucky to sell 40 to 50 per cent of the working time. This is a fact not always appreciated when the hourly rate may look high. The consultant's administration duties include recruitment and training of staff; accounts and taxation; dealing with landlords and suppliers; seeking new business and making presentations to prospects. Proposals for new accounts – in competition with others – are usually prepared free of charge.

Since the profit margin is only a few per cent, the costs of running the business have to be balanced carefully against the number of accounts (clients) the consultant needs to service. A lot of small accounts may be costly to administer, too few big accounts can be dangerous in case one is lost. Wise consultants do not accept clients below a certain minimum fee. A typical consultancy problem is to decide what volume of business one account executive can control, and at what income point employment of another account executive can be justified. In reverse circumstances the consultant has to know when to cease employing staff. These are delicate decisions which can make all the difference between profitability and insolvency.

8. The modern method of charging fees

Rapid inflation has demanded strict attention to cash flow. In the past, consultancy fees were often worked out as a quarterly or monthly division of the annual fee, and charged in arrears. Today consultancies charge one to three months *in advance*. (This is fair since salaries, rents, rates, light and power have to be paid and consultancies cannot afford to have large reserves for credit purposes.)

PR consultancies cannot be compared with advertising agencies whose major cost is the immense bill for space and air time, for which they have to pay quickly under their 'recognition' agreement with the media owners while having to allow their clients credit. A requirement of 'recognition' (which entitles the agency to receive commission from the media) is that the agency does have the necessary cash flow, which amounts to three months' credit. PR consultancies, being mostly small firms, rarely have this sort of financial strength and are vulnerable unless fee charging and receiving is observed with a strict eye to cash flow and profitability.

9. Budgeting fees

This is a preliminary introduction to a subject which will be dealt with in greater detail in Chapter 11, but following the last section it has to be stressed that both client satisfaction and consultancy profitability depend on fair and just fees being charged. It is no use a consultant saying he or she can do a job for some round figure conjured out of the air, any more than a builder can offer a price to build a house until the quantity surveyor has costed it. In the past it has been poor PR practice for PR consultants to quote in round figure terms, so that the client has never properly understood what was to be received for the money and the consultant has over-spent (mainly on time) and made a loss. A PR programme should be scrupulously budgeted so that both client and consultant know what is going to be done and what it will cost.

31

10. The value of budgeting and explaining costs

To take a simple example, if a client receives six press cuttings and a large bill for £X the client may be excused for thinking he or she has been over-charged. But if the client knows that the £X represents:

(a) Researching the story

(b) Writing the story

(c) Seeking approval and perhaps having to produce a revised version

(d) Writing different versions for different classes of journal

(e) Compiling a special mailing list

(f) Printing the releases

(g) Addressing the envelopes and filling them

(h) Postage and despatch; or distribution by fax and e-mail

(i) Payment of the press cutting agency fee

(j) Answering editorial queries

and this is supported by an analysis of the circulation and readership of the journals which printed the story, the bill can take on a very different appearance of good value for money. This is better than an invoice 'for the despatch of fifty news releases', which may raise the question of what happened to the other forty-four?

This cost will be proved effective if it is shown how well the media coverage has contributed to the aims of the campaign. A single report in a particularly important newspaper might be more cost-effective than lots of coverage in less valuable media. This is a useful point to remember when evaluating media coverage on the basis of its equivalent rate-card cost. To pretend it was so much free advertising would be irrelevant.

11. Contact meetings

A PR programme and budget should include an allocation of time and fees for regular contact meetings, at either the client's or the consultant's office. Ideally, these meetings should be at least monthly. On these occasions work done and in progress can be reviewed in relation to the programme and budget, which can be adjusted if necessary. Talking to the client does cost money. Under the advertising agency commission system, this cost does not arise since the account executive's time and advice is covered (except with technical accounts where commissions are small) by the commission which the agency receives from the media. This is not so with PR, and the client has to pay for all time expended on his or her behalf since the consultant has no other source of income.

DOCUMENTATION

12. Reporting meetings

The minutes of a contact meeting are called the *contact report*. The meeting may be called a 'progress meeting' and the minutes may also be called a 'progress report'. The consultant should produce both agenda and contact report, which should be submitted immediately after the meeting in case the

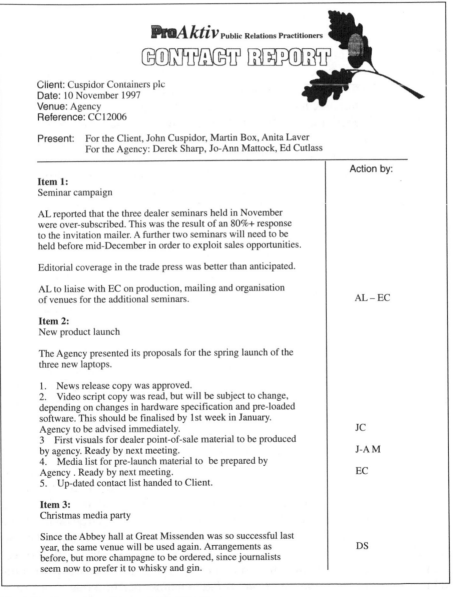

ProAktiv Public Relations Practitioners

CONTACT REPORT

Client: Cuspidor Containers plc
Date: 10 November 1997
Venue: Agency
Reference: CC12006

Present:　For the Client, John Cuspidor, Martin Box, Anita Laver
　　　　　For the Agency: Derek Sharp, Jo-Ann Mattock, Ed Cutlass

	Action by:
Item 1: Seminar campaign AL reported that the three dealer seminars held in November were over-subscribed. This was the result of an 80%+ response to the invitation mailer. A further two seminars will need to be held before mid-December in order to exploit sales opportunities. Editorial coverage in the trade press was better than anticipated. AL to liaise with EC on production, mailing and organisation of venues for the additional seminars.	AL – EC
Item 2: New product launch The Agency presented its proposals for the spring launch of the three new laptops. 1.　News release copy was approved. 2.　Video script copy was read, but will be subject to change, depending on changes in hardware specification and pre-loaded software. This should be finalised by 1st week in January. Agency to be advised immediately. 3　First visuals for dealer point-of-sale material to be produced by agency. Ready by next meeting. 4.　Media list for pre-launch material to be prepared by Agency . Ready by next meeting. 5.　Up-dated contact list handed to Client.	 JC J-A M EC
Item 3: Christmas media party Since the Abbey hall at Great Missenden was so successful last year, the same venue will be used again. Arrangements as before, but more champagne to be ordered, since journalists seem now to prefer it to whisky and gin.	 DS

Fig 4.2　Example of a contact report

client disagrees with it. This report should follow the order of the agenda, state information reported and decisions taken and, in a ruled off column on the right-hand side, specify actions to be taken. The items in the action column should bear the initials of the client or consultancy staff who are responsible for taking these actions, e.g. 'Prices to be supplied – OD' or 'Draft release to be submitted – EB'. Thus, decisions and responsibilities are clearly set out, and copies of the report can be sent to all those present at the meeting, and also to all those on both sides who should be informed. The consultancy files copies of contact reports in a *facts book*.

13. Consultancy time sheets

An essential part of charging on a working-hour basis is to have a simple and efficient system of logging the time spent by staff on behalf of each client. In the course of a day a person will do many independent jobs of short and long duration for different clients. It will be impossible to remember all these separate expenditures of time. There will be telephone calls, letters to read and write, visits to make, callers to receive, creative work to do, photographic sessions, proofs to read and so on, in a busy day. Every day will be different, much will be unpredictable. It is no use trying to fill up a time sheet at the end of the day, folly to attempt to do so at the end of the week.

Moreover, a time sheet should be fit to show a client if he or she disputes a report or invoice. A good idea is to decide on minimum time entries, say 15 minutes as an average for telephone calls. A simple time sheet, as in Figure 4.3, can be kept on a clipboard on the desk or carried in a briefcase, and the time can be totalled once a week by the secretary and the total transferred to a master time sheet. Comparison with the client's total hours time bank will show whether he or she is getting the right amount of service, too much or too little.

14. Identifying each job

To clarify the management of an account, a system of *job numbers* should be introduced so that each separate task – news release, photography, press reception, annual report, edition of a house journal – is given a number prefixed by, say, the initials of the client. If the client's name was John Smith Ltd, the jobs mentioned above would be identified as JS1, JS2, JS3, JS4 and JS5.

These numbers can be used to itemise both the agendas for meetings and the contact reports. Suppliers would be given the numbers on orders and asked to quote them on invoices. This can be helpful because invoices from suppliers may cover items for more than one client. The items can then be transferred correctly to invoices to clients and legitimate charges will not be overlooked. Clients will be able to relate the charges to decisions taken so that they can authorise payment. Taking this system together with the recommendations in **10** above, the consultancy is able to render explicit bills which are unlikely to be questioned. This ensures harmonious client relations and helps to maintain cash flow.

WEEKLY TIME SHEET

Week beginning ---------------- Client --------------------------------

	Mon	Tues	Wed	Thur	Fri	Sat	Sun	Week's total
Daily totals								

Fig 4.3   Weekly time sheet for a consultancy client. Time expenditures are entered as they happen. Each column is totalled daily and a weekly total is taken and compared with the number of hours covered by the fee – the time bank.

SELECTING A CONSULTANCY

15. How to find a consultancy

By studying the PR consultancy sections and client lists in *Advertisers Annual*, the *Hollis Press and Public Relations Annual* and the *Public Relations Yearbook* of the PRCA, and by reading advertisements placed by consultants in the business press such as *PR Week* and the *Register of Members* of the IPR, a certain amount of information can be gained. More personal information may be obtained from business friends, editors, trade associations and chambers of industry and trade. By such methods a prospective client can arrive at a short list of suitable PR consultants.

16. Shopping for a consultancy

One of two things can be done First, invite all those on a short list to submit competitive propositions. Second, arrange to visit each consultancy, and then appoint the one liked best.

17. The competitive method

This can be costly for the consultant because it takes hours to investigate the client's needs, plan a campaign, cost it and present it. If three firms are invited to quote, two will lose anything from hundreds to thousands of pounds in time spent on preparation of a scheme. From the client's point of view it will be unsatisfactory because the investigations made into his or her needs must inevitably be trivial and could be faulty. How can the consultant discover the current image without a survey? Remember the Mexican Statement (*see* 2:4).

18. The selection method

This is the best for both sides – unless, of course, the prospective client is prepared to pay for initial research and the preparation of proposals by all the competitive prospective consultancies. It is best because it gives the consultant the opportunity to be more businesslike, recommend initial (and perhaps continuous) research and so provide a more practical and satisfying service. It is the way one selects most professionals such as doctors or lawyers. It is not like seeking tenders from builders.

This is where the Mexican Statement is so sensible when it says, '*Public relations practice is the art and social science of analyzing trends, predicting their consequences* ...'. But this calls for attitude or image studies or even some inexpensive discussion group surveying. Advertising campaigns are based on initial surveys so why not PR programmes? The answer is *cost*. In advertising the research is small compared to the cost of the total campaign. In PR the cost of marketing research may seem disproportionate, yet without it the modest cost of a PR programme could be money ill-spent.

19. The methods compared

The difference between the 'competitive' and 'selective' methods is that the first can be a gamble, while the second is sound business. The competitive method invites or is satisfied with haphazard, intangible PR; the selective method demands objective-planned PR to achieve specific results. The secret of all this is that the second method reveals that the prospective client is good at business and understands PR, knows what he or she wants from PR, and knows how to buy such a service.

ADVANTAGES AND DISADVANTAGES OF A PR CONSULTANCY

20. Advantages

The PR consultancy:

(a) is an independent adviser, able and willing to criticise

(b) has wide experience gained with many clients requiring a diversity of techniques

(c) is familiar with more media than the staff PR manager in one organisation may be expected to be

(d) has more facilities, and has access to specialist services with whom good working relations are enjoyed – printers, photographers, news release distribution services, research units, translators and so on

(e) has skilled specialist staff

(f) may have a central urban location close to media, venues for receptions and suppliers of services.

21. Disadvantages

The PR consultancy:

(a) is remote from the internal organisation of clients

(b) probably works through only one person in the client organisation, at best through only a few people, and lacks the internal lines of communication open to the staff PR managers

(c) is limited in operations by the size of the fee, unlike the staff PR manager who works full-time for an employer

(d) has to share loyalties among clients

(e) may know little about the client's trade, industry or special interest, and within the limited time represented by the fee may not have time to learn very much.

22. Value for money

The point behind some of the above comments is that the client gets only what he or she pays for. If a consultant is engaged merely to do PR on the cheap, the results are not likely to be pleasing. On the other hand, it is remarkable how much one gets for so little in PR.

23. Would it be cheaper, or as cheap, to appoint an in-house PR manager?

Finally, a mistake is sometimes made by clients who think they can save money by appointing their own PR manager and setting up their own PR department, all for the same cost as a consultancy fee. When it is considered that the PR staff will be working full-time with full-time overhead expenses plus equipment, the in-house cost must be higher. So it may be better to spend more money on a more complete and intimate PR service.

Consultancy services are not expensive, although this view is often expressed quite wrongly by examination students. Perhaps it is thought it costs a company nothing to do PR itself, whereas one has to pay a fee to a consultancy! PR is labour-intensive, and whoever conducts PR – internally or externally – has to be paid.

Progress test 4

1. What is the PRCA definition of a PR consultancy?

2. What services may a client expect from a PR consultancy?

3. Some consultancies specialise in providing certain services: name five of these.

4. Explain the terms 'consultative service' and 'executive service'.

5. How do consultants charge for their services?

6. How do PR consultancies charge their fees?

7. Why should there be regular client–agency progress meetings?

8. What is a contact report and how does it differ in appearance from ordinary minutes of a meeting?

9. What is the facts book?

10. What are job numbers and what is their purpose and value?

11. Describe the two methods of selecting a PR consultancy?

12. What are the merits and demerits of each method of selecting a PR consultancy?

13. What are the advantages of appointing a PR consultancy?

14. What are the disadvantages of appointing a PR consultancy?

15. Is it likely that a client could employ an in-house PR manager for the same money as the cost of consultancy charges?

5

PLANNING PUBLIC RELATIONS PROGRAMMES

INTRODUCTION

In this chapter we shall consider how a PR programme, whether a long-term one for a year's work or a short-term one for a brief event, can be planned so that tangible results can be obtained. Again, we shall talk in the broad scale, but this can be adapted to suit particular or more modest requirements.

1. Four reasons for planning PR programmes

Four important reasons for planning are:

(a) To set targets for PR operations – against which results can be assessed

(b) To estimate the working hours and other costs involved

(c) To select priorities which will control *(i)* the number and *(ii)* the timing of different operations in the programme

(d) To decide the feasibility of carrying out the declared objectives according to the availability of *(i)* sufficient staff of the right calibre; *(ii)* physical equipment such as office machines, cameras or vehicles; *(iii)* an adequate budget.

The words to remember are *working hours*, *priorities*, *timing*, *resources*, *equipment* and *budget*. We are applying economics, that is the study of scarcities, for everything is limited. Constraints are implied, and as we go through the six-point planning model below it will be seen that maximum effort has to be exerted on a minimum number of projects.

Without a planned programme, the PR practitioner would have to operate on a day-to-day basis. The practitioner would always be starting new things and probably never finishing others. At the end of the year it would be very difficult to show what had been done and with what effect. It would be like running a train with no destination, taking no fares and eventually running out of fuel. Unprofessional PR can be exactly like that: purposeless and pointless.

2. Six-point PR planning model

The simple six-point planning model which is widely accepted by professional PR practitioners is as follows:

(a) Appreciation of the situation

(b) Definition of objectives

(c) Definition of publics

(d) Selection of media and techniques

(e) Planning of a budget

(f) Assessment of results.

The application of this model to PR in developing countries will be found in Chapter 21.

APPRECIATION OF THE SITUATION

3. Logical planning

This is planning by objective procedures, but success depends on the skill and efficiency with which it is applied. The kingpin of the exercise is understanding the situation, i.e. asking: Where are we now? What are their misunderstandings?

Before a PR programme can be devised, it is necessary to be clear about its starting point. What image do our publics have of our subject? This follows the military principle of examining the situation before a battle. It calls for 'intelligence' or information. If we make guesses or assumptions or act on a hunch or by instinct, we could be wrong and the PR programmes could be useless.

There is no point in spending money just to get 'favourable publicity' and a collection of press cuttings: that is haphazard, intangible PR, the sort which has earned deservedly harsh criticism of PR. A communications audit, that is a study of both the internal and external situation, is vital.

4. The PR transfer process

The classic PR situation is illustrated in Figure 5.1, where we see what confronts most PR practitioners. Their aim is to convert four negative attitudes into four positive ones. Ultimately, knowledge creates understanding: the principal PR objective is *understanding*. Sometimes this may be even of things people dislike or with which they disagree. For instance, it can be good PR for a Christian to understand Islamic beliefs and vice versa, or for drug addicts to understand those who are trying to help them and vice versa, or for members of different political parties or beliefs to

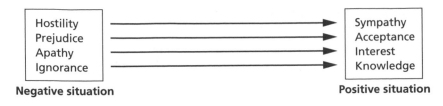

Fig 5.1   The PR transfer process

understand each other. The lion and the lamb may often have to live together. PR is not necessarily about trying to make others think we are wonderful. Tolerance may be an admirable PR objective, but it is difficult to tolerate something which is improperly understood. This is at the heart of race relations PR. Let us consider each of those four negative states in Figure 5.1 from the standpoint of *appreciating the situation*.

(a) *Hostility*. We must ask: To what extent does enmity exist? What form does it take? Why does it exist? Can it and how can it be overcome?

(b) *Prejudice*. The causes of prejudice may be parental, educational, religious, social or class influences, environmental, or just plain misunderstanding. Once there was prejudice in the UK against Japanese goods; now a buyer may prefer a Japanese car, camera or tape-recorder – prejudices change. Leon Festinger's theory of 'cognitive dissonance' may be applicable here. At first, people have conservative attitudes to new ideas and resist change, but once they have become converted to acceptance of a new idea, they become enthusiastic supporters and reject the old idea. The old idea could have been a prejudice. This could be the situation of the owner of a Japanese car who always used to buy British, but now is prejudiced against British cars; that attitude could also be reversed.

(c) *Apathy*. This is the worst enemy of understanding. Disinterest can be the product of selfishness, laziness, lack of imagination, or a result of the subject not having been presented in an interesting and convincing way. People are also very wrapped up in their own interests and unconcerned about other matters. The campaign to encourage the use of unleaded petrol, in spite of its lower price, and irrespective of appeals to preserve the environment, initially suffered from apathy. The secret of successful PR information is that it must – in the words of Ivy Ledbetter Lee – be of 'interest and value' to recipients.

(d) *Ignorance*. This is a common failing. In today's busy world no one can know and understand everything. In overseas markets people will know nothing about many prospective imports or their makers. So we have to accept that it is necessary to compete for a place in people's minds and memories.

It is very easy to imagine that other people are as familiar with a subject as we are ourselves, but such an assumption is often false and dangerous. Ignorance is widespread. An example of this occurs at press receptions when journalists, who have to deal with a hundred-and-one subjects, are confronted by a new one.

5. A necessary compromise

Recognising the difficulties in achieving the transfer process outlined above, the PR practitioner has to be realistic, not optimistic, for he or she cannot expect to be 100 per cent successful. It may be sensible to settle for a certain percentage improvement in, for instance, the number of people who understand, and this percentage may be further improved with successive campaigns over a number of years. Moreover, the PR practitioner has to recognise that new generations are joining the publics all the time. The process is a continuous one.

6. Investigating the situation

To arrive at a helpful appreciation an investigation is required. This may be done by observation, or by a study of existing information and statistics, which is known as 'desk research'. But it may be that no reliable secondary information exists and that original or primary research is necessary. Although research costs money it is an investment – sometimes an insurance – in success. However, the cost need not be frightening.

7. Opinion polls

One method frequently used for PR purposes is the opinion poll or attitude study, where an interviewer questions a sample of people who are representative of the particular public aimed at. From the answers given percentages can be produced of people of different kinds holding certain views. The sample can be made up of, say, men, women, married, single, in different age groups and social grades (*see* Chapter 20).

The result of the first survey would indicate an appreciation of the situation. As the PR programme proceeds, similar surveys can be carried out at intervals of perhaps six months to record changes in people's opinions, attitudes or degree of understanding. The trend can be drawn on a graph. The people questioned would have to be relevant, e.g. for an oil company, the respondents might be motorists, for a teaching aid it would be teachers, while for a baby food it could be doctors, nurses, mothers or expectant mothers, according to the nature of the enquiry.

This emphasises that much of PR is about effecting change, not just creating favourable images.

8. Problem-solving

When the situation is appreciated it is possible to recognise the problem and to recommend a solution. Public relations is often a problem-solving business: how can we achieve better understanding of this or that? Recruitment of staff may be hampered because of negative attitudes towards the employer or the job; people may not contribute to a charity because they do not understand its aims or think that it has been made redundant by the Welfare State; farmers may not use a fertiliser or insecticide because they do not know how to use it safely, economically or effectively; customers may not buy a product because they do not believe the claims made for it. These are PR, or rather *bad* PR, situations which can be corrected only if they are discovered. The existence of these negative attitudes, their nature, or the reason for their existence, may not be suspected within the organisation.

9. Methods of appreciating the situation

The example has been given of the opinion poll, but a fuller list of methods of appreciating the situation may include studies and analysis of:

(a) Opinion, attitude or image surveys

(b) Press cuttings, monitored broadcasting scripts

(c) Sales figure trends and sales report indications

(d) State of competition and effects of imports

(e) Share price, if a public company, stock market opinion, dividends and balance sheet

(f) Industrial relations situation – strikes and wage settlements

(g) State and effect of the weather, if relevant

(h) Customer complaints, product performance and test reports

(i) Discussion with sales force and distributors

(j) Prices and effect of price changes

(k) Market forces: economic, social, political

(l) Attitudes of opinion leaders.

DEFINITION OF OBJECTIVES

10. Definition of objectives

From discussions with leaders of the organisation, a list of objectives can be made. The range of possible PR endeavour may be surprising and formidable, but priorities must be determined. An assortment of possible objectives for a business company might be as follows:

(a) To change the image because the company has adopted fresh activities. For instance, a company which once made railway goods trucks now makes central heating appliances.

(b) To improve the calibre of job applicants.

(c) To tell the little-known story of the company and gain credit for achievement.

(d) To make the company known and understood in new export markets.

(e) To prepare the stock market for a new share issue or because a private company is going public.

(f) To improve community relations following public criticism based on misunderstanding of the company's intentions.

(g) To educate installers, users or consumers about the product.

(h) To regain public confidence after a disaster which had shown the company to be inefficient in some way, the cause having been rectified.

(i) To strengthen the company against risk of a takeover.

(j) To establish a new corporate identity.

(k) To make known the chairperson's participation in public life.

(l) To support a sponsorship scheme.

(m) To make politicians better informed about the company's activities, perhaps because of some impending legislation which could affect the company unfavourably.

(n) To make known the company's research activities.

This topic is discussed more fully in Chapter 6.

11. Factors for consideration in choosing the priorities

Fourteen typical PR objectives for a manufacturer have been suggested in **10**. Very different objectives could be listed for other kinds of commercial or non-commercial organisations – each one calls for a planned programme of action. Some of these activities might be best handled by an internal PR department; others might best succeed through an outside consultancy. However unless the budget is very large, not all of these objectives can be entertained. One possible solution could be to space out activities throughout the year, or involve many of the company's personnel in these tasks, or both.

Taking item **(k)** from the 14 objectives, much depends on how PR-minded the chairman is and how well he can cope with media directly, while item (f) might depend on the willingness of the works manager to cooperate. The PR manager or consultant has to exploit, encourage and integrate communications resources within the company.

To take a simple example, by cooperating with the personnel manager it may be possible to improve the calibre of recruits by improving the style of recruitment advertisements through use of the logo (company symbol), and by inserting copy which explains what the company does.

PUBLICS

12. Defining publics

The listing of publics for different organisations is fully discussed in Chapter 7; the need now is to apply constraints and decide exactly which publics can be reached, and reached effectively, within the limits of the budget, which is crucial information for the choice of media. If the publics are too diverse some may have to be sacrificed, while it may be that several publics can be reached simultaneously through media such as daily newspapers and television. Staff, suppliers, investors, distributors, customers and opinion leaders may all see or be made aware of television coverage. However, television coverage may not be possible or it may be the case that it would be more appropriate to direct special messages to separate publics, in which case television will be unsuitable and even wasteful.

Another difference between public relations and advertising occurs here. Advertising is aimed at target audiences, which may be the few groups of people who are the most likely potential buyers, but in public relations publics can be many and varied, maybe ranging from schoolchildren to Members of Parliament, and not only buyers.

MEDIA AND TECHNIQUES

13. Selection of media and techniques

A medium – note the singular and plural forms – may be the press and a technique may be a press reception. Five comparisons may be made between PR and advertising media as follows:

(a) Different media may be used for advertising and PR campaigns. For example, advertising may be placed in weekend colour magazines to which one would not usually send news releases. It may be possible to introduce PR material into feature articles, or the advertising campaign may concentrate on popular national daily newspapers. At the same time the PR campaign, spread more widely, may also cover regional evening newspapers in which the company is not advertising.

(b) The PR practitioner deals with editors, journalists, TV and radio producers, whereas the advertising practitioner deals with advertisement managers, space representatives and radio or television sales managers.

(c) Advertisement space and air time has to be paid for. Editorial space and programme air time is not for sale and is therefore priceless. Published or broadcast PR material is not free advertising and cannot be evaluated on a rate-card basis. It is wrong to apply this yardstick to coverage.

(d) Advertising campaigns are restricted to those media which may be expected to produce the best results at the lowest cost. There are various sources of statistics relating to the size of audience reached.

Circulation figures are authorised by the Audit Bureau of Circulations and represent the average daily, weekly or monthly net sales of the publications concerned. These ABC figures are obtained by supplying member publishers with audit forms, which are returned with a breakdown of the free and paid-for circulations of each issue. In the case of controlled circulation journals, the return will show the number of copies individually requested, company requested and non-requested.

The Joint Industry Committee for National Readership Surveys (JICNARS) gives figures on the number and kind of people who read newspapers and magazines and the JICNARS figure will therefore be much larger than the net sale or ABC figure.

The Broadcaster's Audience Research Board (BARB) surveys the television audience, a sample of viewers having set meters attached to their receivers to record continuously whether the receiver is switched on and to which station it is tuned and these viewers also complete diaries in which they record their viewing.

Periodic surveys on behalf of BBC and commercial radio stations are carried out by Radio Joint Audience Research Ltd (RAJAR). A panel of listeners keeps a diary of their listening, so that radio audience figures are obtained. These sources are vital in the careful planning of media schedules.

PR programmes generally use a much wider spread of media than advertising, although it is still necessary to build lists with care (*see* Chapter 9). While an advertisement may be placed in the engineering journal which has the best penetration of the market, a news release may be sent to all or most engineering journals. While an advertising campaign may, for example, concentrate on the press, a PR campaign may use many other media including its own specially created private media, such as house journals, films, slides or videotapes. The student should note that the range of PR media (*see* **14**) differs considerably from that available for advertising purposes.

(e) PR uses private media, such as house journals, which in some instances may be necessary because commercial media, as would be used for advertising purposes, do not exist. This might be true of an export market, especially in respect of the trade and technical press, and even more especially in developing countries.

14. The range of PR media

Having evaluated the situation, adopted a short list of essential and practical objectives and agreed which publics to address, communication media have to be selected. The following are the main media used for PR purposes:

(a) *The press*: national and regional newspapers; free newspapers; consumer, special interest, trade, technical and professional magazines, directories, year books and annuals.

(b) *Audio-visuals*: slides and video cassettes (for replay on a television set). Videotapes have superseded 35 mm films.

(c) *Radio*: national, local, international, e.g. tapes supplied to British local radio via Two-Ten Communications (formerly UNS), overseas services of the BBC, COI (Central Office of Information), etc.

(d) *Television*: regional stations, international (via COI). Also Prestel and Ceefax teletext systems by which information can be called up onto a television screen.

(e) *Exhibitions*: special PR exhibitions; PR support for exhibits in trade or public shows, overseas trade fairs, etc.

(f) *Printed material*: educational, informative, prestige, staff induction print of all kinds.

(g) *Sponsored books*: either about the organisation's subject, e.g. do-it-yourself manuals sponsored by power tool firms, cookery books by food manufacturers; ones associated with the product, such as road maps and tourist guides published by petrol, tyre and other firms supplying the motorist; or hobby and sport annuals published by makers of popular products.

(h) *Direct mail*: the advertising medium of direct mail may also be a PR medium, if personal letters are used to convey a PR message, e.g. mailing information to MPs.

(i) *Spoken word*: PR is not only to do with the mass media, and personal confrontation or 'eyeball-to-eyeball' communication can be effective whether over a meal or a drink, in an office, on the telephone or on the workshop floor.

(j) *Sponsorships*: for the arts, sports, expeditions, university fellowships, causes and charities, etc.; sometimes for outright advertising or marketing purposes, occasionally for philanthropic reasons, and sometimes for PR purposes. There is generally a PR element in all sponsorships, since they generate goodwill.

Fig 5.2 Pyramid selling: same product, different presentation. A new sampling pack, distributed to consumers, helps to gain awareness for PG's new pyramid tea-bag during the launch.

(k) *House journals*: once called house organs, occasionally called company newspapers. These are private publications as distinct from the commercial press (whether sold or distributed free). There are two kinds: *(i) internal*: newsletters, magazines, newspapers distributed to employees, pensioners, shareholders, members, subscribers or ratepayers; *(ii) external*: similar kinds of publications distributed to special outside readerships, such as distributors, users, consumers or opinion leaders. A very authoritative external journal may also be supplied to relevant editors and broadcasters with permission to reproduce articles or pictures.

This medium has developed in recent years, thanks to the personal computer, desk-top publishing, electronic mail, and international satellite transmission. The whole process of producing and receiving house journals or internal news has been revolutionised.

(l) *House style and corporate identity*. This can take many forms according to the nature of the organisation but in general it means things which identify the organisation. Airlines paint their aircraft with distinctive liveries, crews wear special uniforms, and a symbol is usually printed or painted on everything a prospective or actual passenger is likely to see. This includes timetables, tickets, luggage labels, check-in points, airport buses, condiment sachets and paper napkins.

(m) *Other forms of PR media.* Novel media also include, for example, the Goodyear airships which have been illuminated with PR messages and flown over Europe and North America; postage stamps to educate drivers and pedestrians about road safety or for other social purposes and first-day covers when new stamps are issued.

15. Media and budget

The PR media planner has to consider which media can be best used to reach the chosen publics, bearing in mind the limitations of the budget. The budget happens to be item five in the planning model, but we may have begun with a given sum to spend.

BUDGET

16. Planning expenditure

The budget is discussed in Chapter 11, and here it is sufficient to mention that PR is labour-intensive and that the biggest single cost is usually working hours. Other major costs can be the printing of house journals and the making of videos. The cost of videos may, however, be spread over more than one budget if, for instance, a construction job is being filmed from start to finish. Also, when made, the video may be shown for several years, so that future budgets will contain items for distribution, maintenance and updating sequences while the benefits of the original expenditure are still being enjoyed.

Videos are lighter and more compact than 35 mm films in their heavy cans, and they have consequently become more versatile in use. This topic is discussed more fully in Chapter 10.

ASSESSMENT OF RESULTS

17. Recording success or failure

This important sixth element of the planning model will be discussed in Chapter 11 but here let us note the following three points:

(a) The research techniques used to appreciate the situation can often be repeated to evaluate the results, the opinion poll or attitude test being a good example.

(b) The methods of evaluating results should be decided at the planning stage. Checks may be desirable or possible while the programme is being executed.

(c) Because the scheme sets out objectives, there are declared targets against which results can be tested, even if they are qualitative rather than quantitative, e.g. a more sympathetic approach by the media.

18. Other examples of PR results

On looking back, after a PR campaign has been concluded, at the list of 14 objectives (*see* 10 above) it should be possible to assess whether the new image is understood, if there is a better calibre of recruit, if the company is better known internationally, whether the new share issue succeeded, if better community relations are now enjoyed and so on. The results could be self-evident and not require special research.

It may be argued that PR was not the only thing to influence some of these results, but that is equally true of the quality of the sales people or advertising. The question to ask is whether the same result would have been achieved without PR. We have often seen or heard of companies surrendering to takeover bids, new products failing, new share issues failing to be taken up and both community and industrial relations worsening through lack of PR. The cost of PR is often fairly modest, and it is generally a good investment – the proof lies in the fact that our most successful organisations are masters of PR. This is frequently because the business leaders or officials are themselves good communicators: to be successful, PR needs to start at the top. The chief executive should be in effect the first public relations officer.

Finally, a planning by objectives approach to PR is something practical which management will understand and appreciate.

Progress test 5

1. Why should a PR programme be planned for a stated period instead of PR being conducted on a day-to-day basis?

2. What are the elements of the six-point PR planning model?

3. What is meant by 'appreciation of the situation'?

4. What is the PR transfer process?

5. Why is understanding so important in PR?

6. How can Leon Festinger's theory be applied to PR?

7. What is an opinion poll?

8. What are the means of appreciating the situation?

9. Suggest some likely PR objectives for an organisation of your choice.

10. How do PR and advertising media differ?

11. Make a list of as many PR media as you can think of.

12. What three points should be noted concerning the assessment of results?

6

PUBLIC RELATIONS OBJECTIVES

1. How tangible and intangible PR differ

The difference between tangible and intangible PR is whether or not there are objectives or whether or not public relations results are measurable. The critic of PR will say that PR is intangible and that it is impossible to measure results. The only reason why results cannot be measured is because there are no objectives to measure them against. Intangible PR derives from unplanned, purposeless PR, and of course that is bound to happen if the only aims are hankering after some spurious favourable image or favourable media coverage, or if the desire is merely to accumulate a collection of press cuttings. Tangible PR means cost-effective PR.

In Chapter 5 fourteen PR objectives were outlined but the list of possible PR objectives could be doubled, although they may not all apply to a single organisation. The examples are given to demonstrate how many different objectives there could be.

At this stage of the programme planning it is necessary to define the possible objectives. It is rather like looking at all the different resorts where we might spend a holiday. Just as we cannot visit every resort and are constrained by time and money, so it is with PR. The number of objectives we can entertain depends on the size and resources of the PR department, or the PR consultancy fee which represents so much time.

2. Defining objectives

How do we discover these objectives? We do not just sit in the office and say let's do this and let's do that. Objectives need to be selected purposefully. There are two ways of defining objectives. The first results from research which has identified problems which need PR solutions, e.g. lack of enthusiasm among retailers or staff ignorance about the company's investment in new machinery. The second results from consultations with department heads to discover their communication needs.

3. Choosing priorities

A number of worthy objectives can now be listed. It could be a formidable list but unless the PR resources are extensive – which is unlikely – priorities will have to be chosen. There are two ways of doing this. Some of the objectives may be of short-term duration, others long-term. More of the first kind can be accommodated than of the second kind.

For example, if a supermarket chain plans to open a number of superstores during the forthcoming year, each event can present a short-term PR objective. On the other hand, if a company plans to export to Japan this could be a long-term PR objective which could occupy much time throughout the year.

4. Objectives versus time

Clearly, there are constraints of time. An in-house PR manager (and his staff) have only so many working hours which can be calculated by deducting all non-working hours (e.g. holidays) from the total number of hours a person could work on a normal five days a week basis. Yes, he or she could work overtime, but for the purpose of the present calculation let us satisfy ourselves with the normal total of workable hours. During this time staff members can usually only do one job at a time or be in one place at a time. There is therefore a physical limit on labour hours. The only variation on this is that the better trained, qualified or experienced person can probably work more quickly or more efficiently than his or her inferior. The same arguments apply to the consultant whose fee represents time and expertise.

5. Objectives versus funds

A further constraint can be that of money. This governs the number of in-house staff and its quality, or the value represented by a consultant's fee. The question of money does not only apply to labour hours but also to other resources such as equipment for conducting PR – word processors, personal computers, cameras, vehicles and so on.

6. Effect of those constraints

Limitations of time, money and resources should mean, if a management-by-objectives approach is taken seriously, that the number and kind of objectives need to be tailored to the realities of physical feasibility. This has to be scrupulously built into any proposed programme when it is presented to management for approval. It is of course related to the budget, which may be pre-set or proposed, but if the budget is cut some objectives may be abandoned, and if management want to take on more objectives the budget must be increased. Any attempt to try to do more for less will result in a dissipation of effort and disappointing final results.

When objectives are set it will be like a railway line with trains being driven to their intended destination – if the driver is induced to turn down other tracks and complicate the journey he will not arrive at the final destination on time. The schedule must be adhered to, and this is a discipline which a professional PR practitioner must obey and the employer or client must accept.

This may seem a purist concept – or is it? When an architect designs a bungalow, and the builder starts building, it would be nonsense if the bungalow was converted into a two-storey house because the client changed his mind after the walls were half built. While it is true that in PR unpredictable things occur and have to be dealt with, experience should show the need to allow some contingency resources to cope with emergencies, but it would be foolish if the PR practitioner merely waited for things to happen before doing anything. Conversely, it may be that a planned PR activity has to be cancelled, perhaps because a prototype product has failed, but changed circumstances should not be allowed to wreck an otherwise planned procedure.

7. Effect of achieving objectives

When an employer or client can be shown the success of a PR programme that employer or client will have confidence in PR and be willing to continue and even expand use of it. This is important because if a PR department or a PR consultancy is in danger of being closed or fired there is something very wrong with its services. It should be irreplaceable and indispensable, unless of course the company or client has gone out of business. This is because PR should be regarded as a necessity and not a luxury. After all, the cost of PR is relatively small compared with that of advertising and sales promotion. Perhaps it is significant that one of Britain's most successful growth companies, Rentokil, has survived and expanded (in spite of periods of recession) with great reliance on every kind of PR technique, but spending very little on advertising.

In a recent report of a survey conducted by *The Economist* and Loughborough University among 1,800 business people and financial analysts, Rentokil Group replaced ICI as No. 1 in the chemicals and plastics sector of 'Britain's most admired companies'. Rentokil was also placed in the top eleven overall, equal sixth with Unilever, on its quality of marketing. It was joint ninth with Wellcome for its responsibility for the community and the environment.

Progress test 6

1. What is meant by tangible and intangible PR?

2. Name two ways by which PR objectives may be identified?

3. How can priorities be decided?

4. How does time affect objectives?

5. How does money affect objectives?

6. What is the combined effect of time and money constraints?

7. What is likely to be an employer's or a client's reaction to successfully achieved objectives?

7

PUBLICS OF PUBLIC RELATIONS

PUBLICS DEFINED

1. Public or publics

Publics are those groups of people, internally and externally, with whom an organisation communicates.

In the IPR definition (*see* 1:2) reference was made to 'publics' (plural). This is because – unlike some dictionary definitions – public relations activities are not directed at 'the general public'. They are aimed at carefully selected groups of people who are subdivisions of the great general public. Moreover, this means that much PR activity is aimed at these different publics in different ways, not broadcast with messages aimed at the mass market through the mass media as is often the case with advertising. Public relations is more discriminating and that often means that it is less wasteful and more successful for communicating certain kinds of message.

Each organisation has its own special publics with whom it has to communicate internally and externally. There are not just two big publics such as employees and customers.

2. Ten basic publics

Although the publics of one organisation may differ from those of another, it is possible to identify ten publics from which other publics may be derived:

(a) The community

(b) Potential employees

(c) Employees

(d) Suppliers of services and materials

(e) Investors – the money market

(f) Distributors

(g) Consumers and users

(h) Opinion leaders

(i) Trades unions

(j) The media.

While this is clearly a larger number of target audiences than one would aim to reach with an advertising campaign, it is still capable of subdivision. It is not entirely relevant to non-commercial organisations such as a local authority, a charity or the police. And it reveals how foolish it is to place PR under the control of either marketing or personnel management (which frequently happens), since PR concerns the total organisation. The PRO or PR consultant should, therefore, be answerable to the chief executive. A commercial organisation has to communicate with many groups of people other than distributors and consumers.

The media can be regarded as the means of communicating with publics, and media personalities and celebrities such as columnists and presenters may then be included among 'opinion leaders'. It is, however, completely justifiable to regard the media as a public in its own right.

3. Analysis of the ten basic publics

The publics outlined in **(a)** to **(j)** above are analysed below.

(a) The *community* will depend on the type of organisation. It will be different for a department store, local authority, nuclear power station, factory, research laboratory, hotel, airport, seaport, educational establishment, hospital, prison, army barracks or police headquarters. Even when different organisations share the same location each will have its own communication needs and problems, e.g. safety, noise, dirt, pollution, strikes, smells, car-parking, inconvenience and so on. A good neighbour policy is wise: PR begins on the doorstep.

(b) *Potential employees* may exist in other organisations, or can be recruited from schools, colleges and universities, or from overseas. They are not likely to seek employment with an organisation, or answer its vacancy ads, unless they understand what the organisation does, and regard it as a potentially good employer. For example, school-leavers may think working in a bank is dull, so banks have made videos for schools, showing how attractive it is to work in a bank.

(c) *Employees* can be of many kinds, some of which are: management and executives; laboratory, factory and warehouse workers; office staff; sales and servicing staff; and transport staff. They may be concentrated in one building or scattered like ships' crews, airline personnel, chain-store sales assistants or field sales people and those in the services. They may represent many different salary, wage, social and ethnic groups.

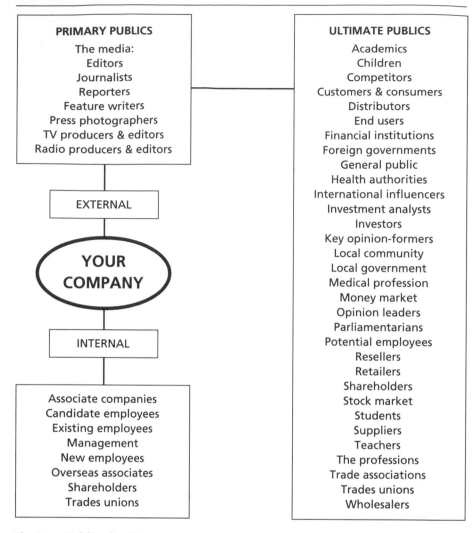

PRIMARY PUBLICS
The media:
Editors
Journalists
Reporters
Feature writers
Press photographers
TV producers & editors
Radio producers & editors

EXTERNAL

YOUR COMPANY

INTERNAL

Associate companies
Candidate employees
Existing employees
Management
New employees
Overseas associates
Shareholders
Trades unions

ULTIMATE PUBLICS
Academics
Children
Competitors
Customers & consumers
Distributors
End users
Financial institutions
Foreign governments
General public
Health authorities
International influencers
Investment analysts
Investors
Key opinion-formers
Local community
Local government
Medical profession
Money market
Opinion leaders
Parliamentarians
Potential employees
Resellers
Retailers
Shareholders
Stock market
Students
Suppliers
Teachers
The professions
Trade associations
Trades unions
Wholesalers

Fig 7.1   Publics for PR

(d) *Suppliers* can be of two kinds, those who supply services such as water and energy, and those who supply raw materials, components, packaging and professional services.

(e) The *financial publics* begin with the local bank and, if it is a public company – its shares being sold on the Stock Exchange – investors will consist not only of personal buyers of securities but also of investment analysts (who advise on share buying) and big share buyers. These big buyers – the 'institutions' – are the pension fund managers, banks, insurance companies and unit trust managers. Willingness to buy shares, or invest in new issues, will depend on what is known about the company's background, performance and prospects. A fall in share price could invite a takeover bid.

(f) *Distributors* – those who handle the goods in bulk between producer and consumer – vary in kind and number according to the organisation. Thus distributors may include wholesalers, factors, job rackers, commission agents, cash and carry warehouses, brokers, retailers, own shops, direct response marketers, discount stores, credit salesmen or tally men, direct or doorstep salespeople, incentive scheme promoters, premium offer suppliers, vending machines, gift catalogue operators, importers and exporters.

(g) Only now do we arrive at *consumers* and *users*, and the latter can include trade and industrial buyers such as 'secondary suppliers', as when the product is used in the assembly or production of another, e.g. tyres for motorcars, milk for manufactured foods. Public relations applied to marketing is often directed at this public only, indicating that marketing deals only with a limited range of PR's potentialities.

(h) *Opinion leaders or formers* comprise all those people whose expressed opinions can harm or help an organisation. According to the organisation, opinion leaders can be numerous and ever-changing, ranging from parents to politicians, priests to protestors. They are part of articulate democracy, but can exist in countries where traditional, military, dictatorial or religious leaders dominate. For example, in some developing countries family planning has won acceptance only after local leaders have become innovators and, in pioneering the new idea, they have, in the PR sense, served as vital opinion leaders. Consumers, environmentalists, newspaper columnists, television presenters, social reformers and others also figure among the galaxy of opinion leaders with whom an organisation may have to contend. This can be a formidable public, often prejudiced and ill-informed, and probably requiring face-to-face communication.

(i) *Trades unions* exert a powerful influence on commercial, industrial and political life in Britain. They no longer have the cloth cap image they may once have had. Today, trades unions employ specialists in every field, just as businesses do: lawyers, accountants, analysts, representatives and lobbyists. No company management can afford to ignore this.

(j) The *media* need completely different treatment from that given to the other publics outlined here. One reason is the fact that the media are your organisation's direct route to your publics. Another is simply that publishers, producers, editors and journalists have total control over what your publics see and hear in their media. A third reason is that every editor, correspondent, journalist and producer is constantly seeking one thing in their professional lives: a good story, relevant to their readers, listeners or viewers. Give them that, and you will always be flavour of the month with the media. It is a mark of your success in PR when editors contact you and ask if you have a story for them!

4. Reasons for defining publics

The major reasons for defining publics are as follows:

(a) To identify all groups of people relative to a PR programme

(b) To establish priorities within the scope of the budget and resources (*see* Chapter 11)

(c) To select media and techniques

(d) To prepare the message in acceptable and effective forms.

5. Results of not defining publics

Some results of not defining publics are summarised as follows:

(a) Effort and funds will be scattered indiscriminately in the attempt to reach too many publics.

(b) The same message would be issued irrespective of its suitability for different groups of people.

(c) Work would not be timed to make the most cost-effective use of working hours, materials and equipment.

(d) Objectives – if defined at all! – would not be achieved;

(e) Management (or the client) would be dissatisfied with the lack of results, and would be justified in regarding PR as being intangible and, worse still, a waste of money or the PR practitioner as being incompetent; the PRO or PR consultant could thus lose his or her job, or the contract.

As we have demonstrated above, and have already considered in Chapter 5, defining the many publics applicable to an organisation is an essential part of planning a PR campaign. Until these publics are determined, and sometimes not until priorities have been decided because it is physically and financially impossible to entertain them all, it is not possible to choose the media and techniques. One public may be reached by the news media, one by video or house magazine, another by mobile exhibition and demonstration, and yet another by word-of-mouth or 'eyeball-to-eyeball' personal confrontation.

PRACTICAL EXAMPLES OF PUBLICS

6. Three examples

Taking our ten basic publics as a model, let us now consider the main publics for three contrasting organisations: a charity, a national tourist board and a food manufacturer.

(a) *Publics of a charity*:

(i) Members, donors, voluntary workers, collectors
(ii) Beneficiaries and users of the service
(iii) Potential supporters and helpers
(iv) Suppliers of services and materials
(v) Politicians, political parties and groups
(vi) Central and local government officials
(vii) Medical and health professionals
(viii) Other charities
(ix) Opponents
(x) Opinion leaders
(xi) Media

(b) *Publics of a national tourist board:*

(i) Own government officials, MPs
(ii) Distributors – travel agents, package tour operators, convention organisers
(iii) Transport operators – rail, sea, air, road
(iv) Banks, credit card and travellers' cheque operators
(v) Hotel owners including international hotel groups
(vi) Motoring organisations – AA, RAC or equivalent
(vii) Visitors – holidaymakers, business people, students, conference delegates, sportspeople, motorists, caravanners, campers
(viii) Opinion leaders – travel writers, politicians, teachers – some of these being in the home country, some overseas.
(ix) Media

(c) *Publics of a food manufacturer*:

(i) Community in vicinity of the factory
(ii) Potential staff – local factory/office labour, technicians from colleges/other firms; management and sales staff from other firms
(iii) All grades of management, office, factory, warehouse, transport, sales staff
(iv) Suppliers of local services, e.g. public services and suppliers of raw materials, packaging, advertising and other professional services
(v) The stock market – city editors, investment analysts, institutional buyers and shareholders
(vi) Distributors – wholesalers, bulk buying chains and supermarkets, cash and carry warehouses, hotels and restaurants, retailers, and exporters
(vii) Consumers – present and potential, including schoolchildren
(viii) Ministers and government departments concerned with food, prices, health regulations and dietary matters; also politicians concerned with import of ingredients, export of products

(ix) Trade unions, trade associations

(x) Opinion leaders – dieticians, food writers, doctors, dentists, health authorities.

These lists of publics are not exhaustive, but there is sufficient contrast between the three examples to show how publics can be determined for every organisation. Especially in the case of the food PR practitioner, the whole organisation is steeped in PR requirements from the managing director to the factory gatekeeper. The PR manager's chief value will lie in advising leaders throughout the organisation on how best to communicate with their publics.

Progress test 7

1. How would you define 'publics'?

2. Why is it wrong to speak of addressing PR to the general public?

3. How do PR publics differ from target audiences in advertising campaigns?

4. What is the point of identifying publics?

5. What would happen if publics were not identified?

6. List the publics for *(a)* a motor-car manufacturer; and *(b)* a youth organisation.

8

THE NEWS MEDIA

INTRODUCTION

1. The international news media

In literate industrial countries the news media – press, radio and TV – are major vehicles for the widespread distribution of PR information. Where, as in the UK, one language predominates, there are multi-million readerships and audiences. This applies to popular magazines as well as to national newspapers. But, in countries where there are many languages and ethnic groups, the readerships and audiences will be smaller (and very much smaller if illiteracy is common), so that communication for the PR practitioner may be more difficult or demand special tactics.

Countries like Britain, Germany and the United States are fortunate in having large numbers of publications, but Britain is unusual and especially fortunate in having national newspapers which reach most readers early in the morning. Some small countries have national papers which are virtually the only papers, while in large countries, such as Nigeria, a newspaper with a circulation as small as *The Times* in Britain does not reach distant parts of the country until next day.

In the UK, the *Financial Times* publishes simultaneously in three centres internationally: London, Frankfurt and Tokyo. This is made possible, of course, by a combination of computer and satellite technologies.

In the USA the major newspapers are localised around cities and state capitals such as New York, Boston, Chicago, Washington, San Francisco, Los Angeles or New Orleans. However, there are newspaper chains and material is syndicated so that it appears simultaneously in numerous newspapers. By means of satellites, and local printing plants, some American newspapers are publishing nationally. This was pioneered by *USA Today*. In Germany, the popular daily picture paper *Bild-Zeitung* has a large circulation but it is built up from regional and local editions.

2. Understanding the press of each country

It is therefore important to realise that the press of each country reflects the history, geography, politics, economics, religions and ethnic groups

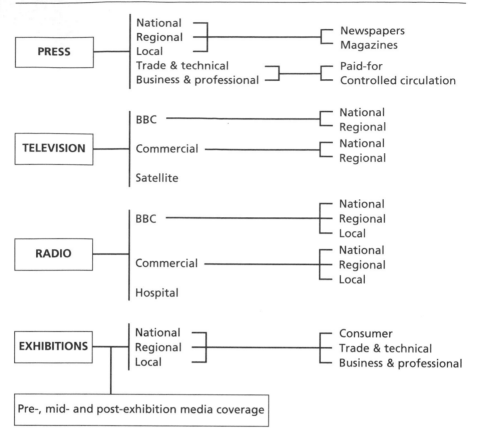

Fig 8.1 PR media

together with educational standards, the size of the country and transportation facilities. The historical background is important. London has been the capital of England for centuries and so makes a natural national press centre, but countries like Germany and Italy are federations of states and kingdoms and the original capitals of these are today's many press centres.

Overseas students may be inclined to believe that *The Times* is Britain's most popular or leading newspaper, and may be surprised to find that its circulation is only a few hundred thousand compared with the millions of the *Sun* and the *Daily Mirror*.

3. Study of media

This is a vital part of the PR practitioner's professional life. It has to be a constant and painstaking study because publications change or come and go, while in the developing countries, such as Nigeria, the press is a growing force with new titles emerging all the time. In recent years, there has been considerable growth in the number of newspapers serving the Middle East. India, which has an educated population as large as the whole population of Nigeria, has a very extensive press. The European press has changed with the advent of the EU, and British publishers have bought interests and developed the European trade and technical press.

Trading nations depend more and more on overseas media for both advertising and PR purposes. International PR has become increasingly important to exporters and a whole new world of media awaits discovery and exploitation, understanding and servicing. In the UK there are many means of enjoying the opportunities for doing this; to mention a few only there are the Central Office of Information, Two-Ten Communications, EIBIS International and publications such as the overseas volume of *Benn's Media Directory*.

But the news media are not limited to the press. The cinema newsreel has been superseded by television news, although it still exists in some parts of the world. Radio has long been a popular medium, and in countries where there is illiteracy radio carries the news to millions thanks to the portable transistor set and rediffusion which is popular in some countries. India probably has more radio sets than any other country in the world.

There is currently a well-engineered, British-made portable radio powered by a clockwork mechanism (Figure 8.2). This is ideal for areas of the world without mains electricity supply, and for group listening where batteries are beyond the pockets of individual listeners.

Fig 8.2   Clockwork-powered radio

In Britain, there has been the development since 1972 of local radio, with independent commercial radio claiming large audiences. Television is to be found in even the poorest of developing countries, programme content and technical standards varying from country to country. But important developments in the Third World have been community viewing, provided there is an electricity supply, and the car battery operated receiver made by the Japanese and widely available in Asia.

ORGANISATION OF PUBLISHING HOUSES

4. Four sides of publishing

Publishers are rather like four different businesses combined under one roof. These four functions or departments are as follows:

(a) *The editorial department.* This department produces the editorial content of the journal and sets its character. Each publication has a special individuality. For instance, at one extreme of the British press the *Financial Times*, *The Times*, the *Guardian*, *The Independent* and the *Daily Telegraph* are very different from each other. At the other extreme, so too are the *Daily Mirror*, the *Sun* and the *Daily Star*. There may be some common qualities such as political and financial news in the first group, and emphasis on gossip, reader contests, and sports news in the latter, but each paper has a recognisable personality.

Those newspapers which use contract printers, or publish internationally by means of satellite, have central editorial offices which send completed pages by facsimile machine (fax) to their printers for plate-making.

A number of British newspapers, such as *The Independent*, have no printing works of their own, but have editorial offices in London and use contract printers in various parts of the country, e.g. the News Centre at Portsmouth.

(b) *The advertisement department.* (Note that it is *advertisement* and not advertising and is sometimes called the *marketing* department.) This is a sales department which earns income for the publisher by selling advertisement space, mainly through advertising agencies, to advertisers. The cost of the space depends on the circulation figures (number of copies sold) and the readership figures (number and kind of people who read the publication) and the value to advertisers in reaching or penetrating certain markets.

(c) *Production department.* Not unlike the production function of a manufacturer, this department directs the printing of the journal which contains the editorial and the advertisements. Working with the other departments (including *circulation*), the production department has to forecast sales and produce the required number of copies which can vary from issue to issue according to contents and seasons and special 'boom' issues aimed at increasing sales.

(d) *Circulation department.* This is another sales department which has responsibility for selling copies through its circulation representatives to wholesalers, newsagents and street vendors, and for organising distribution by road, rail, sea or air. Road transport is widely used in Britain today due to rail strikes in the past and slimming of the network.

5. Editorial and advertising

The PR practitioner deals with the editorial department. There is no need to deal with the advertisement side, which is the business of the company advertising manager and the advertising agency space buyer. However, if the PR practitioner is responsible for both advertising and public relations he or she should remember the distinctions. The PR practitioner should not talk to an editor about advertising or to an advertisement manager about editorial matters. The editor and advertisement manager have separate functions. To explain further – because this can be a problem – the false situations should always be avoided of offering to buy space if editorial coverage is given or agreeing to buy advertisement space because editorial coverage is offered. The two should be kept apart, a PR story being published because it is worth printing and advertisement space being bought because it is worth buying.

6. Advertising features

Is this an editorial delusion? Some publishers devise features and supplements with editorial on a certain topic, the advertisement space being offered to advertisers associated with this topic. Very often the editorial is not produced by the editorial staff, but by journalists or contributors employed by the advertisement department or a special advertising features department. So, some of these features should not be confused with the main editorial content of the journal. Their value must be assessed very carefully by advertisers. While some of these features can be excellent and may be welcomed because of the special focus they place on a subject, others can be of very limited reader interest and a few are no more than revenue-boosting devices of value only to the publisher.

Equally, the PR opportunities need to be similarly judged with care. If editorial space is given only to those who advertise in the feature it is, of course, immediately suspect. Even when a small feature appears in one of our more respectable newspapers it has to be appreciated that the feature is likely to interest only a small proportion of an already small readership.

Advertorials are editorial features which promote products, usually as a reader service when, say, a new lipstick is offered by a women's magazine at a special price. This is a very old idea which was popular 60 years ago,

67

and has seen considerable revival in recent years. If arranged as a PR activity, the PRO or PR consultant must not pay for the editorial. This would be a breach of the IPR Code of Professional Conduct. There are also constraints on advertorials, termed 'advertisement promotions', in the British Codes of Advertising and Sales Promotion.

HOW THE PRESS WORKS

7. Editorial

In this book we are mainly concerned with the editorial function. How does the editor get material? With every kind of publication there is forward planning. For example, a magazine might deal with topical subjects in each issue such as planning holidays, gardening, motoring, holiday clothes, back-to-school, heating and lighting, winter fashions and Christmas gifts. A daily newspaper might have different topics on different days of the week – the Thursday book reviews, the Saturday gardening page and so on. Thus, the editor follows a pattern and has to plan the supply of material for days, weeks or months ahead. The editor does not wait for things to 'turn up'. Even in the case of news which is unpredictable the editor only has certain columns or pages to fill and according to the space available will select from the items which flow in from well-organised sources. The number of pages in an issue will be governed by the cost of printing them and the revenue that may be expected from sales of copies and of advertisement space. It is well for the PR practitioner to understand the highly organised nature of the press and the urgency and constraints under which editors work.

Equally, it is necessary to appreciate that, although a newspaper, or magazine, has a very large number of pages, there are only certain pages or a particular page or even only a feature or a column in which a particular PR story can be printed. Media need to be studied to appreciate this scarcity of space.

8. How news is gathered

The methods by which news, features, pictures and other editorial material are gathered may include the following:

(a) *Reporters*. These are journalists who are directed by the editor to seek information about a given subject. Some may specialise in, for example, crime, politics or sports, others will be general reporters. When a reporter has his or her name printed over a story this credit is called a *by-line*.

(b) *Special correspondents*. These are writers who specialise in subjects such as industry, shipping, science, education and so on. There are also war correspondents and foreign correspondents. These journalists may contribute a regular column or be invited to contribute when their subject is in the news. Some of them may edit weekly or monthly magazines on their subject, and contribute columns to newspapers.

(c) *Stringers*. Newspapers cannot afford to have their own reporters in every town, and so they have arrangements with local journalists (who often work on local newspapers) to cover stories for them. These stringers often feed local stories to the national press.

(d) *Foreign correspondents*. Large newspapers usually retain foreign correspondents in the principal cities of the world. They may work full-time for the paper or act rather like stringers, meanwhile working for newspapers or news agencies in their own countries.

(e) *Feature writers*. Usually staff writers, these are journalists who write articles rather than news reports, perhaps giving in-depth background to the news or specialising in topics such as politics, the arts or fashion.

(f) *Contributors*. These are outside writers who are commissioned (directly or through literary agents) to supply articles, regular features or short stories. They may also be known as freelance writers although freelancers tend to volunteer speculative material.

(g) *Wire services*. A wire service is a central news service which receives, edits and transmits news to news rooms. This used to be done by teleprinter, but is now computerised. In London, the Press Association supplies home news and Reuters supplies foreign news to their subscribers, the newspapers. Also in London, Two-Ten Communications supply the media with news *from* their subscribers, e.g. PR managers and PR consultants, using the PA service since Two-Ten is a subsidiary of the PA.

(h) *News agencies*. These are also firms which specialise in certain topics and sell news and features to the media, or which supply local news coverage. In addition there are foreign news agencies which gather and distribute news for or about their countries, e.g. the American Associated Press (AP) – not to be confused with the British Press Association (PA) – the New China News Agency, and the Russian Tass.

(i) *Picture agencies and picture libraries*. Major news events are photographed by picture agency photographers who, offering a rapid service, submit pictures to editors who pay reproduction fees if they print them. Picture agencies, and photographic libraries, also stock pictures on scores of subjects and can supply selections of prints for illustrating articles. The PR practitioner can invite photo-agencies to cover events, if they are likely to be of sufficient news value to be profitable propositions. This sort of photo-coverage costs the PR practitioner nothing. Photo news agencies supply national and regional newspapers with pictures by computer.

69

(j) *Syndication.* Publishers syndicate or sell the reproduction rights of material such as articles, features, pictures, cartoons and crossword puzzles to non-competing journals. This is an international source of both material and income. For instance, it justifies the high prices paid for sensational life stories.

(k) *PR sources.* Increasingly, editors rely on PR practitioners for news, pictures, interviews, ideas for feature articles or written articles. Journalists will accept invitations to attend press events to obtain news. They will also contact PR consultants and PR managers or press officers when they want information. Their source of reference is the *Hollis Press and Public Relations Annual*, which is the PR practitioner's directory. *Hollis* offers an on-line computerised service. Since the news is often to do with commercial or non-commercial organisations of every sort this liaison between journalists and PR practitioners is an important facet of news gathering which is mutually beneficial.

RADIO

9. The audio medium

Radio has been an important mass medium of information, education and entertainment for more than 60 years, but its importance varies from country to country. Some countries have public service broadcasting, the system being run by a national broadcasting authority like the British Broadcasting Corporation (BBC) or the Radio Authority, the former being non-commercial and the latter commercial. Others have private enterprise radio stations, as in the USA, or a state-controlled system as in countries with one-party or military regimes where the system is less autonomous than public service broadcasting is in Britain. In Nigeria, the NBC carries both non-commercial and commercial material.

Britain has had the novel experience in recent years of being provided with local stations of the BBC plus independent local stations, e.g. Radio Plymouth South in Plymouth, Radio Clyde in Glasgow, Capital Radio in London, which all sell time to advertisers and whose contracts are awarded by the Radio Authority. Hitherto, the only commercial English language radio programmes had been received from foreign stations, e.g. Radio Luxembourg, or, for a short period, 'pirate' stations located at sea.

10. How radio works

Radio programmes consist of the following material:

(a) News programmes: stations may have their own news rooms and rely on sources similar to the press. Independent local radio is served by Independent Radio News (IRN).

(b) Live studio programmes of all kinds including interviews.

(c) Taped programme material, including interviews, prepared in advance, taped in the studio or supplied from outside sources.

(d) Specially produced radio versions of television programmes, either live or taped. In the UK this applies to the BBC. The radio programme could be on a different date or at a different time from the television programme.

(e) Phone-ins, where a presenter – the person who leads the programme – suggests topics and listeners phone in their questions or comments which are answered by the presenter or a guest in the studio.

Except for all-news-and-comment stations, such as LBC and News Direct in London, and Talk Radio, a national station based in London, much air time is 'needle time', taken up by popular music.

Radio programme material, on the BBC national stations particularly, will cover a similar range of topics to that listed later under television, including outside broadcasts. But whereas radio drama can be read from scripts TV drama needs sets, costumes, make-up, action, outside broadcasts and film or telecine sequences.

11. Special characteristics of radio

From the following analysis it will be seen that radio is not only different from the press, but has certain peculiarities and advantages. However, it is ephemeral and, short of making rapid notes or taping broadcasts, it is difficult to retain broadcast material.

(a) Radio has the intimacy of the human voice and the attractiveness of the broadcaster's voice is very important. People will listen to a voice they like, although they may never know what the speaker looks like. However, there is the interesting example of Michael Parkinson, famous for his TV chat shows, who also used to conduct interviews on LBC radio each morning. His voice was unmistakeable.

(b) Programme material can be produced very quickly and inexpensively. A phone-in is instantaneous. An urgent announcement can be broadcast in one of the frequent news bulletins. Some large organisations, e.g. bus companies, have direct links with their local radio station.

(c) The transistor radio and rediffusion have brought radio to millions of people, including illiterates, in developing countries.

(d) In countries with many languages it is possible to communicate with all (or most) ethnic groups in their own language and regional programmes can be broadcast. This can be more successful than vernacular newspapers and can reach people denied television because of lack of electricity. Such broadcasting has been successful in Zambia.

71

(e) However, it is a medium which suffers from the dysfunction that radio listeners may use radio as a friendly, companionable background noise, music being preferred to the human voice. In developing countries there is the problem of broken sets.

TELEVISION

12. Television networks in different countries

Like radio, the system varies from country to country. Hours of viewing may be different; in some Arab countries television is restricted to educational subjects, or commercial TV is a recent development and there are still a few countries in the world without television. In Britain we have 'commercial' television, which means that limited advertising time is sold in breaks in programmes which are produced independently of the advertisers. Sponsored television means that the advertisers sponsor the programmes which include their advertisements. British television is divided into the non-commercial BBC1 and BBC2 stations, and some seventeen regional independent commercial stations, including Channels 4 and 5. These are known as ITV – independent television – although there is no organisation of that name. The authority which awards the station contracts is the ITC, Independent Television Commission. The current contracts were awarded in October 1991.

The contracting companies which run the regional television stations are usually groups of business interests which often include newspapers. They may sell programmes to one another, which are then networked and screened in some or all regions. They also sell air time to advertisers. A networked programme on ITV or a national programme on BBC may be seen by perhaps 15 million viewers. An episode of the popular British sitcom *Only Fools and Horses* attracted 24.35 million viewers in 1996. So, although an ITV programme may be produced in Norwich, Leeds or Glasgow, it may be seen elsewhere in the country at the same or at a different time and it may be seen nationally. On the other hand, local radio (with the exception of Independent Radio News) is purely local in the vicinity of a town such as Portsmouth, Manchester or Birmingham where one may also tune in to the national BBC or the local BBC station.

13. How television works

Television programmes consist of the following material:

(a) National news bulletins, e.g. *News at Ten* on ITV, and regional news bulletins produced by local stations. The ITV national news bulletins are produced by Independent Television News whose international news agency is World Television News (formerly UPITN). WTN has more than 20 overseas news bureaux serving 170 TV stations in 80 countries.

Another source of television news and archival material is Visnews (owned jointly by the BBC, Reuters and the national Australian, Canadian and New Zealand broadcasting interests, with Reuters having 55 per cent majority holding), which supplies international news to world television. Archival material may consist of historical film or stock background material which may have been obtained with PR facilities.

A new development has been the supply by PR sources of short video news releases which can be played during a news telecast, or retained as archival material for future use when the subject is on TV.

(b) Current affairs programmes, e.g. *Panorama* and *World In Action*.

(c) Sports programmes – mostly outside broadcasts (OBs), especially on Saturday and Sunday afternoons.

(d) Series on numerous topics, both informative, e.g. gardening, cooking, and entertaining, e.g. quizzes.

(e) Drama: films, plays and serials.

(f) Music, e.g. Promenade concerts, *Top of the Pops*.

(g) Religion, e.g. early Sunday evening *Songs of Praise*.

(h) Chat shows. The presenter interviews personalities; the presenter may become a 'personality' in his or her own right, e.g. *Littlejohn*.

(i) Children's programmes, e.g. *Blue Peter*.

(j) Science programmes, e.g. *Tomorrow's World*.

(k) Educational programmes, e.g. *The Learning Zone*, including *Languages, Business and Work*, and *Open University*.

Programmes of all kinds have been included to show the versatility of TV because, as with press features, news can be about products and services, interests, hobbies, personalities and all the things that go to make up the kaleidoscope of TV programmes. Topics like new books and theatrical shows often receive coverage on chat shows, when the author or a performer is interviewed.

14. Special characteristics of television

The special features of television as opposed to the audio medium are examined below.

(a) In addition to sound, television has movement, vision and colour, although, of course, there are still many black and white sets and old black and white films are still shown.

(b) In the UK, television is the great mass medium of entertainment, but in developing countries it is largely an élitist medium. However, changes are occurring through the introduction of community viewing in public halls and at workplaces, even though audiences are mostly male. In the West, commercial TV is aimed chiefly at the housewife. In some developing countries TV is regarded as little more than a means of amusing the children, and it is not uncommon to find a TV set on all day in spite of the cost, let alone the waste of precious electricity.

(c) The production of TV programmes is time-consuming and costly, the reverse of radio. But it is possible to make joint venture or cooperative documentaries, costs being shared by two organisations and a TV contractor.

The cost of television has revised attitudes in Britain towards the sponsorship of whole programmes, which on American radio was the origin of 'soap operas'. Now, both BBC and ITV are accepting and seeking sponsorships. Lloyds Bank has sponsored the Young Musician of the Year contest on BBC2, and Croft Port agreed to sponsor the *Rumpole* series on ITV. Currently, Powergen, the electricity company, sponsors the national weather outlook slot on ITV, and First Choice Holidays sponsors the London regional weather slot on Carlton TV. The *Guardian* sponsors *Film on 4*; Midland bank and Coca Cola sponsor drama programmes. In 1997, BT sponsored *Global Challenge*, the round-the-world yacht race; Bell's, the whisky distillers, sponsored Scottish Premier League football. Yet another innovation is the American method (offered in Europe) of 'barter' whereby a programme is supplied free in exchange for free commercials.

Some television shows are live, or are made during the week before showing, but others are made weeks or months beforehand. Advance production can make it very difficult for the PR practitioner to achieve representation of his or her interests, unless it is possible to anticipate production. A big PR consideration is that almost all participation in television takes up an immense amount of time, which is costly. This is due to the process of research, preparation, rehearsal and production.

(d) Being a predominantly visual medium, another serious consideration is that the material or personality must be visually interesting and attractive. In PR terms this means that great care is necessary in choosing people for television interviews, for viewers will be looking at both their physical appearance and their mode of dress, as well as listening to what they have to say. Television can crucify someone who *appears* badly on TV. This has been seen in many elections in North America, Europe and Australia where the sincerity or authority of politicians has been revealed by their appearances on television. 'Election by television' has become a truism.

The opposite is true in African countries. Africans are great talkers. The typical static studio discussions, which may be boring to a Westerner, are popular with African audiences.

(e) A press reporter needs only pen and paper, and a radio reporter needs only a tape recorder, but TV coverage requires equipment and technicians, both being in short supply. Television shooting may also have to take place on its own and at a special time. Camera crews are unlikely to attend a press reception or a facility visit. They will desire a monopoly situation.

DISTINCTIONS BETWEEN RADIO AND TELEVISION

15. How they differ

We have already made some comparisons but the following summarises the major differences between the two broadcasting media:

(a) Radio material can be produced more quickly and less expensively than TV material.

(b) Radio is more immediate, whereas TV programmes often need to be filmed or videotaped in advance.

(c) On radio the voice is important and the speaker is unseen, but on television the speaker is visible which may be either a handicap or an advantage. Dress and use of colour are also important on TV.

(d) Television audiences in industrialised countries can be much larger than radio audiences, which often means that TV programmes are more 'popular', appealing to the mass market C1, C2, D, E social grades (*see* 20:**6(n)**). This could be either excellent or wasteful, the right or wrong audience for PR purposes. Radio tends to appeal to different groups of people at different times of the day. These audiences may be people about to go to work or school at breakfast time, housewives during the daytime, people driving to and from work and people at work, who cannot watch TV. Even the milkman on his round often has a radio on his float! The commuter motorist occupies what is known as 'drive time'.

However, in those developing countries where TV is mainly confined to élitist urban audiences, and perhaps only to areas served by electricity, radio will predominate and have greater penetration of distant and rural audiences.

ALTERNATIVE TV

16. New developments in TV

A number of extensions and changes are occurring which promise to revolutionise viewing. The traditional format of programmes broadcast by a commercial or non-commercial station and, in Britain, commanding multi-million audiences are as doomed as 3,000 seater popular cinemas were by the advent of television. The process began a few years ago of giving the viewer the opportunity to be more selective. We are moving from the era of supplied information and entertainment to that demanded by the individual. There have been extensions to traditional British TV in the form of Channels 4 and 5 and breakfast television programmes provided by ITV and the BBC. However, greater selectivity will result from the increasing adoption of the following:

(a) *VCRs.* With the 8 mm VHS system, viewers can tape programmes and watch them instead of the ones on the air. They can also hire or buy films and other subjects on video-cassettes and watch these instead of the regular TV programmes. And as video cameras become more compact and inexpensive, video 'home movies' will occupy an increasing amount of screen time.

(b) *Viewdata and teletext.* As people more and more buy sets capable of receiving Prestel, Teletext (ITV) and Ceefax (BBC), they seek shopping and general information by calling up pages of computer-held data.

(c) *Cable television.* Again, the viewer is able to view programmes other than those put out by BBC and ITV stations, and will usually enjoy better reception from programmes which are received by cable instead of off-air.

(d) *Satellite TV.* Viewers having their own receivers and dish aerials can receive numerous programmes from British and overseas satellite stations. Some will be highly specialised and will supply minority audiences; some will be pay-per-view. These are referred to as narrow-cast (as distinct from the broadcast programmes of the big stations). Satellite systems exist now in many parts of the world.

(e) *Instant world news* is now provided by the American Cable News Network (CNN), its local camera operators transmitting news as it happens, using satellites. Apart from reporting wars from inside enemy territory, there can be the instant coverage of disasters which can have PR crisis management implications.

(f) *Corporate communications.* Adopted in 1991 by Ford and British Aerospace, this consists of private TV networks which bring constant news to company personnel.

All of these developments, which have been arriving since the early 80s, hold special opportunities as PR media.

Progress test 8

1. Why is Britain unusual in having a national press based on the capital?

2. What are the four sides of publishing?

3. What are 'advertising features' and what are their pitfalls?

4. Explain how reporters, stringers and special correspondents differ from one another.

5. What is a wire service?

6. In what ways do the Press Association and Reuters differ from Two-Ten Communications?

7. How does a picture agency operate?

8. What does syndication mean?

9. Why is radio now a significant medium in Britain?

10. Describe the ways in which radio material is produced.

11. Why is radio so successful in developing countries?

12. What is the relevance of electricity regarding TV in developing countries?

13. What is especially significant about radio being chiefly a sound medium and TV being a visual medium?

14. What is the difference between sponsored and commercial broadcasting?

15. Explain the term 'networked'.

16. What are WTN and Visnews?

17. Why is TV more time-consuming and expensive than radio?

18. Why is it necessary for the PR practitioner to be very careful about TV interviews with members of the organisation?

19. Why do TV reporters and camera crew require different conditions from press and radio reporters?

20. What do you consider to be the main differences between radio and television?

21. What are the various forms of alternative TV and narrow-casting?

22. What is CNN and how does it concern the PR practitioner?

9

PRESS RELATIONS

INTRODUCTION

In previous chapters we have described what public relations practice is, how it should be conducted professionally and how it should be planned by objectives to produce desirable results. Now we shall look at the tools of public relations, beginning with press relations. Because public relations and press relations both have the initials 'PR', it is sometimes wrongly assumed that the two are the same thing: press relations is only a part of public relations. Its importance and popularity depend on the availability of mass media and on the state of literacy. It follows that press relations is more highly developed in industrialised, urbanised nations where the mass media are abundant.

1. Definition of press relations

The role of press relations is to achieve maximum publication or broadcasting of PR information in order to create knowledge and understanding.

Analysis

(a) Press relations is not confined to the press but includes all news media – press, radio, television and cinema newsreels (where they exist). While other expressions such as 'media relations' have never found acceptance, *'news release'* is used in preference to 'press release', as it also recognises radio and television. However, 'press release' is still commonly used and is preferable to 'handout', which is the lay or rather derogatory journalistic term not used by the PR professional.

(b) The object of press relations is to 'create knowledge and understanding', not to print what the client or employer wants to see in print or to gain 'favourable mentions'. No one has the right to expect the media to print or broadcast anything, at least not in a democracy.

(c) As the American PR consultant, Ivy Ledbetter Lee, said in his *Declaration of Principles* as long ago as 1906 – PR is not as new as is sometimes supposed! – all press material should be of 'interest and value'. That should be the criterion of everything the PR practitioner issues to the media and that is how it will be judged. If it is of 'interest and value' to readers, listeners or viewers, the material is likely to be used and the resultant publicity will ultimately please the client or employer.

HOW TO ACHIEVE GOOD PRESS RELATIONS

2. Understanding the media

In addition to supplying publishable material, it is necessary to understand how newspapers and magazines are published and how radio and television programmes are produced. This can be done partly from the outside by examining publications and by analysing broadcast programmes. Visits to publishers, printers and studios are also very helpful. Very often, better understanding of the media can be achieved simply by telephoning the people concerned and asking them sensible questions, such as asking them about the latest date or latest time of day for the submission of PR stories. This is all part of the PR practitioner's continuous job of *finding out*. If the PR practitioner fails to find out, he or she will make blunders such as sending a news release to a publication after it has been printed. Much valuable information is to be found in reference books such as *Benn's Media Directory* or the *PR-Planner*, the first having both UK and overseas volumes, and the latter having UK and European editions.

3. Essential points to know about the press

The following points summarise what the PR practitioner needs to know about the nature of the press:

(a) *The editorial policy* – the journal's outlook and the kind of material it prints. For example, does the newspaper regularly print brief details of business appointments?

(b) *Frequency of publication* – Daily, weekly, twice weekly, fortnightly, monthly, quarterly, annually. The number of editions per day could be important, too.

(c) *Copy date* – what is the last date or time to supply material for the next issue? This depends on frequency and printing process. With national newspapers printed by contract printers outside London, instead of by the old Fleet Street based presses, copy dates can be early in the day.

(d) *Printing process* – is the journal printed by letterpress, photogravure, lithography or flexography (*see* Chapter 17)? Offset-litho has become popular worldwide.

(e) *Circulation area* – is it international, national, regional, urban or sub-urban, and in the case of provincial papers what part of the region does it cover? Satellites have made it possible to circulate journals internationally such as the *International Herald Tribune, Wall Street Journal, USA Today, Financial Times, The Economist*, and some Chinese and Japanese newspapers.

(f) *Readership profile* – what sort of people read the journal – age groups, sex, social grade, jobs, special interests, nationality, ethnic group, religion, politics.

(g) *Distribution method* – bookstall (retail), subscription (mailed), free newspaper (door-to-door), controlled circulation (mailed free, by selection and by request).

4. Principles of good press relations

Some general principles of the means of achieving good press relations are as follows:

(a) *By servicing the media*. With the knowledge referred to above, the PR practitioner will be able to cooperate with the media. He or she will create a two-way relationship.

(b) *By establishing a reputation for reliability*. Accurate material should be supplied where and when it is wanted. Journalists will then know the best sources of accurate information and the two-way relationship will be cemented.

(c) *By supplying good copy*. For instance, supplying good, interesting, reproducible pictures, properly captioned. Also, with computerised direct input, news releases should be capable of being keyed in with little need for rewriting or subbing.

(d) *By cooperation in providing material*. For instance, arranging press interviews with personalities when requested.

(e) *By providing verification facilities*. For instance, allowing journalists facilities to see things for themselves.

(f) *By building personal relationships with the media*. These should be based on frankness and mutual professional respect.

5. Conflicting responsibilities and different loyalties

The last point deserves a little discussion. It has to be acknowledged that the PR practitioner and the journalist have different, and sometimes contrary, aims and loyalties. Their contrasting roles can be analysed as follows:

(a) *The PR practitioner*.

(i) The PR practitioner's first responsibility is to the client or employer, provided that this does not offend against professional ethics, the law and the public interest.

(ii) The PR practitioner's job is to carry out the agreed PR programmes, the aim being to gain maximum knowledge and understanding of the client's or employer's organisation, products or services.

(b) *The journalist*.

(i) The journalist's first responsibility is to the publisher, whose policy he or she must follow, as directed by the editor. Basically, the policy is one most likely to make the publication profitable, the income coming from either the cover price or the advertisement revenue, or a combination of both. Nowadays, newspapers and magazines do not rely wholly on advertisement revenue, if at all. This means that ultimately the journalist has to write stories that sell papers.

(ii) Because of this need to satisfy readers, it is quite likely that what readers want to read – and, equally, what listeners want to hear and viewers want to watch – is not what the PR practitioner wants to publish or broadcast. Hence we have the situation that the media appear to prefer bad news to good. Disasters are often more exciting than successes, and it is perhaps characteristic of British media, for instance, that most audiences crave entertainment rather than serious news. The PR practitioner has to reconcile him or herself to these contradictions and anomalies; this is not being cynical, merely practical. It is known as the adversarial situation.

WHAT IS NEWS?

6. Newsworthiness

Since the PR practitioner wants to publish the news and the material will be judged by its newsworthiness, we may well ask *what is news?* A German reader may well consider that the British press is lacking in 'news', and that only the *Daily Telegraph* matches the *Frankfurter Allgemeine*. The American press is written into the Constitution as 'the fourth Estate', and the *Washington Post*'s exposure of Watergate was a typical expression of the role of the American press. In many developing countries, political news may predominate whereas it might be given little space in a popular British newspaper.

In Britain, a newspaper strong on political news will sell only 400,000 copies per issue, whereas popular newspapers sell four million copies.

The British press, however, is different from that found anywhere else in the world. For one thing, the national dailies appeal to different social classes and print whatever interests these classes. This class breakdown (*see* 20: **6(n)**) is shown by the following analysis (social grades as used by JICNARS):

	Social grade	Newspaper
A	Upper middle class	*The Times, Financial Times*
B	Middle class	*Daily Telegraph, Guardian, The Independent*
C^1	Lower middle class	*Daily Express, Daily Mail*
C^{2}D	Working class	*Sun, Daily Mirror, Daily Star*

In other countries the divisions may be different: religious, e.g. Catholic or Protestant; political, e.g. Christian Democrat or Social Democrat; ethnic, e.g. Malay, Chinese, Indian; or language, e.g. English or French. The point is that different people are interested in different kinds of news.

7. Definition of news

News is information which is not already known to recipients.

Analysis

(a) News is not necessarily about current events. It can be about anything which interests the reader. Sometimes 'serious' news about political or social events is called 'front page' or 'hard news'. It is the kind distributed by news agencies, such as Reuters and the Press Association. But news can also be about a new lipstick, company results or the horse most likely to win the Derby. Subscribers pay Two-Ten Communications to distribute 'business' or 'company' news.

(b) News does not have to be recent – if it has never been published before it is 'news'. Nevertheless, one does have to be aware of *stale* news: a newspaper will seldom report an event that happened days ago. But information about products may be news, however long the products have existed, if information has not been made available until now. Moreover, a PR story about a new product may well appear in a daily newspaper and then in a weekly and a monthly magazine with a considerable time span between each appearance.

THE NEWS RELEASE

8. The test of a PR story

Newsworthiness means that information promises to be of interest to readers and is therefore worth publishing, and these standards should always be applied by the PR practitioner to test all news releases, articles and pictures to be submitted and all press events to which newsmen and women are to be invited. The questions to ask are: *is this story worth printing, will this picture improve the page, why should journalists give up their time to attend this press party?* The PR practitioner must be his or her own judge of newsworthiness.

9. Bad releases are bad PR

A news release creates an image of the organisation in the critical eyes of the editors. Yet, all over the world, nothing is done more poorly in PR than the writing of news releases. Editors everywhere are very disappointed by the quality of the releases they receive, and this can be harmful to press relations as well as forming a bad impression of the sender's organisation. This is a pity because it is not difficult to produce releases that earn the praise of the editors, and some releases do.

A good news release should tell the story as the journalist would have written it, given the same information. It should *not* begin with 'We are proud to announce', nor use pronouns like 'you' nor contain self-praise. A news release must not read like an advertisement. The easiest way to learn how to write a news release is to read a newspaper. Very few of the releases received by editors resemble the reports to be seen in print. We shall return to this in detail below.

10. Good presentation

Four things contribute to the happier relationship:

(a) Releases should be composed in the style used by journalists, which is quite different from essay-writing, the writing of an answer to an examination question or the writing of feature articles. A newspaper report is written in a way peculiar to itself. In fact, good ones often appear below the by-lines (*see* **8(a)**) of journalists who are quite happy to accept PR stories as their own. This is success!

(b) Releases should be set out in manuscript style, not business letter style, obeying printing rather than secretarial rules. The PR practitioner has to instruct the secretary to indent paragraphs, omit full points from initials of organisations, i.e. IPR, not I.P.R., and avoid indiscriminate use of capital letters, e.g. Managing Director should be managing director, as in the *Financial Times*. Then the release has a professional look which is pleasing to the eye of the editor who is saved the trouble of having to make corrections.

(c) Releases should be appropriate to the journals to which they are sent. Technical stories for the technical press should be written in the correct terminology, but there is no point in sending the life story of a business person to newspapers which print only two-line notices of new appointments.

(d) Releases should be despatched to carefully selected journals in sufficient time for the story to be printed. This calls for skilled compilation of media lists founded on sound knowledge of what stories the journals print, the process by which they are printed and the latest date for receiving a copy. Each story requires a new list; standard lists are seldom satisfactory. For example, a standard list might contain monthly, weekly and daily publications, but release of a story might be too late for the monthlies and the weeklies. Their editors might be annoyed at receiving a good story too late to print, and they would be critical of PROs who were ignorant of deadlines.

11. How releases should be written

The easiest way to learn how to write a news release is to study newspaper reports and *observe* how they are written: there is a special technique. The following two fundamental characteristics will be apparent from reading newspapers:

(a) The *subject* is stated in the opening words. In a release the subject is rarely the name of the organisation but what the organisation is doing. For instance, 'A new route to Japan has been introduced by British Airways' rather than 'British Airways have introduced to a new route to Japan'.

(b) The opening paragraph is a *summary* of the whole story, and if no more was printed this single paragraph would tell the whole story in a nutshell.

Busy editors say they have 'one second flat' in which to accept or reject a news release. They receive hundreds daily. The first paragraph can make all the difference between acceptance and the waste-paper bin. The Press Association in London fills two large bins with useless releases every morning.

12. The seven-point formula

Here is a well-tried formula for checking data to be included in a release, for which the author (FJ) is well-known as the creator: the initials form the acronym SOLAADS.

1. *Subject* – what is the story about?
2. *Organisation* – what is the name of the organisation?
3. *Location* – where is the organisation located?
4. *Advantages* – what is new? What are the benefits?
5. *Applications* – what are the uses? Who are the users?
6. *Details* – what are the sizes, colours, prices, performance figures or other details?
7. *Source* – is this different from location, e.g. location might be where the work is done, source will be the head office address.

A layout using this formula is illustrated in Figure 9.1.

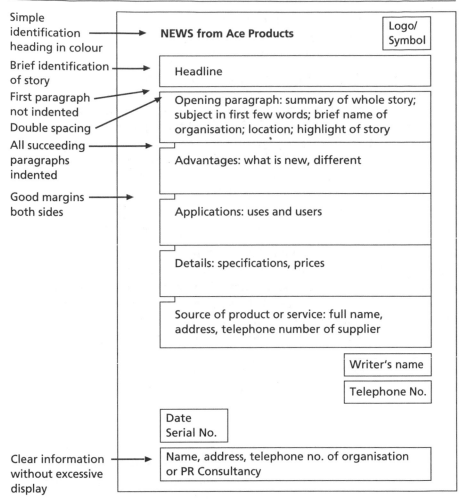

Fig 9.1   Layout of a news release using seven-point formula

13. Value of the seven-point formula

The value of the formula can be summarised as follows:

(a) The formula provides a checklist of data required before writing the release.

(b) It is a plot for the release, indicating the sequence of information, so that like information is presented in the same part of the story.

(c) It provides a checklist to apply after writing the release, so that the writer can see whether any vital information has been omitted. An editor should not have to ring up and ask for some important information which a more thorough writer would have inserted.

(d) The formula does *not* mean that there should be as many as seven paragraphs, or no more than seven paragraphs. It merely proposes an orderly sequence of the information.

(e) The first paragraph should state the subject; the name of the organisation (although not the full business name – Mazda rather than Mazda Car Imports (GB) Ltd, and Meccano, not Meccano Ltd); the location, if necessary or different from the source; and the highlights from the heart of the story. The highlights(s) could be the subject. The story is then substantiated with items 4, 5 and 6 of the seven-point formula.

Nowadays, when only the opening paragraph may be viewed on the VDU of an editorial computer, the 'intro' is all important. Never ever write teasers! Some journalists, when absent from the office, will set up their computer to store the opening paragraph of any relevant stories which come in.

(f) The final paragraph should state the full name, address and telephone number of the organisation, e.g. 'The Red Rose coffee pot is made and marketed by the Old English Pottery Co Ltd, Western Works, Overton, Shropshire, telephone XXXXX.' This paragraph may or may not be printed but it contains a lot of company information which encumbers the opening paragraphs of many bad news releases. After this should appear the name and telephone number of the sender, that is the PR practitioner to whom enquiries should be made. The release should be dated. If releases are issued frequently they should be given serial numbers.

14. Other kinds of news release

The above formula is ideal for a story about a new product or service, or new premises or structures such as colleges, department stores, factories, bridges, docks or airports: it can be adapted to many subjects. There are, however, other kinds of release which do not conform to this discipline.

Six kinds of release are outlined below:

(a) *The publishable seven-point formula release.* Ideally it would be contained on one sheet of paper. Remember how little space there is; remember also that if a long story is cut mistakes could creep in.

(b) *The background information story.* Not intended for publication, this release updates the journalist's information file so that he or she is knowledgeable when next writing about the topic.

(c) *The technical release with summary.* Technical products are likely to require longer releases of perhaps two or three pages, but the editor can be helped if the story begins with a brief summary of the story which follows in greater detail.

(d) *A summarising release to accompany a report or a speech.* Documents such as reports, catalogues and annual accounts, or drafts of forthcoming speeches, should be accompanied by a release which briefly explains what the document is about and draws attention to what is new or most important about it. Unless there is such guidance, the editor may not bother to study the document, and even if the editor does, he or she may not appreciate what is important or newsworthy.

(e) *The extended picture caption.* This is mid-way between a photo-caption and a release. It is used when the picture really tells the story and needs a detailed explanation. A double caption may be used, perforated so that the repeated caption may be detached and used as printing copy or an additional copy of the extended caption may be run off on news release heading.

(f) *The brief announcement.* Releases about simple items such as a new appointment, or a change of address, are best restricted to the single sentence or a single paragraph which the press usually publishes on such subjects. Business newspapers and trade magazines often confine new appointment stories to a few words.

WRITING STYLE

15. News release writing techniques

The news release is probably the most difficult thing a PR practitioner has to write in the sense that it is different from anything else he or she has to write. One of the biggest difficulties is that others – especially those who will authorise the release – may try to convert it into an advertisement or in some way destroy its validity as a news story. Such interference must be resisted on the grounds that it will imperil publication. As the formula makes clear, a discipline has to be applied. The following are aspects of this discipline:

(a) Short paragraphs, short sentences and short words are desirable. Apart from being characteristic of modern publishing style they are difficult to cut or rewrite and so the correct sense can be retained. It is better to say home than residence.

(b) The story should be kept to one page if possible.

(c) Superlatives should be avoided. Adjectives and self-praise can result in a 'puff'. Avoid expressions such as 'the world's biggest', 'the renowned' or 'the brand leader'. A news release must present factual information only.

(d) Avoid vague generalisations and explain everything. Do not use meaningless expressions such as 'economical', 'money saving', 'handy' or 'time-saving', but explain why it is such things, giving facts which imply the advantages. Do not say 'attractive colours', but state the actual colours and perhaps how many there are.

(e) Do not use clichés like 'unique', 'exhaustive research', 'a wide range', 'this point in time', and 'facilitates'. Few things are unique.

(f) Do not quote remarks from leaders unless they have something original to say.

(g) Do not use an omnibus release for all journals. Write different versions for different classes of publication, e.g. local, technical, business and national press all require different treatments with appropriate information.

16. Presentation of a news release

A release is a manuscript. As already stated in **10(b)** above, releases are manuscripts for printing, not business letters. Well-presented releases show that the PR practitioner is a professional who understands what is wanted. This is elementary press relations, a part of servicing the press. The following simple rules for press style should be observed. (Note that the house style of book publishers may differ on some points from that of the press.)

(a) *Printed heading paper*. The release should be produced on a specially designed and printed heading which distinguishes it from a business letter-heading. At the top there can be words such as *'News from'* or *'Information from'* followed by the name and perhaps the logo (symbol) of the organisation. The address and telephone number is best printed at the foot of the sheet. One colour is enough – flamboyant news release headings look like sales letters or advertisements, and so create a false impression. It is the story that matters and the release heading should be as simple and unobtrusive as possible. It must identify the sender but it should not try to advertise.

(b) *Headings*. Your heading should state what the story is about. Clever headings are not wanted; editors write their own headlines to suit the style of their publication, or to fit the space.

(c) *Subheadings*. These are unnecessary as the editor will decide whether they are wanted and where to put them. However, for the sake of clarity, subheadings may be introduced in a long technical story or if there is more than one item, such as Model A and Model B. Generally, subheadings are typographical devices used as part of the design of the page.

(d) *Indented paragraphs*. The first paragraph of the release should not be indented, although a few newspapers indent all paragraphs. Succeeding paragraphs should be indented.

Never use block paragraphs (that is unindented ones) with space between paragraphs. The whole piece should be double spaced, and there should be a good margin on either side.

(e) *Capital letters*. Do not write company or product names entirely in capitals, e.g. Cadbury, *not* CADBURY. Initial capitals should be used for proper nouns only, e.g. Smith, and geographical names, e.g. London, Lagos, Lusaka. Never use capitals for job titles; they should be managing director, chairperson, sales director, and so on. The titles of certain dignitaries are permitted in capitals, e.g. Prime Minister, Secretary of State, President, Professor, Archbishop, Chief Rabbi, Emir or Sheikh, i.e. business titles are not given initial capitals, but most political, religious, military and academic titles are.

(f) *Underlining.* Nothing should be underlined in the text as this is a printing instruction to set in italics, and that is the editor's decision, not the writer's.

(g) *Full points or full stops in abbreviations.* Sets of initials of abbreviations should not be punctuated. Write IPR, USA, IBM, or ITT, *not* I.P.R., U.S.A., I.B.M. or I.T.T. As you can see, these full points are ugly and waste space. However, the abbreviations 'i.e.' and 'e.g.' are given full points.

(h) *Figures.* Conventionally, one to nine should be in words, 10 onwards in figures (except in dates, prices, measurements, or addresses when all figures are used). Larger numbers should be spelt out if it is clearer, e.g. one million.

(i) *Dates.* The press style is to give the month first, and no suffix after the number, e.g. December 23. However, a few newspapers have adopted the style 23 December. Dates are not given 'rd', 'st', 'th' or 'nd' endings.

If the release reports an event, never write 'recently', 'today', 'next Monday' or something equally vague. This can be confusing for editors of journals published daily, weekly or monthly. Avoid using 'recently' as this usually implies stale news! If something is announced 'today', write 'today' followed by the date in brackets as appropriate.

(j) *Continuations.* If there is more than one page, write 'more' or 'continued' in the bottom right-hand corner. At the top of the following page identify the story with a note, such as 'New coffee mixer – 2', numbering each page after the first.

(k) *Quotation marks.* Inverted commas should be confined to reported speech or actual quotations. It is wrong to place quotation marks round product or other names. Publishers have their own house styles and while some may give quotation marks to the title of a book, play or piece of music, most will use italics. In a news release neither should be used, that is neither quotation marks nor underlining. It is now usual to use single rather than double quotation marks.

(l) *Embargoes.* An embargo is a request not to print a story before a stipulated date and time. An editor is not obliged to obey an embargo. Consequently, an embargo should be one which can be respected – because of Stock Exchange rules, or a time difference between countries or because the editor is being given the privilege of an advance copy of a speech or report, e.g. like the government White Papers, which Lobby correspondents receive the day before publication. Editors are entitled to ignore frivolous embargoes. Conversely, there is no point in stating that a release is 'For immediate release' when there is no embargo. If it is not for immediate release, why send it?

(m) *Authorship.* At the end of the release the author should give his or her name and telephone number. Quite obviously, this proclaims the conclusion of the story. There is no need to write 'Ends', which is a hangover from press rooms and the sending down of copy to the foundry on several small pieces of paper, one of which had to be identified as the last.

In Europe, North America and other industrialised parts of the world, it is normal merely to print the writer's name at the end of a release. However, in many African countries, the press expect the writer to sign his or her name at the end of a release. This is to avoid publication of unauthorised releases which may contain false information as has happened in Nigeria.

17. Exclusive signed feature articles

These require a different literary style. A feature article is not a news release and vice versa, nor is it just a longer news release. It is a totally different piece of editorial material requiring a style quite unlike that of a newspaper report. While the same rules apply regarding presentation, an article differs from a news release in the following ways:

(a) It is usually much longer, and so occupies more space.

(b) It is an exclusive, whereas a release is sent to all who may use it.

(c) It is unlikely to be edited or rewritten like a news release.

(d) The author's name is usually published and it might be an authoritative author, i.e. one whose name counts. An article may be written by a professional 'ghost writer' but bear the name of, say, the managing director.

(e) Unlike a news release, the story is not 'blown' in the first paragraph. In an article, the first paragraph should tempt the reader to read on and find out what the article is about; but it should not be a mere introduction, as in an essay.

(f) While the writing style of a release should be coldly factual and free of comment, an article should be imaginatively written, perhaps laced with anecdotes, jokes, reminiscences, questions, quotations, examples, personal experiences and opinions, quotations from interviews and so on. The vocabulary can be much richer, although there should be no 'purple phrases', name plugging should be avoided, and 'puffery' of any kind should not be introduced, although legitimate praise from a satisfied customer would be admissible. Clichés should be avoided.

(g) An exclusive signed feature article has a permanent life which a news release rarely if ever enjoys, being indexed and perhaps becoming part of the literature on the subject. Its life can be further extended by ordering reprints (in good time) from the publisher. Reprints can be used as direct mail shots, material for people in sales to pass on to clients, or as give-away literature for showrooms or on exhibition stands. Provided the information does not date, some reprints may be useful for years.

Feature articles can be produced in the following ways:

(*i*) They can be written by the in-house PRO.
(*ii*) A freelance writer can be commissioned.
(*iii*) A freelance writer can ghost an article for the chairman, managing director, or some other company personality.
(*iv*) Papers and speeches given by company personalities can be offered as articles.
(*v*) A PR consultancy can be commissioned.
(*vi*) They can be produced by Two-Ten Communications (*see* **18**).
(*vii*) They can be produced by EIBIS (*see* **18**).
(*viii*) Facilities can be provided for a staff writer on a journal to visit the organisation and write an article.

Articles can be time-consuming. First, the idea has to be created and this may require seeking the permission of the customer where the subject of the proposed article, product or service is in successful use. Then it has to be negotiated with the editor of a suitable journal. To write the article the subject will need to be researched, and this is likely to involve travel, interviews and first-hand investigation. Then the article has to be written, and drafts checked for accuracy by those who provided information. At some stage, photographs may need to be taken. Finally, the approved article has to be submitted to the editor by the agreed copy date so that it can be printed in the planned issue. All this takes time and accordingly costs money but the article occupies an important place in the journal and has greater status than a news release. Moreover, since it has been negotiated and discussed in advance, a well-written article is unlikely to be altered by the editor.

18. Syndicated articles

Syndicated articles are those which are not exclusive, but which appear in more than one journal. However, they should not be offered to competing journals and in offering such an article to editors it is courteous to stipulate that it is not being offered to editors with competing circulations. A typical example might be a holiday article which is offered to evening newspapers in different cities. Syndicated articles should not be distributed like news releases. It is best to send editors a synopsis and invite acceptance.

A syndicated article service is offered by Two-Ten Communications, using either supplied articles or articles specially written for clients. A basket of titles and intros is sent weekly to some 170 daily newspapers in the UK, whose feature editors can then request the article or articles which interest them. The articles are held by Two-Ten communications on disk for computerised transmission (*see* **23**).

EIBIS prepare articles for overseas distribution, translating them and distributing them to appropriate editors in the countries chosen by the client (*see* **23**).

NEGOTIATING WITH EDITORS

19. Negotiating publication

Articles should not be written speculatively, and then sent to editors hoping that they will publish them. The best method is to select a suitable publication and submit an idea, with the request that if the editor likes the idea, will he or she state how many words are required, if pictures are wanted, when the article will be printed, and when the copy will be required. In submitting the idea, the PR practitioner would vouch for the accuracy of all information contained in the article, promise to minimise commercial references, and make sure that he or she had permission to write about other interests if any were involved. In this way the writer is virtually commissioned to write the article, except that he or she will normally receive no fee. However, some journals do pay for PR articles by authoritative writers.

The negotiation can be by letter or on the telephone – editors do not have to be taken out to lunch! In fact, a busy PR practitioner who writes many articles would not have time to waste on entertaining editors. The editor wants a well-written interesting article delivered on time, not a free meal.

In other words, a PR article should be published on its merits because the editor wants to print it.

PRESS EVENTS

20. Three kinds of press event

There are three main kinds of press event, which are discussed below:

(a) *The press conference*. This is a meeting of journalists who are assembled to receive information which they discuss. It might be called at short notice and it might be held in the boardroom or a hired room. Hospitality would be minimal. Press conferences are often held at airports on the arrival from abroad of a newsworthy person, the facilities of the airport press room often being used, with the cooperation of the airport PRO.

(b) *The press reception*. This press gathering is more of an organised social event with a bar, buffet or lunch and a programme of talks, demonstrations and perhaps an audio-visual presentation. This may take weeks or months to organise.

(c) *The facility visit.* An individual journalist or a party of journalists is taken on a visit to, for example, a factory, an official opening or an outside demonstration requiring transportation, hospitality and perhaps overnight accommodation. This could include overseas visits to see, say, a winery, or to visit a foreign tourist location.

While the press conference is a more simple affair than the other two, all three must have news value and good organising is essential.

21. Organising press events

A badly run press reception is unforgivable so once again we are concerned with good press relations. The PR practitioner should abide by the following essentials of good organisation:

(a) Plan the reception well in advance, selecting a date and time which will make possible publication of the story by all those present. A good rule for times and dates to cover daily newspapers, weekly and monthly magazines is 'early in the day, early in the week, early in the month'. However, this applies mainly to a press centre like London, and other times of day may be more convenient in the regions or overseas.

(b) Choose a convenient venue. Can it be reached by public transport, or does it have car-parking facilities?

(c) State the timetable on the invitation card.

(d) Send out the invitations to named guests in good time, at least two weeks in advance, and provide a means of easy reply. A reply system such as a reply card, fax sheet or e-mail address, enables the PRO to know how many guests are likely to attend. Refusals and no-replies can then be followed up.

If radio or TV representatives are to be invited they are likely to require separate facilities on a different day or at a different time. They are unlikely to sit through a press reception.

(e) Make sure that the catering is good. Food is more important than drink.

(f) Rehearse and time speakers and make sure that everything required is supplied on time – video-cassette recorders, TV sets, videos, overhead projectors, screens, exhibits, samples, photographs, etc.

(g) Provide adequate press information, but do not overload guests with lavish press kits containing irrelevant material.

A mistake is often made of supplying irrelevant press kits in clumsy cardboard wallets, stuffed with material such as the chairperson's portrait, house journals, price lists and sales literature. Journalists show their contempt for such rubbish, dumping kits under their chairs, in the cloakroom or in the taxi back to the office. What they want is a story they can put in their pocket. Photographs can be displayed on a peg board, and supplied on request by the receptionist.

(h) Identify guests with name badges, so that they are easily recognised in the short time available for meeting people. Different colour badges can be used to distinguish staff from guests.

(i) Get on with the business and stick to the timetable – journalists are busy people. In large cities like London more than one press reception may be happening at the same time; it may be necessary to compete for attendance. Journalists will pick the receptions that offer the best stories. Editors of national dailies tend to accept all invitations, but allocate attendances on the day.

(j) Have enough hosts to talk to the guests, but never have more hosts than guests.

(k) Do not mix journalists with other guests such as customers. It can be a temptation to invite business friends to a press reception, but you have no control over what they may say when questioned by journalists.

22. Other aspects of press relations

Photography, photographic prints and captions will be discussed in Chapter 16. The special needs of radio and television are discussed in Chapter 18.

23. Aids to press relations: services and directories

The following are some of the information sources and specialised services which are available in Britain:

(a) *Advance*. Published by Themetree (*see* below). Monthly loose-leaf supplement sent to subscribers, which details under classified headings the forthcoming editorial features which will be appearing in the British press.

(b) *Bacon's Publicity Checker* – USA. For those interested in the US and Canadian press, this two-volume directory covers magazines and newspapers published in North America. It is obtainable in the UK from PR Planner Ltd, Romeike Group, Hale House, 290-296 Green Lanes, London N13 5TP.

(c) *Benn's Media*. Comprehensive two-volume directory of some 15,000 British plus 35,000 international newspapers and magazines, plus BBC and ILR section and media industry services. Benn Business Information Services Ltd, Riverbank House, Angel Lane, Tonbridge, Kent TN9 1SE.

(d) *Editors.* A six-volume directory, with new volumes published at monthly, quarterly, bi-annual or annual intervals. Separate volumes cover newspapers, radio, TV, news agencies; business and professional publications; provincial daily and weekly newspapers; consumer and leisure magazines; town and region local media guide; and writers guilds and foreign correspondents of foreign press. Also, Mediadisk Plus which links the *PR Planner* and *Editors* media database with flexible software. Updated daily by modem, the same link can send copy and media selections to PR Newslink for distribution. Part of Romeike Group. (*See* above.)

(e) *EIBIS International.* Writes, translates and distributes news releases, and supplies pictures and translates feature articles, to overseas press. 120 Wootton Street, London SE1 8LY.

(f) *Hollis Europe.* Covers EC countries, non-EC countries and Central and Eastern Europe. Details of PR consultancies, associates, in-house PR contracts, sponsorship consultants, research and information sources in 27 countries. Hollis Directories Ltd, Harlequin House, 7 High Street, Teddington, Middlesex TW11 8EL.

(g) *Hollis UK Press and Public Relations Annual.* Lists UK companies and their PR contacts; PR consultancies, often with client lists; local government, government and other public sector addresses and PR contacts, voluntary bodies, plus large section on who sponsors whom. Hollis Directories Ltd, Harlequin House, 7 High Street, Teddington, Middlesex TW11 8EL.

(h) *Media Pocket Book.* Annual pocket-book size compendium of media statistics covering national newspapers, regional newspapers, consumer magazines, business and professional magazines, directories, terrestrial TV, cable and satellite TV, radio, cinema, outdoor/transport, direct mail, plus economic and demographic information. Gives details of circulation, readership, audiences. Published by the Advertising Association in association with NTC Publications Ltd, PO Box 69, Henley-on-Thames, Oxfordshire RG9 2BZ.

(i) *PiMS International.* Provides computer-based distribution of news releases, covering media of UK, USA and Europe. Clients supplied with regularly updated media lists from which titles can be selected for specific mailings of stories supplied to PiMS by collection, fax or direct input. PiMS UK Ltd, PiMS House, Mildmay Avenue, London N1 4RS.

(j) *PR Planner/PR Planner Europe.* Directories of media contents and contacts for use by the in-house PRO, published on a subscription basis and supplied in easily updated, loose-leaf ring binder. Covers national dailies; Sundays, local weeklies (by county), consumer, trade and technical magazines; radio and TV networks, programmes, newsreels, news agencies;

editors, correspondents, features and specialist writers by publication. PR Planner Ltd, Hale House, 290–296 Green Lanes, London N13 5TP.

(k) *Press Cutting Services*. Many press cutting services are available such as Romeike & Curtice (same address as PR Planner), while PiMS offer an international financial press cutting service. Other services are listed in *Hollis*.

(l) *Public Relations Year Book*. Public relations annual published by the PRCA. The Association also operates *PReview*, a continuously-updated referral service for organisations seeking a professional PR consultancy.

(m) *Themetree Ltd*. Publishes *Advance* (*see* above); *Advance Feature Search* – fast information service on future editorial features; *Advance Feature Tracking* – on going monitoring of future features; and *Conferences and Exhibitions Diary* (UK and European); Themetree Ltd, 2 Prebendal Court, Oxford Road, Aylesbury, Bucks HP19 3EY.

(n) *Two-Ten Communications*. Provides wire and news release distribution services. Many other support services are provided including City news service, supply of feature articles, picture wire service, radio interviews, editorial assignments, and UK and European media guides (11,000 entries in UK edition), plus international news distribution services. Communications House, 210 Old Street, London EC1V 9UN.

(o) *Willings Press Guide*. Annual which lists in alphabetical order UK newspapers and magazines. Also European edition. British Media Publications, Windsor Court, East Grinstead House, East Grinstead, West Sussex RH19 1XA.

24. Doing the favours

In conclusion, press relations consist of *doing* the favours, not receiving them, and the media would be the poorer if there were no PR practitioners. The media would be uninformed about thousands of topics of interest and value to readers and audiences. PR practitioners help editors and producers to do their jobs and in so doing help to create knowledge and understanding regarding their organisation.

Progress test 9

1. What is the role of press relations?

2. State the two criteria of PR press material, as declared by Ivy Ledbetter Lee.

3. What does the PR practitioner need to know about the nature of the press in order to understand its needs, and so achieve a good working relationship?

4. What are the principles of good press relations?

5. How would you define the responsibilities of the PR practitioner in relation to the media?

6. What are social grades?

7. What is 'news'?

8. What is meant by 'newsworthiness'?

9. What are the two characteristics of newspaper reports?

10. Explain the significance of 'SOLAADS'.

11. There are six kinds of new release. What are they and on what occasions would you use each one?

12. What is a 'puff' and why do editors dislike and reject news releases which contain 'puffery'?

13. What is a cliché? Give some examples of clichés which often spoil news releases.

14. What general rule applies to the use of capital letters in news releases?

15. Why should there be no underlining in a news release?

16. Is it correct to punctuate initials of organisations, e.g. E.C. and U.N.E.S.C.O.?

17. How should numbers be set out in news releases?

18. How would you write 27th June 1997 in a news release?

19. What is an embargo and when should it be used when sending news to the media?

20. Explain the difference between an exclusive feature article and a syndicated feature article.

21. How would you go about getting an article published?

22. In writing a feature article why would you not only avoid name-plugging but promise the editor that commercial references would be kept to a minimum?

23. Distinguish between the various kinds of press event.

24. What are the essential considerations when planning a press conference?

25. What is meant by the statement 'press relations consist of doing favours, not receiving them'?

10

CREATED PRIVATE MEDIA

INTRODUCTION

In order to reach certain publics to achieve particular objectives, the mass media of press, radio and television may not be appropriate, especially if these publics comprise small or specialised groups. One public which immediately comes to mind is the staff (or the membership) who may be best reached by house journal. In this chapter, created private, rather than commercial public, media will be discussed. The main forms are:

House journals
Videos
Slides
Audio cassettes
Educational literature
The spoken word
Seminars and conferences
Private exhibitions

HOUSE JOURNALS

1. House journals

In this section we discuss two kinds of *house journal* (once called house organ and now sometimes called company newspaper), these being the internal (staff or employee) magazine or newspaper, and the external (which should be targeted at a specific outside readership). House journals should not be confused with controlled circulation journals which are commercial publications.

Publications distributed to members or supporters of organisations such as professional institutes, universities, societies, trade unions and charities are best described as semi-externals. While theirs is not a staff readership it is a more intimately involved readership than the users, patrons, customers, dealers, shareholders or opinion leaders to which externals may be directed.

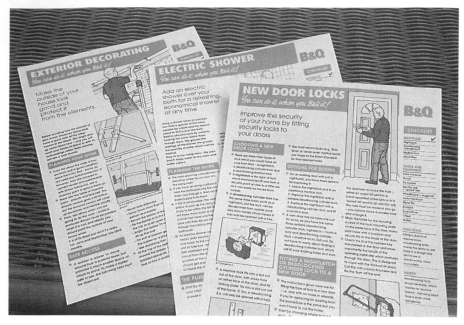

Fig 10.1a   Educational literature: practical ideas and solutions help promote a company's products in a user-friendly way, and enhance its helpful image

Fig 10.1b   Educational literature: helpful material at the point of sale is good public relations, but products mentioned must be in the store

2. Types of house journal

In this section 'journal' will be taken in the widest sense to mean printed media issued regularly.

(a) *Magazines*. This kind of house journal has a magazine format, the favourite page size being A4 (297 × 110 mm). The content will be mainly feature articles and illustrations. The printing process may be lithography or photogravure.

(b) *Newspapers*. Often resembling a tabloid newspaper, the content will consist mainly of news items supported by feature articles and illustrations. The printing process is usually offset-litho, and in the UK this is mostly web-offset-litho (*see* Chapter 17).

(c) *Newsletter*. Consisting of perhaps two to eight pages, a newsletter may be A4 size and contain brief items with or without pictures. It may be printed by lithography or could be produced on an office copier.

(d) *Wall newspaper*. Produced like a small poster and fixed to walls, this is a medium used for both internal and external use. Wall newspapers are often seen outside London Underground stations, especially when there is news to tell about new lines and services. They are also used for similar purposes on rail stations.

New forms of house journal are discussed in **21** below.

CONSIDERATIONS WHEN PLANNING A NEW HOUSE JOURNAL

3. Readership

Who will read this publication? Are different journals necessary for different readers, e.g. management and executives on the one hand, factory staff on the other? The readership has to be recognised and understood just as seriously as with a commercial journal. This will influence the style and content.

It can be a mistake to attempt to make one journal serve too many grades or kinds of staff. Field sales people may not necessarily want to read about the activities of factory staff whom they never meet, and vice versa.

4. Quantity

How many copies are required of each issue? This will affect the method of production and the quality of materials and content.

5. Frequency

The journal should be published regularly and have a known publication date. How often it is to be published: quarterly, monthly, fortnightly, weekly or daily? Daily may seem unusual, but Caltex Pacifica Indonesia did issue a daily bulletin for more than 30 years.

6. Policy

What is the purpose of the journal? Paternal free-gift house organs are relics of the past. Is it to inform readers about the organisation, provide a link for employees or members of a scattered organisation, help dealers to understand and sell the product or to provide a forum for readers' experiences and views? The house journal should fit in with the overall PR programme and be a means of reaching a defined public in order to achieve a definite objective.

7. Title

What is the journal to be called, and what sort of masthead (title design) will it have? The title should be distinctive and characteristic. It could borrow a typical newspaper form like *Ford News*, or be distinguished like the American Express magazine *Departures*. Care should be given to this decision because it is unwise to change titles once one has become familiar.

8. Printing process

Will it be printed by photogravure or some form of lithography, ranging from office machine to web-offset (*see* Chapter 17)? Choice of process will be guided by several factors such as the length of the run, the quantity of pages, use of colour, number of pictures, quality required and whether it is mainly typographical. In some countries only one process, say offset-litho, will be available.

9. Style and format

The size of the page, how many columns to the page, black and white or colour, typography, extent of illustrations, balance of news and features all contribute to the appearance.

Ideally, a house journal should resemble a commercial journal if it is to be credible. It should be as interesting as any journal the reader would normally buy. Credibility can be killed if heavy or shiny paper is used for a tabloid newspaper. It can be foolish to make the journal look prestigious when the real purpose is to get it read. For example, *Ford News* looks very much like the newspapers Ford workers normally buy.

Pages should be designed to make the material interesting, readable and legible. Studio designers can destroy such elementary needs when they use unjustified righthand edges, unindented block paragraphs, few subheadings and reverse type on pale coloured backgrounds.

10. Free issue or cover price

Will it be issued free of charge, or will readers be asked to pay a cover price? This can depend upon the value which readers place upon the journal. Some famous large-circulation house journals are sold like regular newspapers.

11. Advertisements

Will it carry advertisements, e.g. staff sales and wants, company advertising or outside commercial advertising? A good circulation with an influential readership may be attractive to national advertisers. In some journals, employees are invited to insert small classified ads free of charge. They add greatly to the readers' interest. The presence of advertising can add realism to a house journal.

12. Distribution

How will copies reach readers? By post, hand distribution round the premises, with salaries and wages, or at distribution points? Postal distribution to readers' homes is often the best method, with the possible bonus of family readership. However this entails the cost of envelopes or wrappers plus postage, and requires a regularly updated database of addresses.

BUDGETING

13. Cost variables

From the above it will be realised that many factors affect the cost, and these factors offer many variables and permutations. For instance, more copies can be produced of a journal printed less frequently, with fewer pages, on cheaper paper, with fewer pictures or in black and white rather than with a second colour or full colour.

The importance of each factor must be taken into account, but it is possible that the two things which will govern the costings, are as follows:

(a) A given circulation figure because a certain number of employees, members, ratepayers, donors or dealers have to be reached.

(b) The existence of a given budget because it is part of the overall PR budget for the programme of which the house journal is an integral part.

14. Considerations

In such a situation it will be necessary to consider the following points:

(a) How often a journal of a certain number of pages and of a certain production standard can be produced for the money.

(b) To what extent the achievement of the objectives, and the kind of readership will affect all the decisions in **(a)**.

(c) The value of any income, if any, from sale of copies and/or sale of advertisement space, which will offset costs.

(d) The value of the journal as a means of achieving PR objectives. For example, it could be the principal medium for reaching an important public. For an exporter to developing countries where there was a dearth of technical journals, a privately published technical journal could be a most cost-effective part of the PR plan.

(e) Working-hour expenditure has also to be considered. Can the PR manager accept editorship within his or her workload? Or will a full-time editor and even an assistant editor have to be employed? Will an outside designer have to be engaged (*see* **16**)? Or will the whole job be placed with a specialist consultant?

(f) If the journal is to be pictorial, will pictures be supplied free of charge by readers or other suppliers, or will professional photographers or photographic agency fees have to be paid?

PRODUCTION

15. Planning issues and obtaining the material

If an editor sits waiting for copy to arrive, there will soon be nothing to print. In Chapter 8 we described the numerous ways in which commercial editors obtain news, features and pictures and also how future issues are planned. The industrial editor must also plan issues and be sure of the supply of material. The editor needs to know what is going to appear in future issues and where the articles, news stories and pictures are coming from. The outline set out below could be followed:

(a) Each issue can have standard items such as the front cover picture, news from each branch, factory, region or subsidiary company, regular columns on set topics, readers' letters, best sales of the month awards and so on. Regular contributors can be appointed and the editor can arrange interviews or arrange for the writing of articles. Space can be allocated accordingly.

(b) In large organisations the editor can appoint local correspondents who will be responsible for supplying by a given date news about their sections, areas or branches.

(c) The editor can commission photographs of topical events, or to illustrate articles. This may include a seasonal picture for the front cover.

In other words, the editor must know what is wanted and instruct contributors very carefully. It is no use asking someone 'to write an article'. The subject must be discussed with the writer and they must be told how many words to write, what to write about and when the article must be delivered.

Not everyone can write articles, not even senior management. The editor may have to base articles on interviews, tape recordings or notes, virtually 'ghost writing' the article although it will be attributed to the personality.

16. Designing the journal

Mention was made in **14(e)** of an outside designer. This may not be necessary if the PR manager or member of the PR staff is capable of designing print. It is not just a matter of sending copy and pictures to the printer and hoping for the best. A layout (plan for the printer) has to be produced for each page. Headlines have to be carefully positioned. The size, shape and position of photographs have to be decided, including the extent to which they can be cropped (trimmed) for the best effect. For example, a portrait may be improved by cutting out the area of picture below the knot of a man's tie – otherwise the picture looks like a cottage loaf, small head and big body. Columns must not end in blank patches because the copy was short. The typography should be legible with sufficient contrast in sizes and weights of type to make the page attractive.

The appearance of a journal is very important and there should be consistency of style from one issue to the next. If you look at commercial newspapers and magazines you will notice that each one is recognisable and distinguishable from the others. They may change their style over a period of time but not from day to day. *The Times* no longer carries classified ads on the front page as it originally did, but it is utterly different in appearance from any other newspaper. It could be recognised upside-down and without the title being visible.

If an outside designer is used he or she should be a specialist in house journal production. Some are also house journal printers. The designer should not be just an art studio, which may produce pretty designs but illegible typography, like white words on a yellow background! Nor should the designer be an advertising agent who might probably know nothing about PR and produce a flamboyant piece of sales literature. Remember, designers tend to think in terms of how shapes and colours look, not words to read.

Today, many house journals are created by desk-top publishing methods using, say, Apple-Macintosh computers, on which pages are composed and designed, final copy often being sent on-line direct to the printer. In London the Corporate Publishing Division of PR consultancy Dewe Rogerson produces some 35 printed house journals plus a number of electronic publications.

EXTERNALS

17. Non-employee journals

The proportion of externals to internals is constantly increasing. This medium has existed as a major form of PR since the mid-nineteenth century in the USA, when one was issued to customers by the Singer Sewing Machine Company. It is part of the history of public relations. It is also being realised that it will not do merely to distribute copies of the staff journal to outsiders. They are not interested in the domestic affairs of an organisation and the glossy prestige magazine has had its day. Externals have to work hard to achieve set targets. The considerations for house journals listed earlier apply here too, especially the question of well-defined readership. The size of the desired readership could be prohibitive, as when a consumer product is retailed by hundreds of thousands of stockists, making a dealer magazine too costly to entertain.

18. Specific publics and readerships

Seldom is it satisfactory for an external to be dispersed among a mixture of publics and so externals should be pitched at particular readers as follows:

(a) *Distributors* – to familiarise them with the policy of a supplier, to educate them about the product or service and its usage or benefits, to help them with the efficient operation of their business, and to advise them on how to promote sales.

(b) *Users and consumers* – to educate them about the merits and applications of the product or service. In the case of an ingredient or component the user could be a specifier, formulator or designer.

(c) *Patrons* – a journal may be issued as a service to airline passengers, hotel guests, railway passengers, or theatre-goers. There are specialist firms which produce in-flight magazines (which are listed in *Benn's Media Directory*).

(d) *Opinion leaders* – to inform them about the organisation and its story, policy, achievements, research work and so on. Opinion leaders could be politicians, people in business, academics, investment analysts, parents, teachers and others relevant to the PR programme.

(e) *Future customers* – a good example being children who could be taught oral hygiene, road safety, good handwriting and so forth through young people's comics and magazines. In developing countries this is a medium ripe for introduction alongside primary education, for there is a dearth of children's publications.

(f) *Customers of shops* – a number of stores communicate with their customers by the free issue or sale of a store journal. This is a very old form of external, going back to the *Wheatsheaf* issued by Co-ops and *Foylibra* issued by Foyles bookshop.

19. Other types of external

While externals may come within four different types described in 2 above, there is also the kind which occupies either purchased advertising space in the press, or free space provided by a sympathetic journal. An example of the latter is when a trade journal gives space to a bulletin or newsletter from a trade association or professional body.

FEEDBACK

20. Measuring success

The degree to which a magazine is read, enjoyed and has the desired effect should be known if possible and means of recording this may be as follows:

(a) *Readership survey.* Readers are asked to complete a questionnaire, the answers providing a guide to readers' opinions, likes and dislikes. The questionnaire can be printed or inserted in the journal, but a more reliable result would be obtained by sampling readers and surveying them postally or, better still, face to face. A printed questionnaire could be biased since it might be returned by only a minority of interested people.

(b) *Competitions.* The number of entries can indicate the interest taken in the journal.

(c) *Readers' letters.* Whether published or not, the volume of readers' letters can be indicative of interest. They can also reveal attitudes towards the journal.

(d) *Response to advertisements.* Readers' sales and wants advertisements can produce response which serves as a barometer of reader interest.

(e) *Take up of articles.* Some of the more technical externals are sent to the trade and technical press with invitations to editors to reproduce articles and pictures.

(f) *The effect.* This could be on knowledge, understanding, behaviour, dealer cooperation or whatever may be the PR aim. This may be revealed by opinion survey, by observation, or by physical or financial results. Does the staff have a keener appreciation of management policy, are politicians more aware of the organisation's problems, are stockists giving more authoritative advice to customers, are more technicians specifying the product, are more people habitually using the airline or the hotel group?

NEW FORMS OF HOUSE JOURNAL

21. Four new forms of house journal

In recent years four new forms of house journal have given new dimensions to management–employee relations:

(a) *Audio tapes.* News can be recorded on small musicassette tapes for replay by employees on cassette recorders in the office, home and especially in the car.

(b) *Video house journals* such as those produced by companies in their own video studios. The great advantages of these house journals is their realism, making use of colour, sound and movement and bringing people to life to an extent impossible in static print. The video house journal is like a TV news broadcast. It can be shown on business premises or taken home and shown via the domestic VCR on the television screen.

(c) *Corporate video.* A new form of video house journal is the corporate communications private TV network, transmitted by satellite throughout the day to the premises of companies such as Ford Motor Co and British Aerospace.

(d) *Electronic newspapers* which can be transmitted to personal computers with hard copy printers.

22. Desk-top editing

This was mentioned in **16** above but is worth re-emphasising here as a major development.

AUDIO-VISUALS: GENERAL CONSIDERATIONS

23. Audio-visuals (AVs)

These are among the most important, versatile and fast-developing media for the PR practitioner. Unlike the press, radio and TV, they are privately created, owned and controlled media which may be aimed at selected audiences. Even when a video is circulated through a library it is usually shown to private groups, although there may be occasions when a PR documentary is of such wide interest that it will be accepted for public exhibition in cinemas or on television.

24. Initial considerations before making an AV

Before making any kind of audio-visual it is essential to decide on its purpose, audience, likely life span and how audiences will be found. Let us consider each of these four initial decisions.

(a) *Purpose*. The AV is one means of reaching certain publics in order to communicate a special message and achieve a defined objective. If it attempts to be these things to all people it will please no one and be a costly failure. *What is the objective?* Is it to establish an image, show how something works or should be used, depict job opportunities, explain things that visitors will see, discuss and explain company results, advise on safety precautions or help to get export orders? Remember, its purpose can be very practical, serving to achieve some aspect of the overall PR strategy. The mistake should not be made of spending a lot of money on a video merely to achieve something vague like a 'favourable image'.

(b) *Audience*. Is the information presented in the AV and the style of its presentation right for the intended audience? A cookery demonstration will need treatment different from that of a building component demonstration for architects. Can technicalities be presented simply for non-technical audiences – would, perhaps, a cartoon treatment be more suitable? Can the story be told adequately with stills recorded on tape, put in sequence and synchronised? Another audience factor is the size of equipment for the size of audience.

(c) *Life span*. If the AV is to have a long life it is best to avoid shots which quickly date it such as fashion styles or motor cars.

(d) *Obtaining audiences*. Will they be invited, can the video be shown at exhibitions or in showrooms, can it be offered to interested organisations, will the Central Office of Information acquire it for overseas showings, can it be shown to public audiences – what are the prospects of the AV justifying its cost? Will the video be shown in different parts of the world? If so, different formats may be required. However, it is possible to use equipment capable of accepting all formats and systems.

One can transfer film to videotape and vice versa so that either projector or VCR playback facilities can be used in different locations. An international company will usually find it necessary to have all possible versions.

TYPES OF AV MEDIA

25. 35 mm slides

Very popular and ideal for illustrating talks and presentations, slides can be fed into a carousel and operated by the speaker with a remote control push button device. An advantage of slides is that each one is separate and can be replaced by a new or different slide.

26. Synchronised slide-tape projection

A sophisticated and valuable advance on the previous method, slides are synchronised with a taped commentary to which can be added background music. The showing can be operated manually – and interrupted by the presenter – or automatically.

27. Twin-projector cross-fade slide presentation

This is almost the next best thing to a movie. As there is no gap on the screen between slides there is almost the illusion of a film even though the slides are static. This ingenious presentation is achieved by using a pair of slide projectors, side-by-side, focused to fill the same screen area on the one screen and using cross-fade to mix one picture with the other without an interval of blank screen. Large or small screens can be used according to the size of audience and the venue. The only problem is the availability of suitable projection equipment which is not so universally available as the videocassette recorder (VCR). However, slide presentations can be transferred to video for general showings. Thus, the economy of this medium can be combined with the versatility of video.

28. Powerpoint

This is one of the latest – and perhaps most useful – developments in desktop presentation, devised and marketed by Microsoft. It enables the PRO to create material on computer, quickly and easily, and present it either on computer or beamed up onto a large screen. It is the high-tech equivalent of slides or overhead transparencies, but much more versatile and controllable.Virtually any type of material can be incorporated, including pictures, line drawings, graphics and text; in colour and black-and-white. It can also be edited, modified and revised whenever necessary. The software also enables you to create notes both for the presenter and the audience. All this material is stored on computer disk, ready for presentation at any time.

29 Multi-screen presentations

A much more ambitious use of slides and carousels, this method is to programme a large number of projectors so that dramatic effects are achieved on a large screen. All the projectors can combine to show one big picture or the screen can be divided into, for instance, two, four, eight or sixteen pictures according to the number of projectors set up.

The medium obviously lends itself to permanent exhibitions and is not easily transportable. At the Thames Barrier exhibition centre there is a very sophisticated presentation with both front and rear projection. Yet another ingenious presentation is shown in the *Mary Rose* cinema at Portsmouth Dockyard, commentary slides appearing above the main picture.

30. Videocassettes

As the number of videocassette recorders (VCRs) has increased, this first-class medium (playing back on the television screen, or even on a large cinema screen) has become an increasingly useful PR medium. It is especially useful for internal communications such as the induction of recruits but can be used elsewhere such as in shops, showrooms, hotel rooms or on exhibition stands where the small screen can be viewed comfortably. In industry, servicing manuals have been put on to video.

This is one of the most versatile created private media having virtually replaced film (although for some purposes, e.g. TV commercials, a 35 mm film may be shot for the sake of the quality and this is then transferred to video for post-production treatment and the application of computer graphics such as Quantel Paintbox).

In addition to the uses mentioned above videos may be used at press receptions, for explaining the annual report and accounts to staff, or for explaining the amenities of a new venue to which a company wishes to relocate their offices.

31. Overhead projectors

The main advantage of this visual aid is that it can be operated in daylight by a speaker facing the audience. The speaker can lay down ready-made sheets of film bearing charts, statistics or other information that is less easily presented verbally. Or the speaker can write or draw on a blank piece of film as he or she speaks, projecting the image on a screen as and when required. But it is essential that the material to be projected is bold enough for it to be visible to the audience. Word-processed or handwritten messages can be indistinct if the attempt is made to use an overhead projector in too large a room with too big an audience. This can be very irritating.

However, excellent OHP films can be made on, say, a photocopier with enlarging facilities, and special paper-interleafed OHP film. Thus small items can be copied and blown up for the final transfer onto OHP film. These images can be given a long 'throw' to appear on a large screen and be visible to a fairly large audience.

32. Eidophor screen

This giant version of closed circuit television (CCTV, *see Note* below) has the advantage of a huge screen and three uses of it are of special interest in PR.

First, an event may be difficult to cover by the media. This may be because of distance or awkward location; or because Royal Protocol restricts the number of media representatives. Event and press reception could be hundreds of miles apart. The event can be filmed on the spot with a TV camera, and the picture transmitted by landline to a venue where

Fig 10.2 Multi-media projectors add impact to presentations. Leading-edge systems, like the LitePro 210, are compatible with PC and Mac graphics standards, and work into hi-fi sound systems.

journalists are conveniently and more comfortably gathered. The picture is then shown on the giant Eidophor screen.

The second use is at a conference where CCTV is used so that the speaker is shot and shown simultaneously on the big screen. This is useful in a large auditorium and particularly useful when the speaker wishes to demonstrate small objects which would otherwise by unrecognisable by the audience.

Third, speeches and performances can be shown to overflow audiences in additional halls, and – using BT landlines – the scene can be shown on Eidophor screens in other towns, even in other countries. Eidophor screens are also used in television studios to display large pictures of programme material received from overseas by satellite, or from another television studio.

Note: CCTV (closed circuit TV) is the process of shooting subjects and showing them, all within the same premises, there being no broadcasting to outside viewers.

USES OF AV MEDIA

33. The many uses of AVs

The above descriptions have already suggested some of the ways in which AVs may be used by the PR practitioner. The following is a more detailed list:

(a) *Invited audiences.* Presentations can be made to invited guests in private cinemas, business premises, hotel rooms or hired halls. These presentations can augment talks, demonstrations or exhibits.

(b) *Libraries.* Videos may be placed in libraries which will catalogue, handle requests, distribute and maintain them in good condition. There are also libraries which stock 'library' shots, e.g. airliners in flight, for use in feature films and TV series.

(c) *Catalogues and advertising.* Regular makers of videos, e.g. ICI, BP, Shell, produce catalogues and advertise the availability of them on loan.

(d) *Press receptions.* Most press conferences can be enhanced by the showing of a short, relevant video.

(e) *Exhibitions.* AVs of various kinds can be an attraction on an exhibition stand, especially if the rest of the exhibit is static. Movement can be an asset on stands.

(f) *Employee communications.* AVs provide attractive and intimate communications, e.g. overcoming the remoteness of management who may be located elsewhere, even overseas. Ships' crews can be communicated with in this way.

(g) *Rural audiences.* If audiences live in country or scattered locations, AVs can be taken to or sent to them. Farmers can be given video performances at agricultural shows by means of mobile cinemas. The 'road show' method of showing videos in market squares can be used.

In developing countries, where 80 per cent of the population may be rural and also illiterate, the mobile film show can be both a welcome and a necessary form of communication. These mobile shows are carried by a vehicle such as a Land Rover, the screen is mounted on the roof and hundreds of villagers gather in the open to enjoy the performance. It is important, however, that the films used should be short and simple and not extend beyond the comprehension and experience of people who may be unfamiliar with urban, let alone foreign or Western, life. Such films require a content to which the audience can relate, otherwise attention will wander and the message may have to be repeated to achieve impact, understanding and memorability. The ideal length for such films is ten minutes.

During the mid-80s, video replaced film for mobile shows in some countries. The Malaysian government information service, which takes shows into villages to explain new legislation and for other official information services, has adopted video. In Malawi, the Whitehead textile company tours video fashion shows.

(h) *COI and government information services.* Most government information services provide international distribution of videos which may be official ones or documentaries produced by national organisations and companies. The British Central Office of Information has an Acquisitions Department which adopts company videos, provided they have no advertising content, for distribution to overseas television companies and for loan through British embassies and consulates. For this purpose the overseas copyright is acquired.

OTHER CREATED MEDIA

34. Educational literature

Not to be confused with sales literature, educational literature consists of all printed material which helps to explain or encourage the use of a product or service, or is of associated interest and value.

Included in this broad category are recipe leaflets and cookery books; information on the control of garden pests or advice on how to grow a perfect lawn; maps and guide books and other publications.

35. The spoken word

The giving of talks, perhaps supported by AVs, can be an important PR activity. Some organisations employ full-time speakers who address clubs and societies, but otherwise suitable personnel from the organisation may give talks.

36. Seminars and conferences

Making use of some of the media already mentioned (AVs, spoken word) events may be organised to which appropriate publics are invited as guests. These could range from receptions in hotels to large gatherings in conference halls. The aim of such PR events is to make presentations to selected people. They should not be dressed up with sales and trade displays, the object being educational rather than selling. For example, at one time Rentokil organised a series of one-day conferences throughout the country to explain developments in modern pest control to medical officers of health. A number of pharmaceutical companies have organised such events to explain new drugs to doctors.

37. Private exhibitions

These can be permanent on company premises or at special sites, or they can be mobile – either travelled by caravan, bus, train, aircraft or ship – or portable for erection in venues such as forecourts, libraries, hotels, shop windows and so forth. To these exhibitions PR publics can be invited.

Progress test 10

1. What is meant by internal and external house journals?

2. What are the five types of house journal?

3. Why is it necessary to determine the readership of a proposed journal?

4. What is meant by the 'format'?

5. List the methods by which house journals may be distributed.

6. What factors enter into the budgeting of a house journal?

7. What is involved in the design and production of a house journal?

8. How can an editor plan issues and rely on getting material?

9. Give some examples of specific publics to whom external company magazines can be addressed.

10. How can feedback be obtained and measured?

11. What is an electronic newspaper?

12. What is desk-top editing?

13. What four initial decisions should be taken before producing an audio-visual?

14. Describe the medium of synchronised slide-tape projection.

15. Explain the merits and demerits of twin-projector slide presentations.

16. What is Powerpoint? Explain its advantages.

17. What is a multi-screen presentation?

18. How can videos be used for PR purposes?

19. What is a film library, and what are 'library' shots?

20. What are the special requirements of films or videos for showing to unsophisticated rural communities in developing countries?

21. How can government information services help in the distribution of industrial videos?

22. What is meant by educational literature?

23. How can seminars and conferences serve as PR media?

24. What is a private exhibition?

11

BUDGETING

INTRODUCTION

1. Reasons for budgeting

Budgeting is imperative for the following reasons:

(a) To learn what it will cost to carry out a PR programme.

(b) Alternatively, to learn what sort of programme can be carried out for a given sum of money.

(c) Having agreed a programme and its estimated cost, the budget provides a checklist of tasks which have to be performed. These can then be organised in the form of a timetable (*see* Chapter 5).

(d) The budget sets a discipline for both expenditure and over-expenditure, for it is as necessary to spend as planned as it is to control excessive expenditure.

(e) After completion of the campaign, results can be measured against the budget (as well as against the programme itself) to consider whether enough, too little or too much was spent and whether individual allocations for particular activities were correct.

PR DEPARTMENT AND CONSULTANCY BUDGETS

2. The difference between department and consultancy budgets

The only difference between budgets for PR departments and PR consultancies is that the latter must include profit.

3. The four elements of a PR budget

A budget consists of the following four elements:

(a) *Labour.* This includes the salaries not only of PR practitioners but those of all supporting staff such as secretaries, clerks, accountants, receptionists, messengers and others in either a PR department or a consultancy. Since PR is labour-intensive, this may be expected to be the biggest item in the PR budget.

(b) *Office overheads.* These are mostly the fixed costs of rent, rates, insurance, central heating, air-conditioning, lighting, and cleaning, but also include variable costs such as telephone and client liaison.

(c) *Materials.* All physical items are included here such as stationery, postage, print, visual aids, mobile exhibition stands, photographs, slides, audio and videotapes.

(d) *Expenses.* Out-of-pocket expenses such as fares, hotel bills and hospitality are included here, together with the special expenses to do with organising PR events which may involve catering and various hire charges for microphones, VCRs, TV sets, screens, vehicles, marquees, chairs, umbrellas and so forth.

4. Computing charges

When a consultancy computes its hourly or daily rate, it amalgamates salaries and wages with overheads and profit, and estimates materials and expenses separately since it is usual to charge them at cost, unless it is agreed that the consultancy may retain any discounts. It is not usual for consultancies to add a percentage to the prices it pays for materials and expenses – unlike advertising agencies. The principle is that the income should be derived from fees based on time and skill. The latter is reflected

---

Budget for a PR consultancy programme

12 progress meetings	$12 \times x$ hrs $\times £x$	£xxx.xx
12 news releases	$12 \times x$ hrs $\times £x$	xxx.xx
Official opening of HQ	x hrs $\times £x$	xxx.xx
Preparing annual report and accounts	x hrs $\times £x$	xxx.xx
Editing/designing quarterly house journal	$4 \times x$ hrs $\times £x$	xxx.xx
4 feature articles	$4 \times x$ hrs $\times £x$	xxx.xx
2 interview tapes for radio	$2 \times x$ hrs $\times £x$	xxx.xx
Contingency, say 10%	x hrs $\times £x$	xxx.xx
		£xx,xxx.xx
Estimated material costs:	News releases	£xxx.xx
	Printing annual report	x,xxx.xx
	Printing house journal	x,xxx.xx
	Postages, stationery	xxx.xx
	Radio interview tapes	xxx.xx
Expenses:	Official opening	xx,xxx.xx
Contingency fund, say 10%		xxx.xx
	Total	£xx,xxx.xx

---

in the salaries which have to be recovered, and some consultancies have hourly rates directly related to the salary of the individual account executive so that the client pays according to the experience hired. A possible form of budget is shown on the previous page.

Analysis

(a) Progress meetings are the client–consultancy meetings to be held monthly.

(b) 12 × x hrs × £x means 12 meetings multiplied by the estimated number of hours involved times the hourly rate. Thus if each meeting lasted three hours, and the hourly rate was £85, the item would read 12 × 3 hrs × £85 making an annual total of £3,060 for regular meetings with the client. The budget and the fee must allow for these meetings: it is not confined to actual work done. However, £85 should not be taken as a standard rate right across the industry. It could be double that or more.

(c) The workload consists of news releases at the rate of perhaps one a month; the organising and running of the official opening of a new headquarters; writing and designing the annual report and accounts; researching, writing and publishing four feature articles in newspapers or magazines; and organising two interviews for tapes for distribution to local radio stations.

(d) To give some idea of what this means, the working hours might total 500 hours. If the hourly rate were £85, for instance – the rate would be higher for a London consultancy than a provincial one and in Europe the rate would be higher, but less in, say, Africa or Asia – the total fee would amount to £42,500. To this would have to be added the costs of materials and expenses, major items being printing and the hospitality connected with the official opening. Very roughly, the total cost for fees, materials and expenses might be in the region of £85,000. This would, of course, depend on the catering costs of the official opening which could be high if there were many guests. Normally without such an expensive item, working hours (fee) would be the major cost of a consultancy service.

(e) A contingency fund is a sum of money which has not been allocated for a particular use, but may be drawn upon if more money is required, possibly because of a price increase. It is a safeguard against unexpected costs. It does not have to be spent.

(f) Given such figures it is possible for the client to decide whether he or she wishes to accept the budget, spend more or less, carry out the scheme as proposed, extend or reduce it. Both sides know where they stand, what has to be done, what has to be spent, and the consultant is responsible for working within these constraints.

5. Allocations

Within this budget are several subsidiary budgets or allocations, and only their totals are shown in the programme budget. The official opening, the annual report, and the house journal require their separately detailed budgets.

The costs for the official opening would be subject to the location, number of guests, style of programme and the extent of catering, hospitality, overnight accommodation, transport, and hire charges for things like marquees, chairs, microphones, and part-time staff. Again, the budget may control the number of guests or a given number of guests will control the budget.

The annual report costs would cover writing and designing, printing and distribution. These costs would be governed by the number of pages, number of copies, page size, colour or black and white printing, illustrations, quality of paper, together with distribution, which could include envelopes, addressing, filling and postage.

The house journal costs would follow a similar pattern to that already described for the annual report, with probably more money being spent on photography and artwork.

6. Calculating a PR department budget

Now let us look at the hypothetical budget for an internal PR department. Here we are not dealing with an hourly rate which has to cover salaries, overheads and produce a profit. The mistake that can be made, however, is that of recognising only salaries and forgetting to allow for depreciation on furniture and equipment and to calculate sums to cover the rent and rates of the offices, heating, air-conditioning, lighting, cleaning and a share of company services, such as the telephone switchboard operator.

It is easy to think that an internal PR department is cheaper than a consultancy service simply by comparing staff salaries with fees forgetting that the PR department also has to be equipped, accommodated and serviced. Everything in a company operation costs something, although this may be shown more critically in a small consultancy than in a big organisation, where it is easy (but wrong) to take it for granted that the premises are there anyway. It can therefore be much costlier to operate an in-house department than to hire a consultancy, whose services would be only part-time. Students often make the mistake in examinations of claiming that consultancies are expensive.

Deliberately, the following budget is for a large organisation, so that many activities can be itemised, but for the smaller organisation the activities will be fewer. Moreover, for simplicity and avoidance of supplementary budgets, all costs are run together within each item.

Budget for a large organisation with its own PR department

Salaries: PR manager, assistants, house journal editor,
photographer, secretaries, etc.   £xxx,xxx.xx

Overheads: rent, rates, lighting, heating, air-conditioning,
cleaning, share of telephone switchboard, etc.   xx,xxx.xx

Depreciation: furniture and equipment (word-processors,
personal computers, copiers, cameras, office printing
machines, vehicles)   xx,xxx.xx

Insurances: car, all risks on equipment, travel, pensions,
private medical   xx,xxx.xx

Press receptions: materials, catering, hire charges   xx,xxx.xx

Staff journal(s): editing, designing, photography, artwork,
printing, distribution   xx,xxx.xx

External journal: ditto   xx,xxx.xx

Slide presentation: treatment, script, photography, music fee,
production, copies, distribution, maintenance   xx,xxx.xx

Video: treatment, script, actors, music, shooting, editing, post-
production, copies, distribution, maintenance, synopsis
leaflet   xx,xxx.xx

News releases: research, writing, production, compiling
mailing lists, distribution   xx,xxx.xx

Feature articles: research, negotiation with editors, writing,
reprints   xx,xxx.xx

Press cutting service: fee, mounting, copying, circulation   xx,xxx.xx

Information service: maintaining information, distribution,
kits for school projects   xx,xxx.xx

Radio tapes: interview fees, copies, distribution with scripts   xx,xxx.xx

TV properties: supply of sample products to property
managers of TV studios for use on sets   xx,xxx.xx

Printed literature: production of leaflets, folders, brochures,
wall-charts, calendars, reports, histories   xx,xxx.xx

Sponsorships: prizes, awards, bursaries, sponsorships,
hospitality   xx,xxx.xx

Trade/technical conferences/seminars: materials, catering,
accommodation, hire charges, expenses, travel   xx,xxx.xx

Photography: shooting, blow-ups, prints, captions,
card-backed envelopes   xx,xxx.xx

Facility visits: transportation, accommodation, catering, press
information, materials, hire charges, expenses   xx,xxx.xx

Exhibitions: (mobile, private, PR support for trade and
consumer) display panels, blow-ups, models (mechanical,
human), etc.   xx,xxx.xx

Vehicles: cars, vans   xx,xxx.xx

Stationery: letter headings, news release headings, photo

caption headings, envelopes and general stationery	*xx,xxx.xx*
Telephone, telex, fax:	*xx,xxx.xx*
Postage:	*xx,xxx.xx*
Travelling expenses: car allowance, fares, hotel bills, hospitality	*xx,xxx.xx*
Contingency: say 10%	*xx,xxx.xx*
Total	*£xxx,xxx.xx*

Analysis

Once more it will be seen that many items, e.g. press receptions, house journals, videos and facility visits, are represented by the sums of supplementary budgets. Thus, this overall budget represents several other calculations, and in presenting a budget together with proposals for the year all the supplementary arithmetic would need to be appended. Note that expressions such as 'editing' and 'writing' refer to costs involved and not to time which is already covered by salaries, unless outside help is engaged. This budget also indicates the complex range of PR activities which the full-time in-house PR department may undertake. Generally, it is much more comprehensive than that conducted by a consultancy on behalf of a client.

7. Use of budgeting by management

Given such specific costings, management can see that the PR manager (or consultant) operates in a businesslike way, costs can be related against their productive value, and deletions, additions or amendments can be made *before* the work begins. Moreover, such budgeting will show what can and cannot be done with existing personnel and resources. The working hour aspect is important in both consultancy and PR department budgets. The salaries in the PR department budget must represent enough working hours of the right standard to carry out the proposals.

For example, it is no use recommending the production of a house magazine unless someone has both the time and the ability to edit it. This could be a case where it may be economic to augment the in-house PR department with the part-time services of a PR consultancy which has a design studio and desk-top publishing computer equipment.

8. Budgeting priorities and constraints

The above logic may conflict with a typical management attitude that, having employed a PR manager, he or she may be expected to do anything that is asked irrespective of the workload. This can only result in too many things being attempted at the same time and none of them being accomplished well. Budgeting brings out the priorities and places constraints on ineffective work so that cost-effectiveness is achieved. It is then feasible to make fair judgement of results against objectives and costs. Once again we see how the Six-Point Planning model (*see* Chapter 5) introduces state-by-stage constraints so that a cost-effective programme results.

Progress test 11

1. Why is it wise to budget a PR programme?

2. How do budgets for PR departments and PR consultants differ?

3. Which may be the largest item in the PR budget?

4. What is the difference between 'materials' and 'expenses'?

5. What are overheads?

6. What are the four elements of a budget?

7. What are progress meetings?

8. What is meant by the consultancy's hourly rate?

9. What is a contingency fund?

10. What is the purpose of budgeting?

12

EVALUATING RESULTS

NATURE OF RESULTS

1. Two kinds of results

There are two kinds of results:

(a) *Qualitative.* Many results of PR activity will be of this kind, that is they will not be measured statistically but by experience and self-evident qualities, e.g. the evidence that the job applicants are better educated, more proficient or in some other way more suitable than in the past.

(b) *Quantitative.* These results might show, for instance, a percentage increase in awareness, a reduced number of complaints, a larger number of job applicants, oversubscription of a share issue or a recorded number of mentions or sightings of the company name in the press and on the radio and television as a result of sponsoring a sports event.

2. Self-evident results

These are results where nothing has to be spent on a marketing research survey to check, i.e. they are to be seen or experienced. If a trade relations exercise has succeeded, the sales force will be better received and orders will be more forthcoming. The results will be evident in increased orders compared with the previous experience with the same product, sales-people, stockists and similar advertising support, but *no* trade relations programme. The monetary value of the extra business can, of course, be assessed quantitatively, but the self-evident result is beyond doubt anyway, for a change has to be admitted.

Again, suppose complaints had been received because customers were misusing the product and after an educational PR programme the complaints ceased: the result would be obvious.

Or supposing the government of a developing country decided to introduce primary education and there were problems about encouraging attendance because, firstly, parents were illiterate and did not appreciate the value of education and, secondly, children were wanted to work on the parents' farms, resulting in a PR programme being put into operation. If, as happened in similar circumstances in Nigeria, demand exceeded supply and unexpectedly large numbers of children enrolled, it would be self-evident that the PR effort had more than done its job.

These examples are given to show that sometimes the facts can be so plain that, given clear objectives, PR cannot be intangible and unaccountable. Results can literally stare you in the face. The accountability of PR rests on the existence of objectives in the first place and these as demonstrated in Chapter 6 are an integral part of the PR plan.

SOME METHODS OF ASSESSMENT

3. By enquiries received

When media coverage produces direct enquiries their numbers can be totalled, and if they are converted into sales their value can also be calj126 culated.

4. By statistical data on audience numbers and ratings

Press, radio and television coverage can be assessed not merely in volume of column inches or centimetres or by time, but by exposure based on the readership figures and audience ratings (*see* 5:**13(d)**). Thus it can be calculated how many people and, using the demographic profiles given in readership and audience surveys, what kind of people had the opportunity to read, hear or see the message. Readership figures can be more interesting and helpful than circulation figures; for instance, a newspaper like the *Financial Times* has a fairly small circulation but a large number of readers per copy. Usually, the type of person who reads the *Financial Times* is different from a *Daily Mail* reader. The same number of column centimetres might be obtained in both papers, but the value of that space would not be its volume (still less its illusory advertisement value!) but the relevance of the readership, that is its *quality*.

In the previous paragraph reference has been made to three forms of evaluating: *volume of media coverage*, *opportunities to see*, and the *quality* of the coverage meaning the importance of the medium carrying the story. A fourth form of assessment is *tone*, that is how was the message conveyed? Was it garbled, hostile, sympathetic or well-informed?

5. Evaluation by source

Another method of evaluating media coverage is to give values to each newspaper or magazine and so arrive at a score for each news release issued. For an engineering story the *Financial Times* could be given value of five, but only one for the *Daily Mirror*, but for a household product story the values would be reversed. Once again we see how a volume measurement could be deceptive whereas a value judgement could be more accurate. A media evaluation chart would look like the one in Figure 12.1.

Title	Value	News release 1	News release 2
Daily Times	5	X	X
Daily Echo	5		X
Daily Bugle	4	X	X
Daily Telephone	3		
Daily News	2	X	
Daily Voice	1		
Score		11	14

Fig 12.1 Media evaluation chart; values given according to importance of journal to sender of news releases

6. Opinion polls

The shift of opinion or the extent of awareness can be measured by means of an opinion poll (*see* 5:7). If samples of relevant publics are interviewed at intervals of, for example, six months, it is possible to measure the upward or downward trend of these shifts. The target may be to secure a certain percentage shift: when the situation is surveyed initially it may be found that only 20 per cent of respondents or interviewees understand what the organisation does and the target for the PR programme may be to increase this awareness to 50 per cent over the course of the year. Surveys at six-monthly stages might produce a graph as in Figure 12.2, showing shifts over time.

If the increase after six months was forecast as 5 per cent, at six months the result is on target. At twelve months, however, there is a shortfall of 5 per cent on the 50 per cent target. This calls for analysis to see what went wrong.

Was the programme faulty? Was the budget too small? Were there any outside influences which prevented achievement of the target? Thus a new

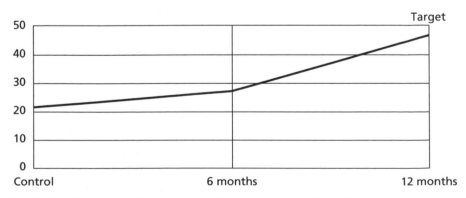

Fig 12.2 Graph showing results of three opinion polls conducted at six-monthly intervals

appreciation of the situation can help with the planning of the next leg of the campaign. Should new tactics be adopted or should the first ones be intensified? Does this call for a bigger budget? Has the environment of the organisation changed? Are there new conditions, situations or influences to contend with?

Alternatively, had there been a shortfall at the intermediate six months stage, the programme could have been reviewed and changed or extended to improve the performance of the PR effort and so bring about the target figure of 50 per cent awareness.

In such ingenious ways, PR activity can be checked on a quantitative basis. Without this investment in research the PR practitioner would be working in the dark, at best relying on hopeful assumptions, but never knowing what progress, if any, he or she was making. Those spending money on PR are entitled to know what return they are getting. More than that, responsible management should want to know the cost-effectiveness of PR.

7. Evaluation by direct statistical feedback

If an advertising campaign follows a PR programme of educating the market, the success of the advertising can be judged. Does the take-up of the product meet expectations and are retailers re-ordering? Better still, are sales better than when a previous new line was launched without preliminary PR?

If a video is made about, for example, the company's construction of a dam, and it has been shown to prospective clients, have more new contracts resulted from the confidence created by this video?

Similarly, if a bank with branches all over the country was anxious to recruit school-leavers, made a video about the bank's services and opportunities for young people and loaned the video to schools and clubs, the success of this venture could be measured by the increase in applications for junior jobs. Application forms could actually ask if and where the video had been seen.

Again, if a bank was keen to service more farmers and showed a suitable video at agricultural shows, gymkhanas, Young Farmers Club meetings and other rural events, the success of the video could be measured by the number and value of new accounts opened and other business conducted with farmers. Results would depend, of course, on any advertising campaigns running at the same time.

8. Media feedback

If the media have shown misunderstanding, scepticism or hostility in the past does feedback (press cuttings, monitored broadcasts) show that the media are now well-informed and more sympathetic? This could be the result of PR activities such as news releases, photographs, feature articles, a press information service, press receptions and facility visits.

9. Assessing increased understanding

As a result of publishing a dealer magazine, are dealers now better informed about the product, explaining it to customers more efficiently, giving it more display space, using display material to greater advantage, receiving the company's sales representative more warmly and placing more frequent or larger orders?

10. Desired results

From the above examples, it will be seen that the results are ones which are sought after, not casual or unexpected benefits. In other words, a PR programme should be undertaken to do something positive which is capable of being recognised when it has been achieved. Results depend upon objectives.

Fourteen hypothetical objectives were set out in 5:**10**. The success or otherwise in achieving such objectives can be measured by observation, experience and marketing research.

Progress test 12

1. What are qualitative and quantitative results?

2. What are self-evident results?

3. How can exposure to readers, viewers or listeners be calculated to show the true value of press, television or radio coverage?

4. How can shifts of opinion or awareness be measured over time? Draw a graph to demonstrate your answer.

5. Assume that your organisation has made a documentary video to demonstrate the value of its product or service. After showing the video to target audiences, how would you measure its success?

6. When the media have been hostile how can the effects of PR activity be assessed?

7. How can the effectiveness of a dealer magazine be judged?

8. Upon what do results depend?

13

THE ETHICS OF PUBLIC RELATIONS

THE ROLE OF ETHICS

1. 'Ethics are good economics'

This is not a glib, cynical phrase but another way of stating that 'it pays to be honest'. A business is more likely to succeed if it is trusted. In PR, credibility is vital. Not only must it be believable but it must be true. PR is about knowledge and understanding and that leads to goodwill and reputation, which depend on faith.

Consequently, to apply another saying, 'honesty is the best policy' – it follows that PR will not work unless it is believed. This is different from propaganda, for instance, when people are indoctrinated to accept a certain religious, social or political creed, or advertising which aims to persuade people to make purchases. In PR we are responsible for producing factual information, accurately and without comment. The receiver of this information must decide what to do with it. For example, if the facts show that a piped water supply is purer and healthier than water from a river or a well, it is expected that villagers will accept the piped water.

2. Ethics and behaviour

Ethics apply particularly to the way PR practitioners behave. Personal integrity becomes a part of their professionalism, as with doctors, teachers or accountants. Public relations officers have to do PR for themselves in that they will be judged by the way they act. They give expert advice; they do not bribe and corrupt; they publish stories on their merit, not because they entertain journalists; they are *professionals*.

3. Unethical instructions

Equally, if employers ask PR practitioners to do something unethical they have the strength of their professional code of practice to support a refusal to act unprofessionally. Professional PR practitioners therefore find it advisable to seek qualifications such as the British CAM Diploma in Public Relations, or to be accredited by the examinations of the Public Relations

Society of America or the International Association of Business Communicators, and to seek election as a member of the British Institute of Public Relations (or a similar body in their own country). Consultancies may have corporate membership of the Public Relations Consultants Association. Membership of the IPR is based on age and experience plus possession of the CAM Diploma or its equivalent.

CODES OF PROFESSIONAL CONDUCT

4. Value of codes and international codes

A code of professional conduct is valuable only provided it is effective in regulating the conduct of professional practitioners. (It can do nothing about the cowboys and cowgirls outside its orbit, that is who do not belong to their professional body.) Since there are so many willing critics of PR who, out of prejudice but chiefly ignorance, enjoy maligning it, it is essential that a code is seen to work. This is not to say that there are no dubious operators, but the same may be said of other professions.

There are certain international codes such as the admirable Code of Athens of the International Public Relations Association which originated in Athens in 1965 and was modified in Teheran in 1968. The emphasis of this code is on 'human rights'. IPRA has members in 70 countries. Therein lies both the code's strength and weakness. Its sentiments are splendid and cannot be disputed, but the tenets of the code are impossible to administer, and there is no recorded case of an offending member ever having been investigated, let alone penalised. The IPRA code has gums but no teeth.

In contrast the Code of Practice of the British Institute of Public Relations is made and seen to work. When a person is elected to membership he or she undertakes to uphold the code. There is a Professional Practices Committee to which complaints may be sent in writing via the director, and a Disciplinary Committee has power to act without ratification by Council, which is a very serious matter. Such cases are rare but there have been some suspensions and a published reprimand.

The Public Relations Consultants Association had a similar code which was concerned with the regulation of its consultancy (corporate) members, whereas the IPR Code applies to individuals. In 1990 and 1991 radical changes occurred in the structure of the two codes. First, the PRCA converted its fairly terse code into a more detailed Charter which not only spelt out what should *not* be done but what should be done. In the same year, 1990, the IPR reversed its controversial and nonsensical clause 9 forbidding payment by results. (The author was once brought before the Professional Practices Committee for criticising this ambiguous clause which was capable of a double meaning!)

Originally, the clause had said that there should be no payment contingent upon achievements. The intended purpose was to ban the

129

racket whereby fringe operators offered, say, 100 press cuttings for £100 when such a guarantee of publication of news releases was impossible. The ambiguity lay in the fact that a PRO could lose his job or a consultant could lose a client if he failed to produce results, the false implication being that PR was intangible. However, events have defeated the original object of the clause, for some people such as those involved in take-over bids and government privatisation are, in fact, paid by results and there are bonuses for success, while local government PROs are given performance awards. Consequently, clause 9 was reversed at the AGM in April 1990.

At the AGM in 1991 the old code was replaced by one resembling that of the PRCA so that there is no compatibility between the two British codes. The IPR Code of Professional Conduct reads as follows:

(1) Conduct towards the practice of public relations

A Member shall:

1.1 Have a positive duty to observe the highest standards in the practice of public relations and to deal fairly and honestly with employers and clients (past and present), fellow members and professionals, the public relations profession, other professions, suppliers, intermediaries, the media of communications, employees and, above all, the public.

1.2 Be aware of, understand and observe this Code, any amendment to it, and any other codes which shall be incorporated into it; remain up to date with the content and recommendations of any guidance or practice papers issued by IPR; and have a duty to conform to good practice as expressed in such guidance or practice papers.

1.3 Uphold this Code and cooperate with fellow members to enforce decisions on any matter arising from its application. A Member who knowingly causes his or her staff to act in a manner inconsistent with this Code is party to such action and shall be deemed to be in breach of this Code. Staff employed by a Member who act in a manner inconsistent with this Code should be disciplined by the Member.

A Member shall not:

1.4 Engage in any practice nor be seen to conduct him or her self in any manner detrimental to the reputation of the Institute or the reputation and interests of the public relations profession.

(2) Conduct towards the public, the media and other professions

A Member shall:

2.1 Conduct his or her professional activities with proper regard to the public interest.

2.2 Have a positive duty at all times to respect the truth and shall not disseminate false or misleading information knowingly or recklessly, and take proper care to check all information prior to its dissemination.

2.3 Have a duty to ensure that the actual interest of any organisation with which he or she may be professionally concerned is adequately declared.

2.4 When working in association with other professionals, identify and respect the codes of those professions.

2.5 Respect any statutory or regulatory codes laid down by any other authorities which are relevant to the actions of his or her employer or client, or taken on behalf of an employer or client.

2.6 Ensure that the names of all directors, executives, and retained advisers of his or her employers or company who hold public office, are members of either House of Parliament, Local Authorities or any statutory organisation or body, are recorded in the IPR Register.

2.7 Honour confidences received or given in the course of professional activity.

2.8 Neither propose nor undertake, or cause an employer or client to propose or undertake, any action which would be an improper influence on government, legislation, holders of public office or members of any statutory body or organisation, or the media of communication.

(3) Conduct towards employers and clients

A Member shall:

3.1 Safeguard the confidences of both present and former employers or clients; shall not disclose or use these confidences to the disadvantage or prejudice of such employers or clients, or to the financial advantage of the Member (unless the employer or client has given specific permission for disclosure), except upon the order of a court of law.

3.2 Inform an employer or client of any shareholding or financial interest held by that Member or any staff employed by that Member in any company or person whose services he or she recommends.

3.3 Be free to accept fees, commissions or other valuable considerations from persons other than an employer or client, if such considerations are disclosed to the employer or client.

3.4 Be free to negotiate, or renegotiate, with an employer or client terms that are a fair reflection of demands of the work involved and take into account factors other than hours worked and the experience involved. These special factors, which are also applied by other professional advisers shall have regard to all the circumstances of the specific situation and in particular to:

 a The complexity of the issue, ease, problem or assignment, and the difficulties associated with its completion.

 b The professional or specialised skills required and the degree of responsibility involved.

 c The amount of documentation necessary to be perused or prepared, and its importance.

 d The place and circumstances where the work is carried out, in whole or in part.

 e The scope, scale and value of the task and its importance as an activity, issue, or project to the employer or client.

A Member shall not:

3.5 Misuse information regarding his or her employer's or client's business for financial or other gain.

3.6 Use inside information for gain. Nor may a member of staff managed or employed by a Member directly trade in his or her employers' or clients' securities without the prior written permission of the employer or client and of the Member's chief executive or chief financial officer or compliance officer.

3.7 Serve an employer or client under terms and conditions which might impair his or her independence, objectivity or integrity.

131

3.8 Represent conflicting interests but may represent competing interests with the express consent of the parties concerned.

3.9 Guarantee the achievement of results which are beyond the Member's direct capacity to achieve or prevent.

(4) Conduct towards colleagues

A Member shall:

4.1 Adhere to the highest standards of accuracy and truth, avoiding extravagant claims or unfair comparisons and giving credit for ideas and words borrowed from others.

4.2 Be free to represent his or her capabilities and service to any potential employer or client, either on his or her own initiative or at the behest of any client, provided in so doing he or she does not seek to break any existing contract or detract from the reputation or capabilities of any Member already serving that employer or client.

A Member shall not:

4.3 Injure the professional reputation or practice of another Member.

(5) Interpreting the Code

5.1 In the interpretation of this Code, the Laws of the Land shall apply

5. BAIE Code of Professional Conduct

The brainchild of Les Holloway, chairman of the British Association of Industrial Editors in 1988–89, the 'seven commandments' of this short code apply to house journal editors. The code reads as follows:

(1) Integrity of communication

Members shall make every effort not to publish or otherwise disseminate false information.

(2) Confidential information

Members who are given or obtain information in confidence during the course of their professional duties shall not publish or otherwise disclose such information except as required by law.

(3) Injury to other members

A member shall not maliciously injure the professional reputation of another member.

(4) Reputation of the profession

Members shall not conduct themselves in a manner which is likely to be detrimental to the reputation of the Association or the practice of internal corporate communications.

(5) Legal requirements

Members shall seek to ensure that the communications media for which they are responsible comply with the legal requirements, in particular those concerning copyright, libel, and publishing imprints.

(6) Breaches of this Code

If a member has a reason to believe that another member has engaged in practices which are in breach of this Code it shall be his/her duty to inform the Council of the Association, through its current Chairman or Vice-Chairman or the Chief Executive of the Association. Council shall take whatever action is considered appropriate in the circumstances, as specified in the Articles of Association. A member affected by such rulings shall have the right of appeal to the Senate of the Association, in accordance with the Articles of Association.

(7) Upholding this Code

A member shall uphold this Code of Professional Conduct and co-operate with other members in so doing.

6. Legal requirements

The BAIE lays stress on copyright, libel and publishing imprints, and since BAIE members are publishers these legal matters are very important. An imprint is the identity of the publisher and printer, often printed in small type at the end of a piece of print, which provides legal proof in the event of a dispute.

Progress test 13

1. Why do the ethics of public relations apply particularly to the behaviour of the PR practitioner?

2. What is the procedure for reporting breaches of the IPR Code of Professional Conduct?

3. What has the code to say about conflicting interests?

4. Explain what clause 3.6 means about the confidentiality of information.

5. Explain the meaning of clause 3.9.

6. Why does the BAIE stress 'legal requirements'?

14

MANAGEMENT AND EMPLOYEE RELATIONS

GENERAL CONSIDERATIONS

1. Internal PR

As we have already seen in Chapter 10 regarding house journals, internal PR is just as important as external PR. If money terms are the yardstick, the one can aid profitability just as much as the other. Staff relations are not quite the same thing as industrial relations (with their emphasis on wages and working conditions), but industrial relations are influenced by effective employee communication.

Internal communications can be of three kinds: downward from employers to employees; upward from employees to employers; and sideways between employees.

The effectiveness of internal PR calls for a combination of:

(a) Candid management

(b) Recognition by management of the value and importance of employee communication

(c) A communications manager (PR manager) who is not only skilled and experienced, but who is backed by modern technical resources; some of these resources have been described in Chapter 10.

The title 'communications manager' is used here. He or she may be the PR manager as discussed in Chapter 3, or a staff newspaper editor, whose task has broadened to cover the other internal PR activities – titles matter less than the job specification, and the status given by management to the internal PR role. The communications manager is likely to be the kind of specialist who is a member of the British Association of Industrial Editors and the International Association of Business Communicators (which has a British chapter).

2. Range of media and techniques

The variety of communication aids is immense, but any one organisation will probably use only those few methods which suit it best. Much depends on the nature of the organisation, its kind and range of personnel and the location of the workplaces. Obviously, a department store is very compact compared with a shipping line or multinational company, but also very different are the personnel of, for example, computer hardware and pickled onion factories. The range of media and methods is outlined below.

INTERNAL PR AND TECHNIQUES

3. House journals

See Chapter 10.

4. Noticeboard

Standard noticeboards can be placed at vantage points throughout the organisation so that all personnel are given the same information at the same time. Items may be printed poster fashion and attached to the board or the board may consist of sections or clips for each type of news item. No other items should be fixed to these boards.

Ideally, items for noticeboards should be given to a controller (e.g. PRO) who reproduces the items in an attractive form, and is responsible for positioning them. Only this person (or his or her representatives) should be allowed to place items on the noticeboards.

5. Videotapes and closed circuit TV

The television screen, which has become an everyday feature in many people's lives, is a medium for personalised messages, either on prepared tape or live. This modern medium gains the face-to-face communication which can help bring closer understanding between management and staff.

6. Radio station

The famous example was United Biscuits, who had the problem of maintaining job satisfaction among factory staff, mostly immigrant, in noisy factories where conversation was difficult or impossible. The solution was to fix a large number of loudspeakers at points where the radio could be heard, above the din of the machinery, by very small groups of workers. The radio programmes were produced by the company's own radio station and included news bulletins, sports results, record requests and personal messages. The company had nine factories in London, Manchester and Glasgow – hundreds of miles apart – and the programmes were relayed by BT landlines. Today, local radio programmes have replaced the company station.

7. Phone-in news service and ideas

A daily company news bulletin can be tape-recorded and members of the staff may dial a house telephone number to listen to the bulletin. In reverse, employees may phone-in ideas which are recorded. This may be linked to an incentive scheme whereby payment is made according to the contribution the idea makes towards efficiency. Prizes may also be awarded.

8. Ideas box

Boxes are placed at strategic points throughout the premises and staff are invited to place ideas, complaints or comments in the box.

9. Speak-up schemes

This American method of getting feedback from the workshop floor and elsewhere uses a variety of approaches (such as 7 and 8 above), but may also include the right to telephone the chief executive officer direct, the managerial 'open door' technique (*see* below), the writing of letters to management and the use of printed 'speak up' forms with a collection box.

The 'open door' technique may need a little explanation: the 'my door is always open' offer is a form of open management which helps to break down the concept of secrecy, remoteness and aloofness which creates an artificial barrier between management and employees.

10. PA broadcasts

Management may broadcast to employees over a public address (PA) system. This is flexible, so that in large factories messages can be conveyed while everyone is working. It does not have the visual intimacy of video but the smallness of the television screen can be a handicap when large numbers of people have to be addressed.

11. Shop-floor talks

Actual eyeball-to-eyeball talks are among the most effective form of open management. The advantage over broadcasting and video is that employees can ask questions and express views. The facility for staff to communicate upwards and for management to listen and receive feedback is vital in good employee communications. Management should not regard employee communications as monopolistic like political broadcasts.

12. Works councils and committees

It has been proved in Europe that strikes rarely, if ever, happen in companies which have worker directors on the board, works councils and committees. When there is worker participation or involvement the employees know and understand what is going on. They can influence the management of the organisation and are unlikely to 'kill the cow that gives the milk'. It is a lesson which old-fashioned British management has yet to learn. The works council (with many committees) has been used very successfully in ICI.

13. Video/slide presentations

These AV's can be used for purposes such as induction of new staff, explaining safety measures, describing company progress, explaining the annual report and accounts, recruitment, demonstrating how a new product works or describing the amenities of a new venue to which the company is relocating.

Now that so many companies – and especially nationalised industries which have been privatised – have encouraged employees to become shareholders, the video version of the annual report and accounts has become an important medium of management–employee relations.

14. Induction literature

For new staff, the story of the organisation, how it works, and the family tree of management and functions can be told in an introductory booklet.

15. Staff conferences and area meetings

Meetings of staff, at HQ or in local offices, or at national conferences, are useful gatherings which help to unite staff and create good management–employee relations. Again, face-to-face communication occurs.

16. Visits by management

In organisations which have many locations or branches, visits by HQ management can create good relations, and remove the bogey of management remoteness. These visits can often coincide with a social function to celebrate a promotion, award or personal event concerning a member of the local branch.

17. Staff visits

Staff should not be isolated in units so that they never know what is happening in other parts of the organisation. The other units can be brought to employees through house journals, films and video, but actual trips and visits can be enlightening. For instance, those on the production side can be shown the distribution side, e.g. company shops, and shop assistants can be shown round the factory.

18. Staff events

Parties, anniversary dinners, outings and sports tournaments – which include families and friends – also help to cement good relations.

19. Exhibitions and displays

Permanent, mobile and portable exhibitions and displays can be used to demonstrate and explain company history or policy, what the company does and how it operates. Displays may tell the story of the manufacturing process, show how the company operates worldwide or describe a forthcoming advertising campaign. Permanent exhibitions made up of scale and sometimes working models can serve a dual purpose since they will be of interest to visitors.

20. Clubs and societies

Well-established in many companies, the encouragement and sponsoring of hobby and sports societies and the provision of premises and sites such as sports grounds has moved from its paternalistic origins to a fringe benefit of many organisations.

TASKS AND OBJECTIVES OF EMPLOYEE COMMUNICATIONS

21. Face-to-face and upward communications

Experience shows that while printed communication is good and still has an important place, face-to-face communication is vastly superior. This suggests that the videotape often makes an excellent compromise between print and shop-floor meetings.

Employee communications have moved a long way from the paternal house journals of yesteryear and the idea that a house journal was a form of charity. The belief that a house journal is a one-way, i.e. downward, form of communication, with management telling employees what it wants them to know, is also out of date. The modern employee newspaper has won independence, invites readers' opinions and is prepared to publish criticism of the organisation. It has moved from a management pulpit to a staff forum. It has developed into a more truly PR medium of two-way communication (instead of management propaganda), partly as a result of legislation which requires management to be more informative and partly because it has been realised that too many strikes were based on grapevine rumour. In this volatile atmosphere the modern staff journal has to satisfy the suspicions of articulate trade unionists on the one hand and induce the candour of cautious management on the other.

But as we have seen, the house journal is not the only medium and there are today many direct and personalised techniques. In a sense they are not all that modern: what they do is revert to the close relationships that existed between masters and their journeymen and apprentices of the craft guilds of the Middle Ages. The guilds were very jealous of their public relations and had codes of practice for the production of goods. Quality standards depended on face-to-face communication.

22. The complexities of management–employee communications

It would be a foolish oversimplification to suggest that employee communications were only to do with explaining company policy or with providing a forum for complaints. It is true that good communication is superior to a grapevine of rumour, one of the most common causes of lightning strikes. But the following analysis suggests the diversity of tasks and objectives which call for efficient employee communications.

23. Explaining company policy and how management is managing

Employees are entitled to know whether the company is worth working for, what level of security there is and if there are prospects for advancement in either pay or position. This is the essence of job satisfaction. It is very much an area of confidence based on knowledge and understanding, the classic PR situation.

24. Explaining the annual report and accounts

Companies are nowadays expected to tell employees about financial results. Most employees expect their companies to make profits, but do not always realise what a tiny fraction of a company's turnover results in gross profits and how little of profits goes into dividends. The largest sum of money that companies have to recover out of sales is the cost of labour. Well-explained financial results can be a revelation. House journals do this very well, but in recent years some employers have adopted video. Well-known personalities, who specialise in business films, have been used to present company results in interesting down-to-earth terms.

25. Integrating staff following an acquisition

Misunderstandings and jealousies can occur between the staff of the acquiring company and that of the acquired. A major bad employee-relations situation may exist, which might be resolved by good communications using some of the media techniques described in 3–20.

This is a very real problem because 'old-hands' and 'new-hands' may have conflicting traditions and standards, and uniformity has to be established.

26. Explaining new technology

Many industries face great technological changes – automation, robotisation or computerisation with microelectronics and the silicon chip – which may appear as threats to job security. Some changes are inevitable, some will provoke redundancies and some will herald greater prosperity. Amicable industrial relations depend on good employee communications and not only on trade union negotiations. The setting up of committees of shop stewards to study new processes or sending them on familiarisation visits and courses and, of course, greater worker participation and profit-sharing schemes are all part of this communication process. Industry has been changing ever since power looms were invented: internal communication has not always matched the same march of progress.

27. Safety

Many industries have perils which can be averted if staff are not only instructed but reminded about safety precautions such as the wearing of special clothing, use of safety guards and the correct handling of dangerous materials. This education can be a continuous process because there are always new staff and new hazards, while some people can be fatalistic, apathetic, forgetful or careless. Some firms display notices stating accident figures or better still the safety record. Some excellent safety videos have been made, for instance in the steel industry, where dramatic visual presentation increases the impact of information.

28. News about staff

In organisations where employees are scattered among many locations or tend to move about as in airlines and shipping companies, the house journal and other media may be welcomed by employees who seek news of friends and colleagues. Retired staff also look for news of this kind. Many companies continue to send the house journal to their pensioners.

29. Management structure

Charts showing who holds which position and is responsible for what function are useful means of familiarising staff with the identities and roles of management at different levels.

30. Shares and share issues

The stock market activities of a public company are also employee business. Why is there a new share or rights issue or, perhaps, why is a private company 'going public'? Many companies offer shares to their employees, or tell them how they can participate in a share issue. If employees own shares, they will need to understand stock market activities and be able to understand how share performance can be a measure of company performance to which they contribute.

31. Employee benefits

Pensions, Christmas bonuses, incentive schemes, sales contests, educational awards and training schemes all need to be communicated properly if they are to be appreciated or supported.

32. International marketing

If the company exports, has overseas subsidiaries or royalty and licensing agreements for overseas manufacture, these undertakings can be of interest to the staff, offering prospects of greater prosperity and jobs abroad.

33. Employee speakers

Public relations efforts extend to everyone in an organisation provided they are well-informed and able to speak with authority. Every member of the staff can thus be an ambassador, especially those who have contact with customers whether they be secretaries, accountants, clerks, telephonists, transport drivers, sales staff or service staff. In this way the multiple image can be avoided and everyone can present a similar image of the organisation.

34. Legislation

When new laws affect an organisation their meaning and implications should be explained.

35. Feedback and results

Finally, an important objective – which, in itself, can stimulate good employee relations – is to encourage the workforce to feel that its voice should be needed and heeded. This concerns not only the topics which may rightly belong to the trade union sphere but opinions on advertising, house style, the company name, packaging, distribution methods and other matters with which staff are familiar.

Generally, good employee communications can increase productivity for productivity is not only about people working harder but working willingly, enthusiastically, knowledgeably, proudly and efficiently. This can lead to fewer quality control rejects, fewer customer complaints and product recalls, greater customer satisfaction, recommendations and thus better business and fuller employment. This is a cordial circle. People work better when they understand what the company is doing and why. Similarly, absenteeism – due to poor motivation and boredom – can also be overcome. Management owes it to itself to communicate effectively, which is why responsibility for PR should start at the top and why PR is very much a management technique.

Progress test 14

1. What three requirements are called for if internal PR is to be effective?

2. How did the United Biscuits radio station operate?

3. What is a speak-up scheme?

4. In what way are shop-floor talks superior to other forms of internal communication?

5. How can worker participation demonstrate that good communications improve industrial relations?

6. Why is it necessary to tell workers about financial results, and how can this be done?

7. How can communication techniques help to reduce accidents?

8. Suggest some ways in which feedback can create employee involvement in company affairs.

9. How can good employee communications contribute to job satisfaction and help to increase productivity?

15

EXHIBITIONS AND CONFERENCES

USES AND TYPES OF EXHIBITION PR

1. The use of PR for exhibitions

Most public and trade exhibitions form a below-the-line advertising medium, since their objective is to make known in order to sell, and a great deal of selling and order-taking occurs at exhibitions. All the same, PR concerns exhibitions in the following ways:

(a) Exhibition promoters use PR on behalf of their shows – to inform potential exhibitors and visitors and to support participants in the show – and the press office is an important service to both exhibitors and the media. During the run of the show the exhibition press officer organises radio, TV, wire service and photographic coverage. News releases and pictures are displayed in the press office and supplied to visiting journalists. There is usually a press day or a preliminary press opening ceremony. If the official opener is a personality who makes news, the event is well publicised in the media.

(b) Exhibitors can extend the value of their stand or booth by taking advantage of the press officer's services. Advance publicity, and further stories and pictures published during and after the show, can attract visitors in the first instance and, in the second, spread the message to thousands of people at home and abroad who do not attend. In these ways, exhibition PR is like ripples produced by a stone dropped into a pool, spreading outwards.

(c) Some stands may be used for PR purposes, the opportunity being taken to create knowledge and understanding rather than to advertise and sell something. Non-commercial organisations, trade and professional bodies use exhibitions in this way, while cinema shows, exhibits and demonstrations are given at agricultural shows and gymkhanas by the police, the armed forces, dairy and other food promotional boards.

2. Kinds of exhibition

In Europe and North America, where the weather is unpredictable or temperatures are low, the majority of public and trade shows are held indoors, but in warmer countries or ones with more stable climates, these events are more often held out-of-doors. Exhibitions may be divided into the following types:

(a) Public exhibitions such as the *Daily Mail* Ideal Home Exhibition.

(b) Trade exhibitions usually limited to ticket holders and *bona fide* business people, e.g. the Toy Fair. There are some events which interest both the public and the trade, with special days for each, e.g. the Motor Show and the Furniture Exhibition.

(c) Outdoor exhibitions such as the Royal Agricultural Show and county agricultural shows which combine show-ring events with a trade exhibition, or outdoor shows for building equipment, caravans or aircraft.

(d) Private exhibitions, held on own or hired premises, to which guests are invited (*see* **(h)**).

(e) Overseas trade fairs, to promote the products of a country, attract importers, or provide an international showplace with national pavilions and stands. The International Motor Show and the various 'Expos' are typical examples.

(f) Joint ventures, i.e. those organised by the British Overseas Trade board to subsidise the grouping together of British exhibitors on one stand.

(g) Mobile shows, the exhibition being transported by trailer, train, special vehicle or aircraft. Ships have also been converted into floating exhibitions which have toured ports, numerous firms displaying their goods on board.

(h) Portable exhibitions, which can be taken from place to place and set up in public halls, foyers of various buildings, libraries, hotel rooms, station forecourts and so on. They may be either public or private.

(i) Small exhibitions for shop windows, hotel foyers, railway station and airport concourses. They may be housed in glass cases or mounted on display panels or specially set up in an allotted area. They may include samples, models, photographs, charts and lettered panels.

(j) Shopping Weeks sponsored by governments, trade associations, manufacturers, tourist organisations and other bodies. Shopping Weeks are held in large stores in foreign towns and cities. They are usually supported by window displays and in-store demonstrations and may be linked with theatrical events such as cinematic shows and stage shows consisting of national singers and dancers. Food and wine tastings, fashion shows and similar attractions may be associated with the week.

(k) Special exhibits, which can include the laying of carpet at railway terminals and airports so that they have to endure being walked on by thousands of travellers – Monsanto's carpet at Brussels Airport was a good example and aroused much interest and valuable enquiries.

NATURE OF EXHIBITIONS

3. Special characteristics

The modern exhibition is based on the old trading marts of sixteenth-century Europe which were great occasions for business coupled with entertainment. This happy atmosphere still prevails even in the austerity of conventional exhibition halls. A visit to an exhibition or fair is still an outing which visitors expect to enjoy. Those participating must not disappoint visitors. Special characteristics of these events are as follows:

(a) They bring the exhibits to the notice of unknown people, who are attracted to the show as if it were a magnet. The medium has its own special lure.

(b) Person-to-person contact is offered. Since the exhibitor and the products are there and ready to be criticised, this frankness invites credibility.

(c) Entertainment is an inherent factor and therefore the exhibitor must not be dull. Even the most static subject – such as banking – needs to be enlivened by some form of movement. It might be a representative in national costume – if it was an international event – or a film, video or slide presentation, or perhaps a moving model. Many a stand has been brought to life by a toy train set!

4. Conferences and exhibitions

Sometimes conferences and seminars are run in conjunction with exhibitions, while alternatively an exhibition may be mounted for the benefit of conference delegates: the first is a means of attracting visitors to the show, the second is a service to those attending the conference.

The PR practitioner may be able to arrange for a representative of his or her organisation to address a conference sponsored by exhibition promoters, and this speech may be publishable in the press.

Film shows may also be held during the run of an exhibition, and this can be another PR opportunity if a participant has a suitable film for inclusion in the programme.

PLANNING FOR EXHIBITION PR

5. A PR plan for exhibitors

Anyone taking part in an exhibition has many PR opportunities, if prepared to carry out a proper scheme of activity. Merely to supply news releases to the press room is to neglect the very real PR possibilities which exist with most exhibitions. The plan of PR action should be decided *as soon as the stand space is booked*, which may be as much as a year in advance. An ideal procedure might be as outlined below:

(a) Contact the exhibition press officer immediately the contract for stand space has been signed. Questions to ask the press officer are as follows:

(i) What is required to help with advance PR for the event? Information about the exhibitor? Pictures? (At this early date the nature of the actual exhibit may not be known, but at least information can be supplied about the organisation and what it does, makes or sells.)

(ii) What will be the press day arrangements?

(iii) Who will be the official opener? Is this person likely to be interested in the exhibitor's particular products or services? If so, an invitation can be sent direct to the official opener with the suggestion that the stand should be included in the itinerary of his or her tour of the exhibition. This may have to be done through the VIP's PRO. Only a limited number of pre-selected stands can be visited in this brief tour.

(iv) What will be the press office facilities? Usually there will be a stated number of releases and captioned pictures, maybe 50 or 100, which the press officer is prepared to accept and display. A single, numbered picture may be displayed, the other prints being stored in a filing cabinet. Sometimes sales literature may be laid out on a table. Lavish press packs are discouraged by those exhibition press officers who do not want the trouble of having to dispose of them when the show closes. Journalists do not arrive with suitcases: what they want are good, brief, news stories and attractive pictures, which they can put in their pocket, or briefcase if they happen to be carrying one.

(b) For the exporter there are further opportunities through the services of the Central Office of Information which distributes overseas stories about interesting British exhibits. The COI also makes videos of exhibitions for overseas television and tape interviews for overseas radio. It pays to inform the COI two or three months in advance. This extra publicity costs nothing, or, rather, it is paid out for out of taxes and is there for the asking.

(c) Information about exhibits should be sent to journals which are previewing the event. This information is often invited by editors and it is not necessary to buy advertisement space, although an astute advertisement manager will obviously try to win advertising support.

(d) The exhibition catalogue entry should be submitted by the prescribed date.

(e) If a private press reception is to be held on the stand (or elsewhere) during the run of the show, catering arrangements and the dispatch of invitations must be made in good time.

(f) If there is to be no private press reception, individual invitations can be sent to the media to visit the stand. This may include an invitation to attend a demonstration.

(g) In certain cases, retailers, agents and other distributors may be invited to visit the stand, not only to see new products but so that they can meet company personnel. Admission tickets will have to be ordered from the exhibition promoters.

(h) Reference to the company's participation should be featured in the house journal.

(i) Similarly, local media should be informed.

6. Part of overall PR plan

For various exhibitors there may be other and different opportunities which will be apparent to a wide-awake PR practitioner. The point is that taking part in an exhibition calls for a special PR programme which should begin as early as possible to achieve maximum coverage and results. The rewards are there to be gained. This special PR programme should be dovetailed into the total programme, and the necessary working hours, finance and resources must be calculated.

7. Conferences

In **4** reference was made to conferences associated with exhibitions, or vice versa, but many conferences are organised for PR purposes which are independent of exhibitions. These were also mentioned in 10:**27**.

The organising of a PR conference is similar to that for a press reception (*see* 9:**21**) except that it will be of longer duration (at least a whole day); more guests will be invited and catered for; the programme will be more extensive with more speakers and more use of AVs; and of course it will be more costly. A special conference venue will be required such as a conference hall or the ballroom of a hotel. Catering will include either a buffet or sit-down luncheon. The speakers may be company personnel or outside authorities, papers will need to be written and reproduced, and rehearsals may be necessary. Guests should receive a printed programme.

Progress test 15

1. How does PR concern exhibitions?

2. What is the difference between public and trade exhibitions?

3. What governs whether a show is held indoors or out-of-doors?

4. What is a joint venture?

5. Describe some of the means of transporting mobile exhibitions.

6. What is a Shopping Week?

7. Describe the special characteristics of an exhibition.

8. In what ways can conferences be associated with an exhibition and be of PR value?

9. Draw up a plan, with a timetable, for PR activities to support an exhibition which is to take place in six months' time.

10. How many working hours do you estimate the plan for Question 9 will require?

11. In what ways is a conference different from a press reception?

16

PHOTOGRAPHY

IMPORTANCE AND USES OF PHOTOGRAPHY IN PR

1. The importance of photography in PR

Photography is one of the most important aspects of public relations because PR information may need to be well-illustrated and pictures can sometimes be more informative than words. It is, therefore, essential that the PR practitioner should have a good working knowledge of photography and know how to work with professional photographers in order to get the best possible pictures.

It is also sensible for the PR practitioner to know how to use a camera and be able to take good pictures when a professional photographer is not immediately available. Opportunities for PR pictures can occur at unexpected moments. But if the PRO does take his or her own pictures it should be remembered that black and white film has to be used as most pictures printed in the press are not in colour.

Proper instructions are vital when commissioning photographers. Poor photographs can result from bad briefing. The mistake is too often made of assuming that the photographer will automatically know what is wanted. Photographers are not mind-readers.

The PRO should regard the camera as a communication tool just like a pen, word-processor, personal computer, telephone and the spoken word. In other words, the PRO should know how to communicate through a camera lens, that is how to tell a story with a camera. This will also result in the production of publishable pictures which will please editors and readers, and also enhance the interest and quality of any print for which the PRO is responsible. A good picture may get a story published.

2. PR uses of photography

Photographs may be used for PR purposes in the following ways;

(a) To build a photographic library so that prints are available to meet requests and for general use when pictures are needed

(b) To supply with news releases

(c) To illustrate feature articles

(d) As picture stories, sometimes in sets

(e) For window and showroom displays

(f) For display in travelling exhibitions and on portable display panels at seminars, press receptions and other events

(g) For display – as enlargements ('blow-ups') – on exhibition stands

(h) For illustrating house journals

(i) For illustrating PR literature and visual aids, including educational leaflets, folders and booklets, posters, company histories, staff induction handbooks, annual reports, instruction manuals, and technical data sheets: good PR literature may also be used as sales literature and for advertising purposes such as direct mail enclosure

(j) For stills as used in television studio backgrounds to speakers or during TV news bulletins. In this, colour transparencies are advisable.

(k) For conversion into 35 mm slides and for use in slide-tape presentations: these may be colour-slides taken on colour film. Videos can be produced too on the slide-on-film principle.

3. Functions of pictorial material

Whilst not every picture will serve the same purpose, it is worth remembering the possible variety of future uses when a photographic session is being booked or is in progress. The pictures for a news release, the house journal and for enlarging or 'blowing-up' for exhibition and showroom use, may have to be taken differently. For instance, the news release picture may need a consumer interest, the house journal picture an employee interest and the exhibition stand picture an industrial interest. Again, the chance to take certain pictures may never happen again and it will pay to exploit the occasion fully. It should also be remembered that for most press relations purposes, black and white pictures will be required, while colour slides may be needed for other purposes. The photographer may have to use two cameras, one with black and white film and the other with colour slide film. Beware of photographic firms which offer colour prints 'for PR purposes': never send a colour print with a news release, even though some publishers can convert them into black and white.

WORKING WITH THE PHOTOGRAPHER

4. Preparatory work

The photographer is a professional in his or her own right. He or she will know about the technicalities of producing pictures, but cannot know what messages the pictures have to convey, how the pictures will be used and who is likely to see them, nor how they will be reproduced – *unless told*. The photographer could take a prize-winning picture which could be useless for public relations purposes. Therefore, the PR practitioner must know what sort of pictures are wanted, and be able to explain the exact requirements to the photographer.

It may be helpful to sketch the desired composition, necessary to stage-manage the subject or wise to supervise the shooting session. All essential preparations should be made to assist the photographer, such as clearing scenes of irrelevant items or making sure that people to appear in pictures are available and are correctly dressed, e.g. it may be wrong for people to be smoking, not wearing safety gear or be working in a jacket instead of in their shirt-sleeves.

It is the PR practitioner's responsibility to look after such details; the photographer cannot be expected to think of them. Whenever possible, the PRO should be present at the photographic session.

5. Avoiding problems

A common fault is for the photographer to invite the wrong people or too many people to pose in a picture without realising that, for instance, four people working a labour-saving machine makes a nonsense of the picture. If a good working relationship is achieved, the photographer will be appreciative because his or her work will turn out better and both sides will be satisfied.

COMMUNICATING WITH PICTURES

6. Introduction

It is true that pictures can often tell more than words. Editors welcome pictures which help to make their pages look attractive, but the mistake should not be made of introducing irrelevant material. The quality or interest of a picture does not end with the photographer: pictures can be improved by 'cropping' or trimming. Portraits often include the torso when a better picture is one which has been trimmed below the throat with enlargements made of the desired area of the negative.

7. Practical tips

Some practical hints for producing good pictorial material are given below.

(a) *Presentations and handshakes*. Avoid a gap between the two figures as when arms are extended across a table during a presentation or when two people are shaking hands. It may be better to ask the subjects to pose again later when they can stand closer together.

(b) *People at work.* Never have the subject looking up from his or her work to stare or smile at the camera. The subject should be seen, perhaps in profile or even from behind, concentrating on the job.

(c) *Human interest.* If this would look natural, introduce people into pictures, e.g. a hotel room looks better if there are guests or staff present: if there is no life it will look as if the place is up for sale. But many a PR picture has been ruined by the use of a pin-up who is irrelevant to the subject.

(d) *Large objects.* Some large objects will actually look small if the photographer has to stand back to get the whole subject in. A portion can give an impression of the whole, or the subject can be taken at an angle to gain a three-dimensional effect. These remarks have particular bearing on photographing buildings and large subjects such as ships or aircraft.

(e) *'Busy' pictures.* Avoid unnecessary detail or irrelevant surroundings which detract from interest in the subject, or make reproduction difficult. Fancy wall-paper designs, trees and shrubs, factory interior backgrounds and so forth can be a nuisance. Good photographers usually carry with them white sheets or rolls of white paper which they can hang to obscure unnecessary backgrounds, e.g. when a piece of machinery is being photographed in a factory. Special problems with background and surroundings can occur when fashion pictures, for instance, are being taken out-of-doors.

(f) *Light or pale subjects.* White or light-coloured subjects, such as dresses, fabrics or curtains, can be very difficult to reproduce and it is important to secure contrasts, either in the background, or by means of folds or shadows or in skin tones. Ideally, for example, a white bathing costume or dress would be best modelled by a black model and vice versa.

(g) *Perspectives.* Be careful of 'railway line' effects as when work benches taper off into the distance.

(h) *Colour pictures.* Except for 35 mm slides or special illustrations like a front cover picture, colour pictures are not required in press relations work. The situation will, of course, change when colour pictures become common in newspapers, but for the moment most journals require black and white pictures. However, when colour pictures are to be used, a variety of colours should be sought; red is always an interesting colour to have in a picture if possible. This is important because so many everyday colours are dull greys, browns and greens, and yellow, orange and red are generally absent. They are wanted by TV as can be seen by the dress of newscasters and presenters.

(i) *Flat or profile pictures.* Pictures are more dramatic if given a three-dimensional effect of depth. This is easily done by turning the subject (or positioning the camera) so that a front and side view is obtained.

(j) *Impression of size.* If the size of the object is not obvious it pays to introduce something of known size, such as a hand or a full figure, which will indicate how small or how large the subject really is. Otherwise, in the case of a well-shaped object, for example, it would be impossible to tell whether it was as small as a cotton spool, of medium size like a tape reel or huge like a cable reel. Hackneyed devices such as coins and matchboxes should not be used.

(k) *Name display*. Avoid the temptation to turn the picture into a blatant advertisement by introducing name displays on packages, vehicles and other objects. This may either be difficult to avoid or identification may be required, e.g. the name or insignia of an airline on an aircraft. On other occasions the hint of a name, for instance just a few letters, may be sufficient to suggest a full name.

(l) *Loss through printing*. Limitations can be imposed by the problems of reproduction. Remember that in most printing processes a dot screen is superimposed on the pictures (*see* Chapter 17) so that the picture is made up of dots (often very visible on newsprint) and there is bound to be a substantial loss of definition and detail. The paper used is generally dull, whereas the original print is glossy, and newsprint has a blotting paper quality, so that the ink spreads, while pale subjects can be ruined by show-through from printing on the reverse side of the paper. This applies particularly with big circulation newspapers which are printed at great speed. Alternatively, unless there are good highlights a dark subject can reproduce as a patch of solid black ink. When having photographs taken and when supplying them to the press, it is important to imagine what will happen to them under printing conditions and processes. For letterpress printing, a 'soot and whitewash' (high contrast) picture without middle tones of grey is best, while for lithographic printing a more detailed picture with gradations of tone (from pale grey to black) is likely to reproduce well. But for photogravure, rich, 'velvety' pictures are best as dark tones are reduced to solid areas without definition.

One of the effects of printing London national newspapers on offset-litho instead of letterpress machines has been the increase in picture quality. This is because the dot screen is usually twice as fine as that used for letterpress printing. Consequently, these newspapers can accept – and require – pictures with grey tonal qualities and containing more detail such as landscape scenes rather than close-ups.

Printing processes are explained in the next chapter.

CAPTIONS

8. Content

All pictures *must* be captioned when sent to an editor, supplied to an exhibition press office or sent to anyone making a request for pictures. The caption should contain the following information (*see* Figure 16.1).

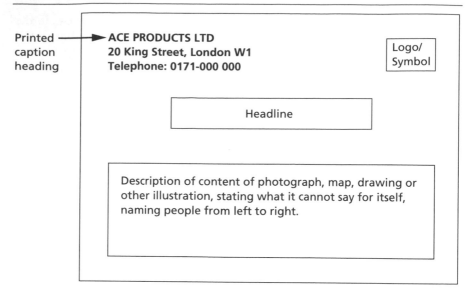

Printed → caption heading → **ACE PRODUCTS LTD**
20 King Street, London W1
Telephone: 0171-000 000

Logo/ Symbol

Headline

Description of content of photograph, map, drawing or other illustration, stating what it cannot say for itself, naming people from left to right.

Fig 16.1   Layout of photo caption or caption to any other illustration

(a) The name, address and telephone number of the *sender*, who should be the copyright owner (printed caption headings are ideal).

(b) The text of the caption should have a brief headline which identifies the subject.

(c) The text should state what the picture cannot say for itself. This wording should describe the picture. It should not be something lifted from a news release (*see Note* below).

(d) Copyright ownership must be stated, and permission to reproduce *free of fee* may also be declared, but on no account should there be a statement that the sender owns the copyright and therefore reproduction must not be made without permission. It happens, but it is nonsense. Normally, an editor will assume that if a picture is received from a PR source he or she is entitled to print it free of charge – otherwise, why has it been sent? For this reason, the PR practitioner must own the copyright of all the pictures that he or she submits. The PR practitioner must not distribute other people's copyright pictures: editors will not print them because they will not wish to pay reproduction fees to the original copyright owners.

(e) To avoid confusion, the photographer's rubber stamp must *not* appear on the backs of prints. The sender may apply *his* or *her* rubber stamp in addition to the caption, which is useful if the caption comes off or is removed.

Note: The caption should not be included in a news release, nor should the text of the release refer to accompanying pictures. Picture availability can be mentioned

154

after the close of the story together with the author's name and the date. In an editorial office, it must be remembered, different people at different times will handle the release and the picture so that each must be independent of the other. A picture without a caption is therefore an incomplete and confusing piece of information which may well be rejected. It is always possible that while a news release may be rejected the accompanying picture may be retained in the photograph library, for which purpose a caption with identifiable source will be essential.

9. Fixing captions

A caption should be fixed so that it is not easily torn off, leaving the picture naked of vital information. Captions may be fixed firmly with a strip of clear adhesive tape top and bottom, or attached as a flap so that the caption can be dropped and read while viewing the picture. The merit of the first is that the caption is secure, while that of the second is that caption and picture can be studied together. Both methods are commonly used. But since the caption will not be sent for setting because the art editor or journalist will write his or her own caption based on the information given and according to the journalist's style and the space available, the security of the fixed caption outweighs the handiness of the flapped and easily ripped-off type. It is not wise to glue captions on, as this can have a crimping or corrugating effect on the print.

A third method, used when a large number of pictures are being sent out simultaneously – as happens in the entertainment world – is to duplicate the caption directly on the back of the picture.

Photographs should not be pasted onto a sheet of paper with the caption typed below, because when the picture is removed for plate-making it will have no identification on the back. Nor should a picture be pasted in the middle of a news release. Both practices do occur but they infuriate editors.

OTHER TECHNICAL CONSIDERATIONS

10. Size of prints

Editors prefer large prints so that they can crop them as they wish. If the subject fills the picture, either because it was composed like this in the viewfinder or because the picture was cropped or masked before being enlarged, the editor will have little waste area to trim.

Very large prints, even when protected in card-backed envelopes, are often folded in half by postmen who like to contain all the post for one address in an elastic band, nylon cord or a piece of string. This postal peril can be overcome by using half-plate (16.5 × 12 cm) prints which suit the postman's bundle without being bent. Card protection is still required. If large prints are demanded or desirable, they are best hand-delivered.

11. Avoiding damage to prints

Finally, photographs must not be attached to other items by means of a paperclip that will produce a dent which will show up during plate-making at the printers; nor should pictures be stapled to accompanying material: these habits can destroy pictures. Again, if pictures accompany items such as a two- or three-page news release or an article or report, the stapled edge should be tucked inside when folding so that no damage can occur to the picture while it is in the post.

While photographs should have a glossy and not a matt surface, they should not be specially glazed. Such pictures crack and attract fingerprints and are useless for editorial purposes.

Progress test 16

1. Why should a PR practitioner practise photography him- or herself?

2. List five PR uses of photography.

3. Explain how the same subject could produce pictures for very different purposes.

4. Why is it necessary to have a good working relationship with the photographer?

5. How can pictures be given appropriate human interest?

6. What is meant by a 'busy' picture?

7. How would you demonstrate the size of a giant boiler?

8. Why should blatant name displays be avoided?

9. What are the essentials of a photo caption?

10. Why is it best to fix a caption so that it cannot be removed?

11. Why should pictures be protected in the post, and what is the best size for a print?

12. How can photographs be damaged and therefore made useless to editors and non-productive for the PR practitioner?

17

PRINTING PROCESSES

BACKGROUND AND TERMINOLOGY

1. Usefulness of the knowledge of printing

It is necessary for the PR practitioner to have a knowledge of printing processes.This is because he or she has a lot to do with dates, print, printers, press dates, printing methods and requirements. This is essential when, for example, compiling mailing lists for news releases, and when timing their dispatch. The printed word predominates in PR, even in developing and less literate countries, where newspapers may not be as dominant as in the West. Even a simple leaflet or poster calls for some knowledge of printing.

Principally, it is important at least to be able to distinguish between the six main processes, know something about the kind of work they can produce and understand what kind of material the printer requires in each case. The six main processes are: letterpress, lithography or litho, photogravure or gravure, flexography, screen and digital.

It is always helpful to visit print shops and see practical demonstrations. However, each printer may be equipped to produce only certain kinds of work such as books, newspapers, calendars, stationery, business forms, labels, packaging, advertising brochures, or general jobbing work. You will need to visit a great number of printers to get a comprehensive impression, but opportunities to make visits should never be missed.

One thing is basic to all printing: the transfer of an image to paper or other surface. Each of the processes does this differently:

(a) Letterpress and flexography print from a raised surface (relief).

(b) Lithography prints from a flat surface (planographic).

(c) Gravure prints from a recessed surface (intaglio).

(d) Screen printing uses stencils.

(e) Digital uses a toner-fusion technique.

Before discussing the technicalities of each process, we will look at the areas common to all printing.

2. Typography: the point system

In conventional letterpress printing, words are usually set in metal type. Typefaces (individual type designs) are measured by a 'point' system. This was conceived in Chicago in 1892. There are 72 points to the inch (25.4 mm). Typical type sizes are 6 point, 12 point and so on. Newspaper text is mostly 8 point, book text about 10 point. This is the vertical measurement on which the letters are set. Getting more white space between lines of type in letterpress can be achieved by interspersing with non-type-high strips of metal called *leads* (pronounced leds). This name derives from the metal they are largely made of. Alternatively, the space can be included in the depth of the body of the type, hence expressions such as '10 on 11' meaning that 10 point type is carrying 1 point of leading to provide a 1 point space between the lines of type.

However, as will be seen in **10**, most typesetting today is computerised, and type sizes do not necessarily follow the point system. Type can be enlarged, reduced, expanded or condensed electronically by the keyboard operator, or when plate-making a typeset page can be expanded or reduced to suit the format of the publication.

3. Faces, founts and families

The design of a type is called a *face*, and typefaces have names such as Perpetua, Times, Gill Sans, Bodoni, Goudy, Palatino, Univers or Baskerville. A sans serif face is one (like Gill or Univers) without serifs or short lines at the ends of the strokes (look at the ts and ds, for instance). For contrast a sans serif face may be used for display lines or headlines, a serif or book face for text or body matter.

Too much sans type is difficult to read – a mistake often made in advertising print. Sans faces are also less easy to read on shiny paper than serif faces. The text in this book is printed with a serif face: all this reading matter would be difficult to read if set in sans type, whereas it is ideal for the bold titlings.

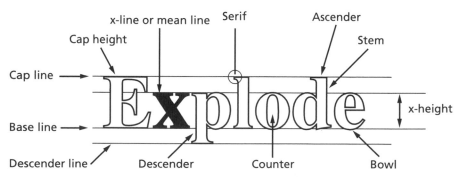

Fig 17.1 Typeface characteristics

Medium or regular	Explode Serif face
Bold	Explode Sans serif face
Extra bold	Explode Slab serif face
Italics	Explode Fancy face
Condensed	*Explode* Script
Expanded	

Fig 17.2   A typographical family   **Fig 17.3   Some basic type styles**

If the serif is the same thickness as the strokes of the type, it is called a *slab-serif* or Egyptian. Such faces often have Egyptian names like Cairo and Karnak, although the best known is called Rockwell.

A complete set of characters including alphabet, numbers, punctuation marks and signs is called a *fount*. There are two historic origins of the word. It is said that in the early days of printing by monks, a whole alphabet of type was kept in a spare fount, as used for baptisms. But a fount (also spelt and generally pronounced 'font') can also be taken from the Old French word *fondre*, meaning casting from or melting which is somewhat related to type.

Variations in the thickness of type are called *weights*, and different weights are described as light, medium, bold and extra bold. A complete set of alphabets in the various styles of face is called a *family*.

In some faces there will also be condensed and expanded varieties. Upright type is called *roman*, sloping type *italic*, while faces resembling handwriting are called *script*. Other faces resemble typewriter characters or the old hand-tooled characters.

There are many hundreds of typefaces and they are multiplied by the special versions of a style as created by different typefounders for copyright reasons. Before specifying any typeface, the printer should be asked what faces can be supplied. Ordering small quantities of a special face, perhaps for display or headline work, is called *buying sorts*. Computerised typesetters now offer a vast choice of typefaces.

4. Printing papers

A large choice of papers may be used in letterpress printing, and some of the varieties are:

(a) *Newsprint* – a cheap, absorbent paper suitable for printing newspapers.

(b) *Supercalendered* – a cheap but mechanically polished paper suitable for printing magazines.

(c) *Antique* – a bulky, absorbent, rough surfaced paper sometimes used in book production.

(d) *Imitation art* – a polished paper with a china clay content.

(e) *Art* – a high-class paper with a coating of china clay or similar substance on one or both sides which is highly polished.

In rotary offset-litho printing the choice of papers is limited to those available in reels or webs, usually newsprint, supercalendered or special litho papers. A greater variety of papers can be used for sheet-fed litho. There are special litho papers.

TYPESETTING

There are several ways of setting type for letterpress, and these are outlined below. In the UK, Europe and the USA, most of them have been superseded by computerised setting.

5. Hand composition

This is used in small letterpress jobbing work, for display lines, headlines and corrections. The compositor takes type characters out of a type cabinet, with trays called *cases*. He or she composes in a stick held in the hand. Small type letters are arranged in the *lower case*, capitals in the *upper case*, hence these printing expressions denoting the letters, although upper case is usually called 'caps'.

6. Linotype and Intertype

These are letterpress typesetting machines which set type in metal *slugs* to the column width required. A slug is a line of type as a single metal unit. Slugs are used for the setting of letterpress-printed newspapers. The operator sits at a keyboard, and, when a key is depressed, a matrix or mould is brought down from the magazine where they are held, lined up with others and, after spaces have been inserted, the line of type is moulded in molten metal. The machine operates so rapidly that while the operator is setting one line, the previous line is being moulded, and the matrices for the line previous to that are being returned to the magazine. Each magazine holds a particular fount of type and they are interchangeable. The Intertype is similar to the Linotype and is found in many print shops overseas.

7. Monotype

Whereas the Linotype and Intertype machines set slugs or solid column-width lines of words, the Monotype sets single characters similar to those used by the hand compositor. This system of typesetting is used mainly for book-printing or other work containing formulas and mathematical or technical settings. A single character can be corrected instead of having to reset a whole line. There are two machines, a keyboard which produces a small roll of paper with the copy coded into punched holes, and a caster which sets the type in response to compressed air being blown through the perforated roll of paper.

8. Ludlow

This is a machine for casting newspaper headlines.

9. Phototypesetting

The opposite to hot metal setting since no metal type is used, photo-typesetting has revolutionised printing to the extent that computerised phototypesetting can produce a completely made-up page, complete with pictures, in photographic negative form ready for printing down on the litho plate. All this can be done with equipment which can set and lay out, store information for present or future use, replay for correction, and provide camera-ready copy.

10. Modern computerised newspaper production

There are many computerised typesetting, editing and layout systems. These range from desk-top computers such as the Apple Macintosh, and software such as Adobe PageMaker, to large, sophisticated systems used by national newspapers. Direct-input editorial offices may be many miles away from the printing plant, but with on-line linkage pages can be edited and designed in one place and transmitted by telephone line to another for setting, plate-making and printing. For example, some London newspapers edit in London but use contract printers dispersed regionally throughout the country who both print and distribute, e.g. the News Centre in Portsmouth.

Modern typesetting is clever and has many advantages over hot metal setting. However, it has its own problems and characteristics. The style of, say, a page will be programmed, but if there is faulty programming the same error will recur. Keyboard operators may depress a key for, say, italics, and omit to release it so that unnecessary italics are set. There are two styles for completing lines, with or without break words, and the line will not be spaced out on the machine as was the case with Linotype slugs. When proofreading it is necessary to watch out for the idiosyncrasies of computerised setting. Yet another problem is that keyboard operators may

161

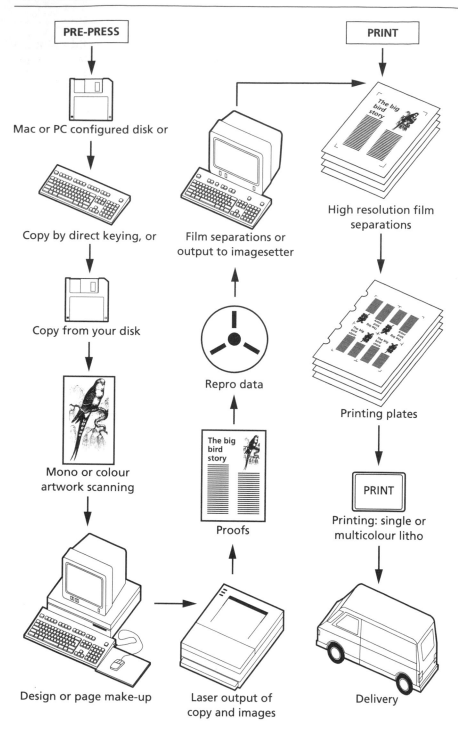

Fig 17.4 The anatomy of a litho print job, from disk to delivery

be careless about errors simply because they are so easily corrected, but the proofreader has to find them!

One of the best-known newspaper systems is made by ATEX, a Kodak company, which is of American origin but available worldwide and used by some 600 publishers. It was first created in the 1970s as a text processing and information handling system, and now provides a cost-effective, integrated electronic publishing system. ATEX can create all textual and graphic elements including halftone material, line art, screens, tints, borders, rotated type, and output full pages with these elements in place ready for plate-making. Electronically, it replaces the old letterpress foundry with its hot-metal typesetting machines, making up of pages with metal type, blocks, rules and spacing, and the making of metal stereos to place on the plate cylinders of the printing machine.

It is possible to work from inputting editorial material to printing in a matter of minutes if necessary. For example, the production of sports pages, with scores of results coming in from all over the country, to production of a Saturday evening sports edition can be done in about 15 minutes.

Briefly, ATEX systems offer publishers four integrated services as outlined below:

(a) *For text editing*, ATEX permits users to create text and fit headlines, track copy, and edit and fit copy to pages, all by computer keyboard and visual display unit. An editorial office consists of numerous desks with small computers. There are no typewriters in the 'paperless newsroom'.

(b) *For design purposes*, ATEX systems simplify page building, providing on-screen feedback about the impact of the design process on the editorial process.

(c) *In the preparation of newspaper advertisements*, the ATEX system allows users to create, manage, and track the production of all advertising on a single database. Correct price quotes, automatic credit checking and quick access to accounts information is provided. This is particularly useful when classified advertisements are phoned in or there is a telesales operation.

(d) *For production purposes*, ATEX permits electronic paste-up and out-putting of fully paginated pages. It also gives production management the means of monitoring and expediting the flow of work.

11. The News Centre, Portsmouth

Portsmouth Publishing & Printing Ltd is a subsidiary of Portsmouth & Sunderland Newspapers plc and its News Centre at Portsmouth (about 80 miles from London) is one of the world's most modern newspaper printing plants. Not only does it print six weekly papers and four editions of the Portsmouth evening paper *The News*, all distributed over a large circulation area. It also prints numerous special souvenir publications on themes like

Her Majesty's 60 Years. It produces paid-for and freesheet newspapers and house journals for companies like IBM and British Airways, and other magazines.

The quality of its printing far exceeds old Fleet Street letterpress standards with more legible type and better reproduced pictures.

High-tech methods are applied to both advertising and editorial sections.The News Centre runs Goss Metroliner offset litho presses seven days a week which can produce up to 192 pages of tabloid or 96 pages of broadsheet in one high-speed pass. Up to 32 pages of full colour can also be printed.

More than 650 people are employed, and printing occupies 22 hours a day. The Metroliners can print 70,000 copies per hour. Nobody is to be seen in the machine room of the print hall as the whole operation is controlled by computers. To enter the machine room one has to wear ear-muffs because the noise is 103 decibels two feet from the folders.

A Dainippon colour scanner SG737 uses laser technology to achieve pin-sharp definition when producing screened negative separations for printing in colour.

A specially adapted computer system scans the page negative produced for plate-making. Information on densities is transmitted to the Digital Equipment Corporation PDP 11/44 minicomputer. This sets the correct ink adjustments to speed press start-up and reduce paper wastage from spoils, and so produces good copies immediately.

There are computer consoles in the press hall which make fine adjustments to the ink flow and printing register. In addition, the printer uses a visual display system terminal and can command the computer to make other adjustments to the presses while they are running. The printer can display press operating data, either on screen or by calling up typed copy from a line printer. All changes made during the print run are logged by the computer.

These control operations take place in a double-glazed noise-protected and air-conditioned cabin which runs the full length of the press desk, separating the two Metroliner presses, with air-lock double doors at each end. The printers rarely have to leave the cabin while the presses are running. If a printer wants to see a copy off the press it can be supplied automatically by a hatch in the cabin. Each press is sealed by sound-proof glass panels, so that a stilled machine can be attended while the other is running.

Counting, stacking, film wrapping and strapping of publications is controlled by Muller Martini and Signode equipment in the despatch department. This also controls the quantity of newspapers to be packed for delivery to each newsagent.

Reels of newsprint are delivered to an area like an aircraft hangar, large enough to take three of the largest and longest articulated lorries.

In 1991-92, Portsmouth Publishing and Printing replaced its DEC editorial system with a 120-terminal system from the Danish company, Dansk Data

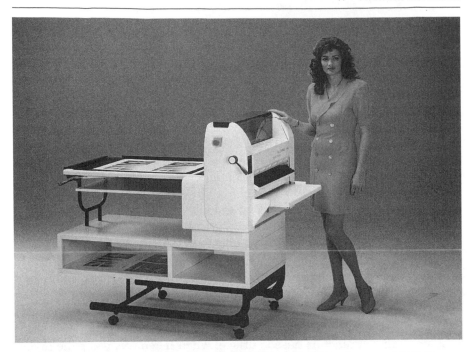

Fig 17.5 Dry colour proofing: the Cromalin EasySprint system uses toners rather than ink; special colours can be added

Electronik (DDE). The system, costing in excess of £1 million, allows subeditors to design their pages on screen. This has led to full page output with all the elements – text, pictures and advertisements – in position.

1997 saw the introduction of a new advertising system from MILES 33, allowing advertisement reps and operators greater flexibility in booking and processing customers' advertising.

LETTERPRESS

12. General background

For a long time letterpress was the most popular printing process in Britain. Vast improvements in offset-litho printing (a form of lithography in which the ink is not transferred direct from the image to the paper), and the introduction from the USA of the web-offset-litho newspaper press (which prints at high speed on continuous rolls or webs of paper rather than sheets), have transformed the British printing scheme in recent decades. It is more economical to print newspapers by web-offset, combining the advantages of offset-litho with the use of huge reels of paper.

In the late 80s the national press of Fleet Street changed from letterpress to litho printing, either by moving to new plants in the East End of London,

165

or by using contract printers outside London. The Daily Mail Group introduced flexography at their new plant in 1988.

Well-printed newspapers, produced by offset-litho and often in full colour, had been common for many years elsewhere in the world. This type of production was slow to arrive in Britain due to trade union resistance. The process does require fewer operators, but it has been possible to retrain and absorb many former print operatives.

By the late 1990s, conventional letterpress had almost completely disappeared from the UK printing scene. The national daily and Sunday press had gone over to web offset litho and flexography. Most magazines were printed web- or sheet-fed litho, or gravure. The only printers still using letterpress were a relatively few jobbing specialists.

However, outside the newspaper world letterpress has fought back, especially with heat-set machines which mean that colour work can be quickly dried on the machine with heat-boxes. The versatility of this process retains its popularity for jobs as varied as business cards, stationery, books and high-quality colour work. Paper varying from newsprint to art may be used and, according to the grade of paper, so pictures can be reproduced with halftone screens ranging from coarse to very fine (*see* **14**).

In letterpress, a relief or raised surface, when inked, *impresses* the image onto paper. This is similar to the effect of a typewriter character or date stamp. Letterpress work is sometimes recognisable by the feel of the impression on the back of the paper or by a slight halo round the edges of each printed character.

13. Halftones

Flat, tonal subjects such as photographs or paintings can be reproduced only if the printing plate can receive and transfer ink. If the picture was merely re-photographed onto a metal printing plate, this plate, when inked, would produce only a shape equal to that of the plate, i.e. the whole plate would be inked and would print as a black area.

A halftone printing surface is created by converting the photographic full-tone image into dots. These are of different sizes, depending on the light, medium or dark tones to be printed. Larger dots create an optical illusion of dark tones; greater areas of white round smaller ones creates an illusion of lighter tones. The final image is an illusion of overall tonal shading.

The dots are created by placing a ruled screen between the lens of a process camera and a printing plate which has been sensitised to light. The term 'halftone' comes from the use of the screen, which eliminates half the original image in order to reproduce tone. The finer the screen and the dot size, the better the illusion, as in good quality magazines, whereas on coarse newsprint the dot size is such that the dot structure of the picture is often visible.

The halftone system applies to letterpress, flexo, litho and screen printing, but not to gravure.

14. Halftone screens

The screen consists of two pieces of glass cemented together. The pieces of glass are ruled with lines at 45° in opposite directions, so that when they are put together a screen of tiny diamond shapes is created. Screens vary from 65 lines to the inch (25.4 mm) for newsprint to 200 lines to the inch for art paper (which is higher quality paper). (See Figure 17.6.) The fineness of the screen used depends largely on the paper quality, but also on the ink and the process.

The platemaker photographs the picture which is to be printed and the light is broken up by the screen so that the picture is received on the plate in dots. Because the screen is set at a little distance from the film in the back of the camera, the diamond shapes are distorted into round dots. The pattern of dots is transferred from the film to the plate and by chemical-etching processes the waste material around the dots is removed, resulting in a letterpress printing plate with a raised dot surface, capable of transferring to paper a picture consisting of dots of various sizes. For litho printing a screen is placed in contact with the film and a screened print is produced. The screened picture is pasted down with the typesettings for platemaking.

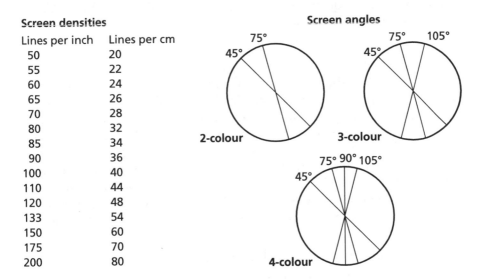

Screen densities

Lines per inch	Lines per cm
50	20
55	22
60	24
65	26
70	28
80	32
85	34
90	36
100	40
110	44
120	48
133	54
150	60
175	70
200	80

Screen angles

2-colour — 45°, 75°

3-colour — 45°, 75°, 105°

4-colour — 45°, 75°, 90°, 105°

Fig 17.6   Halftone screens

15. Colour printing

For full-colour continuous tone reproductions, such as transparencies and paintings, colour printing is known as 'four-colour process printing' because the picture is built up of the three primary colours: magenta (red), cyan (blue) and yellow; and black. For four-colour work of this nature filters are used so that the plates can be made for each separate colour and then each colour is printed down in register with the others. Because the screens for each colour have lines set at different degrees, the dots print in different positions, blending colours but not obliterating or mixing them.

16. Duplicate plates

A problem with letterpress is that the metal printing surface wears because it is constantly touching paper and so imperfections develop. To overcome this or to print large quantities, copies are moulded from the original plates. Duplicate plates include *stereos*, which are cast using a papier mâché mould from the original plate, and *electros*, which are better class duplicates made by the electrolysis process by which the mould is electroplated with copper and sometimes surfaced with nickel or chromium. The type of duplicate metal surface determines the life of the plate on the printing press. Chromium-surfaced electros have a very long print-run life, but other duplicates might be cheaper if a shorter run is required. Letterpress printed newspapers are printed on rotary presses requiring curved plates and the made-up pages of flat type and illustration plates are converted into curved plates by the same stereotyping process. For litho printing, the final thin plate is made by photographing the pasted-up material on to it, so duplicates are unnecessary.

17. Line blocks

To reproduce a line drawing, chart, signature or other design not having gradations of tone as in a photograph, but having solid black areas only, the artwork is photographed without the screen used for halftones (*see* **13**). Again, the waste material of the sensitised plate is etched away so that a printing plate is produced with relief just like type. In fact, a piece of type such as a letter is really a tiny line block in effect. Plates, whether halftone or line, are then attached to metal or wooden blocks to make them the same height as the type for printing the words – this standard height is called *type high*. A mounted plate is called a *block*, i.e. halftone block or line block.

18. Make-up: the chase and the forme

When ready for making-up into pages, the various items are placed on a metal-surfaced bench called the *stone*. Many printing terms derive from the early days of printing, when much printing was done in monasteries and churches. In those days, what is now a metal composing table was a flat stone. Another expression with a similar derivation is 'father of chapel', a printing union shop steward. *Make-up* describes the operation of arranging all the printing material satisfactorily and locking it tightly into place in a *chase*, which is rather like a picture frame with tightening devices, called *quoins*. The material might include, as well as text and blocks, lines for dividing columns or forming borders, known as *rules* and standing type high, and metal (occasionally wooden) spacing material, called *furniture*, which is not type high in order to permit white space between the words, pictures and rules. When all the material is secure in the chase, the whole *forme* can be picked up, placed on a flatbed machine for printing or moulded to make a matrix for casting stereos or curved plates to wrap round the plate cylinder of a rotary letterpress machine.

Finally, the complete *forme*, as printing material locked up in the chase is called, can be stored until required again. Storage is referred to as keeping the type *standing*.

From the above it will be realised that all this hot metal work, occupying the foundry of a letterpress printing plant, required a large staff of highly skilled operatives. All that has now gone with newspapers being printed by either offset-litho or flexography.

LITHOGRAPHY

19. Planographic printing

The principle of litho printing is that grease and water will not mix. Thus, if the area to be printed has a greasy texture, the water will wash away the excess ink leaving the image on the greasy area only ready for printing onto paper.

A thin plate is used today, but originally printing was made from a slab of limestone from the Jura mountains in Germany, the word litho being taken from the Greek *lithos*, meaning stone.

Stones were used for flatbed work, but modern rotary presses require a printing surface that can be placed round a cylinder and use mainly metal plates. The original limestone was porous, retaining moisture, and the litho artist had to draw (in reverse) directly onto the stone. Most of the famous pictorial posters of pre-Second World War days were created like this.

20. Offset-litho

This form of lithography is rotary and therefore very fast. To understand the process three cylinders have to be imagined (*see* Figure 17.7). The first is the *plate cylinder* round which is wrapped the thin metal plate bearing the material to be printed. The words and pictures have been processed photographically so that the image is flat on the surface of the plate, not raised as in letterpress. A dot screen is used for photographs and other full-tone illustrations. Water and ink are applied to the printing plate. The second cylinder is the *blanket cylinder* which has a covering of rubber or other suitable flexible material. The third cylinder is the *impression cylinder* which conveys the paper and impresses it on the blanket which in turn prints – or offsets – onto the paper. The plate never touches the paper:

instead, it prints on the blanket which in turn prints or offsets on the paper. The paper may be individual sheets fed into the machine mechanically or a continuous reel (*see* below). Flat-bed litho is used for those print jobs which cannot be printed from reels, e.g. magazine covers on heavy paper and large posters consisting of several pieces.

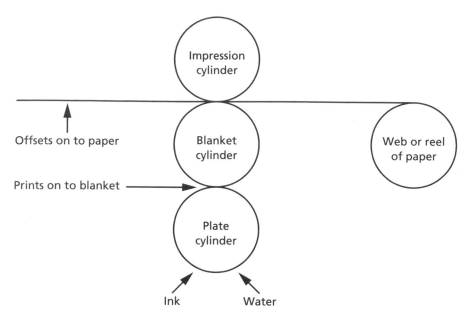

Fig 17.7   Diagram of a web-offset-litho machine principle (in four-colour process printing each colour printed has a bank of cylinders on this arrangement with driers between each bank on heat-set machines)

21. Web-offset

This means that instead of printing on separate sheets of paper, a continuous reel or web of paper is fed as with rotary letterpress machines. This gives very fast lithographic printing suitable for large runs of newspapers or magazines. In fact, it is so fast that owners of such machines invariably have capacity to accept many smaller jobs such as house magazines.

22. Special characteristics of lithography

A combination of developments and innovations has popularised offset- (and web-offset) litho in the UK and elsewhere, although it was popular much earlier still in the USA. The process rescued many local weekly newspapers which in post-war years could not afford to replace worn-out letterpress machines, but found it economic to use a specialist offset-litho plant. Many new evening newspapers (such as the Thompson series) were launched in Britain because of the introduction of web-offset machines. Such is their capacity that one strategically located printer will print several local newspapers, a number of national magazines, and fill in any spare machine time with house journals and other jobs. The process revolutionised house journal design so that the tabloid became popular, but with the introduction of webs of better quality paper, the A4 magazine format is also popular. In the section on phototypesetting (*see* 9) reference has already been made to the preparation of camera-ready copy, that is line artwork and typesetting mounted ready for photographing as, say, a complete advertisement, but tonal pictures being supplied separately so that a screen may be applied.

Litho machines range from office printing machines to giant newspaper presses, and camera-ready copy as opposed to the sophisticated ones already described.

While litho is popular one does see some very poor litho in some developing countries where print of all kinds lacks the perfection of European litho. There are at least four reasons for this, and they tend to be related to local conditions. They are:

(a) Poor photographs, lacking in definition and suffering from poor processing.

(b) Poor quality hard or coarse paper, due to the high cost of importing paper.

(c) Paper stretch, which can distort colour pictures, printing them out of register.

(d) The effects of humidity. A good litho printing plant needs humidity control. Humidity is often high in these countries and printers rarely have humidity control systems.

23. Advantages of lithography

(a) Paper-makers now produce well-finished papers for litho printers, when not so long ago hard papers such as cartridge were typical.

(b) Fine halftone screens, 133 to 200 lines per inch (54 to 80 lines per centimetre), ensure better gradation and more detailed images. The almost unrecognisable pictures which one expects to find in letterpress-printed newspapers are unheard of in modern web-offset, even on newsprint (litho newsprint is a little harder than letterpress newsprint). From the PR point of view this does mean that very different qualities of picture are required for letterpress and litho printed publications. This is one of the reasons why it helps to understand a little about printing. Since litho printing is so common today, it is even more important to provide the press with first-class pictures.

(c) Because expensive halftone blocks do not have to be made (and sets of four-colour halftone letterpress blocks *are* very expensive), offset-litho and web-offset lend themselves to pictorial and colour picture work. Examples are motor car and package tour brochures, while many house journals can afford colour when printed by litho. Text and illustration are on the same printing plate, and will both print onto most grades of paper, whereas in letterpress illustrations are often printed in a separate section on extra-quality paper.

(d) Full-colour work is obtained by the heat-set system of drying each colour on the machine before it passes to the next printing. This automatic drying process is quick, provides good register of one colour on another and avoids shrinkage of paper.

(e) Glossy inks with a large proportion of pigment result in excellent, rich colour work, as seen in sales folders and pictorial catalogues, calendars and picture books.

(f) Text matter is clean and almost perfect. Each reproduction of the same character is identical, thanks to computerised typesetting. The type is not impressed into the paper: it sometimes looks as if it could be scraped off the surface with a knife. No longer do we have irregular type, as occurred with Linotype settings, nor battered type resulting from metal characters being damaged.

(g) The machines are more compact than letterpress machines, even when set up in batteries for colour work. This offers economies in print-shop planning, and has made possible the setting up of litho plants in urban areas where the tendency had been for letterpress printers to seek more economical locations outside town.

24. The British newspaper revolution

With the arrival of *Today* and *The Independent* newspapers in Britain in 1986, and the subsequent switch from letterpress to web-offset by other London newspapers in 1987, the special qualities of lithography have become familiar to British readers. The *Daily Mail* went further. It introduced flexography and water-based inks, achieving even better reproduction (*see* **30**).

PHOTOGRAVURE

25. An intaglio process

Sometimes called 'rotogravure' (being rotary with cylindrical plates known as sleeves) or 'colourgravure', the photogravure process is different again from the letterpress and lithographic processes. It resembles the etching process. Whereas in letterpress the printing surface is raised and in lithography it is on the surface, in photogravure it is below the surface, that is etched into the plate, the recesses holding ink.

There are two classes of photogravure – high-class photogravure as used for producing postage stamps and prints of paintings, and the cheaper, mass production kind used for the printing of large quantities of full-colour catalogues, multi-million circulation magazines and some of the weekend colour magazines published by newspapers. For a comparison of quality it is interesting to study the quality of British colour magazines still printed by photogravure with those which enjoy the superiority of lithographic printing with its more detailed pictures and clearer text. However, the merit of photogravure lies in its economical printing of mass circulation full-colour magazines on super-calendered paper which is comparatively cheap but with a better finish than newsprint. It made possible the printing of large-circulation women's magazines, such as *Woman* in the mid-30s.

26. How the process operates

The distinguishing features of photogravure are outlined below.

(a) The surface of the cylindrical plate is pitted with square cells 150 to the inch (400 to the inch for high-class work such as postage stamps), and the surface is therefore given a grid effect, from the walls around the cells, called the *resist*. The cells are deeper or shallower according to the quantity of ink that is required for printing darker or lighter areas.

(b) Unfortunately, this grid effect extends over the entire printed area, text as well as illustrations. The type has a ragged look, the effect of broken edges, which can be seen with a magnifying glass.

(c) A special liquid ink with a high spirit content is used. It is applied to the plate sleeve, filling the tiny cells. The *doctor blade* then scrapes the surface or resist clean of surplus ink, and the paper passes through, sucking the ink out of the cells. Because it is a volatile ink, the pigment remains on the paper and the solvent evaporates and is reclaimed. Photogravure print can often be detected by the smell left by the ink.

(d) A rich velvety print effect is obtained but it tends to eliminate detail and produces dark masses. Highlights disappear. This lends itself to slightly blurred pictures which would look bad if printed by letterpress and especially by lithography.

(e) It is not a process which the PR practitioner is likely to use for printwork, but it will be encountered in some magazines although many today are printed by offset-litho, or by a combination of gravure and litho. The PR practitioner has to remember that the process is limited to a number of large printers who specialise in producing magazines. Because of the long print runs, four-colour production and large numbers of pages, these journals take much longer to print than letterpress-printed ones. Copy (e.g. news releases and feature material) is required two to three months in advance.

27. Hard dot photogravure process

The newer German photogravure system, the Klischograph, is superior to the old method described above. The hard dot cylinder consists of cells made up of square dots of varying surface area, instead of cells of varying depth. This overcomes the ragged look created by the square-grid resist or surface of the original type of photogravure cylinder or sleeve, and gives excellent definition instead of the velvety look characteristic of photogravure. Work produced by the Klischograph process may be mistaken for offset-litho printing, and is actually superior to offset-litho.

SCREEN PRINTING

28. A stencil process

This is a versatile process which does not compete with other processes to any great extent. Often, it can be used when the other processes cannot. In particular, screen printing is carried out on a great variety of materials such as paper, board, metal, acetate, fabrics, foils, rubber, wood, vinyl and glass. It is also done on unusual surfaces and shapes such as bottles and ashtrays. Screen is used for printing posters on paper and vinyl; book-jackets, transfers, drip mats and carrier bags. It will print ties, T-shirts, caps, balloons and other promotional material.

29. How the process works

Screen printing is based on the stencil principle, using a screen mesh usually of nylon. The image is produced photographically. The area to be printed is open to the mesh, allowing ink or paint to be squeezed through the space. The process is very old, a Chinese invention. Human hair was used in early times; silk was used until modern technology took over.

Small presses will be found in factories where dials are required for clocks and instruments or control panels have to be printed for electronic equipment. Typical publicity work consists of posters and showcards, often using fluorescent inks. Good quality photographic posters can also be produced for outdoor advertising. However, halftone screens cannot be as fine as litho; it can be only as fine as the screen mesh used.

FLEXOGRAPHY

30. Flexography

Best known, with its rubber plates, for printing on delicate materials such as foil confectionery wrappings, flexography was adapted to newspaper printing in the USA. When the *Daily Mail* left Fleet Street for a new plant in

South East London, flexo machines were installed, using water-based inks rather than oil-based ones. Colour and halftone reproduction was an improvement on offset litho, and the ink did not transfer to the reader's fingers. That indeed was the theme of the *Mail*'s re-launch: the newspaper that lets ideas come off into your head, not onto your hands. Good differentiation and excellent branding.

It is a rotary web letterpress process which uses flexible rubber instead of metal plates, and quick drying solvent or water-based inks.

For newspaper printing purposes, photopolymer plates and special inks are used. Flexo inks are brighter than offset inks (which themselves are brighter than letterpress inks).

DIGITAL PRINTING

31. Background

Among the most important of the changes in the world of marketing communications is the rapid development of short-run colour printing technology. At the leading edge is digital printing, which is becoming the main contender for short-run and on-demand printing.

In recent years, there have been substantial improvements in short-run colour production, mainly in offset litho and electrostatic printing. Today, the demand for improved output, in terms of quality, quantity and speed, is becoming more intense and competitive.

The development of digital printing is bringing about a fundamental change in printing technology. It came from the need of print buyers and others who needed high-quality four-colour process printing on demand in relatively small quantities. They needed print runs which would be uneconomical to produce using conventional litho.

Conventional offset	Digital printing
Electronic page layout Scanning Film exposure Film processing Stripping Colour proofing Platemaking Make-ready Printing Finishing	Electronic page layout Printing Finishing

Fig 17.8 Digital printing: savings in time and costs

32. Digital printing technology

Digital printing is a technology which allows printed material to be produced without printing plates, image-setting, film, stripping, halftone screening or scanning. The colour quality is as good as, or better than, high-quality conventional litho printing.

Digital printing allows the marketer and PRO to create, for example, promotional material targeted to small groups of recipients, or even individuals.

One of the most important features of digital printing is that it is a system which accepts computer-generated data. Basically, it converts computer-generated data into an image.

The job is produced on a company's own PC or Mac in any PostScript application. After everything has been finalised, the job is saved on disk and sent for printing, on disk, by modem or ISDN line (Integrated Systems Digital Network, a high-quality data transmission system). The films go straight from the printer's computer to the press.

More technically speaking, the system accepts data in PostScript form, either direct from a disk or via ISDN. It converts the data into a bitmap image via a Raster Image Processor, then reproduces the image direct onto the printing substrate.

One of the best-known digital printing systems, or 'engines', is made by Xeikon. Digital presses based on Xeikon are web-fed machines using uncoated or coated paper. The press does not use printing ink, but dry toner, and is capable of producing print in monochrome or full colour.

Other companies manufacturing digital systems include Xerox, MicroPress and Heidelberg. Research programmes by Mitsubishi, Man Roland and Océ, using their own technological techniques, could be under way during the lifetime of this edition of *Public Relations*.

33. Features and advantages

Typically, a digital colour press can produce over 2,000 double-sided colour pages an hour. It needs no film or plates, and make-ready is limited to loading the press with the paper to be used. This gives the printer or in-house print manager the opportunity to complete a job 60% faster than conventional offset litho. On 4-colour runs, it can also be more economical.

One London printer using this technology offers to turn round high-quality, four-colour brochures within a day, at a fraction of the cost of conventional methods. They report having printed 40 copies of an eight-page, four-colour brochure, digitally, and delivered them within two hours of having received the files via ISDN from a customer.

One of the unique features of digital printing differentiates it from conventional methods: every single page can be different. Even parts of a page can be personalised, so that no two news releases, sales letters, house journals, leaflets, booklet and posters, for example, need be the same. The variable data is imported from a database and merged with the elements of the page which do not need changing. There are no limitations on the type of data to be merged, so that text, line illustrations and halftone images can be carried on each copy printed. This of course is ideal for personalised PR communications. It opens up a vast range of new opportunities for the marketer and PR department.

Special papers have been developed for digital printing. Paper specialists Robert Horne, for example, market a range of *Royal Digital* and 'silk' papers, which meet the high-quality criteria for digital printing. These are designed to withstand the high temperatures generated in the digital printing process, and produce curl-free pages.

New papers are constantly being developed. The current range includes weights from 60 gsm to 250 gsm; including a 'crack-back' stock for four-colour adhesive labels. In addition, the digital press also prints on plastic.

For Xeikon-based printing, the maximum width is 320 mm. However, because the press is reel-fed, the printed length can vary up to 840 mm. This makes four-colour process printing very economical, on any job from a simple compliment slip to a 96-page brochure, even for small quantities. It can be used cost-effectively for quantities as low as ten copies. With a little creative thinking, myriad other applications can be devised.

An interesting additional tool offered by Xeikon is its in-line finisher. This is designed to work with its digital colour press, finishing folders,

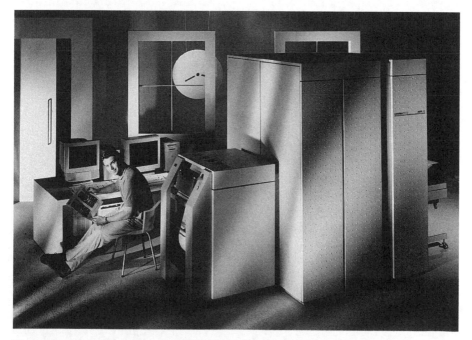

Fig 17.9   Digital printing: ideal for high-quality short-run work; Agfa's IntelliStream system prints full colour direct from disk

booklets and brochures without operator assistance. This includes collating, folding and stacking. The whole job is therefore untouched by human hand from start to finish.

One of the first digital colour presses was Agfa's Chromapress, designed for short runs up to 5,000 copies. The version launched in 1997, Intelli-Stream, enables complete jobs to be printed straight from computer.

The system can produce micro-runs, e.g. 200 company fact sheets in ten languages in a single run. With its Electronic Collation feature, Intelli-Stream enables you to produce, say, five 126-page brochures as a preview for a trade exhibition. In the past, this complex operation would have been too costly and time-consuming.

Instant reprints is a further IntelliStream option. This enables past print jobs to be retrieved from the computerised archive, and reprinted on demand.

Progress test 17

1. Give some of the reasons why it is useful for a PR practitioner to have a working knowledge of printing.

2. What are faces, founts and families?

3. Explain the terms serif face and sans serif face.

4. What are the main differences between Linotype and Monotype hot-metal typesetting machines?

5. What is so revolutionary about computerised phototypesetting?

6. Explain the term 'heat-set'.

7. Letterpress is described as a relief process. What does this mean?

8. How is it possible to reproduce photographs by letterpress?

9. What is a stereo?

10. What is a line block?

11. In letterpress printing, what is meant by the stone?

12. What is the name given to the blocks, type and other metal when they have been assembled ready for printing and have been locked up in the chase?

13. What is the principle of lithography?

14. In lithography, what is meant by the stone?

15. What is the purpose of the blanket cylinder?

16. How does web-offset differ from ordinary offset-litho?

17. In what ways does modern lithography become a photographic process?

18. Name the important developments which have helped offset-litho become so popular.

19. For what sort of printing is photogravure chiefly used?

20. Explain the terms resist and doctor blade.

21. What are the defects of photogravure?

22. What sort of work can be produced by screen printing?

23. Describe the principle of the screen printing process.

24. What is flexography?

25. How is it superior to offset-litho printing?

26. What is digital printing?

27. What are its main features and advantages?

18

SPONSORSHIPS

INTRODUCTION

1. Types of sponsorship

Sponsorship, in the sense of providing financial support for worthy subjects, causes and individuals, stems from the patronage given to artists and musicians by wealthy royalty and aristocracy. Beethoven and Mozart would not have survived without such patronage. Later, wealthy industrialists and financiers such as Tate, Carnegie, Ford and Morris endowed many institutions.

Today we have three kinds of sponsorship which in turn may be undertaken for three different purposes, namely advertising, marketing or PR.

First, there is the form of advertising whereby a company sponsors a radio or TV show. It began with the soap operas (literally advertising soap) on American radio in the 1920s and 1930s. In Europe, programmes were also sponsored on Radio Luxembourg (the first 'popular entertainment' programmes to be received in Britain on a Sunday). This was, and in many parts of the world still is, a typical way of producing revenue for radio and TV companies, although it was not permitted in Britain by the former IBA. In Singapore, for instance, one may watch the English football Cup Final on TV, sponsored by a cigarette company.

Second, there is the new kind of British sponsorship which had begun to appear in BBC and ILR programmes in 1990 but became permissible on BBC, ILR and ITV whereby a whole programme is sponsored and credit is given to the sponsor. This will be discussed later.

Third is the kind of sponsorship which is the modern commercial counterpart of old-time patronage by wealthy benefactors. Here, a sport, art exhibition, theatrical show, literary prize, expedition, educational bursary or an individual may be given financial support. The reward for this is usually independent media coverage as when Grand Prix motor racing cars are sponsored by, say, Canon, Marlboro or Goodyear.

BENEFITS AND REASONS FOR SPONSORSHIP

2. Benefits of sponsoring

Since nobody wishes to gain an award from a disreputable or even unknown or undistinguished patron it follows that those who make public awards need to be reputable and well-known. Consequently, sponsorship bears a mark of approval which is good PR in itself. As explained in 1, sponsorship is the modern form of patronage, industry replacing the wealthy benefactors of the past. But industrial sponsors are rarely philanthropic: they usually expect a return for their money.

They may not be as fortunate as Cadbury-Schweppes, whose racehorse 'Schweppeshire Lad' won six of its seven races and was second in the seventh, proving to be a self-liquidating investment. Nevertheless, commercial sponsorship has been in the public interest, for example, in achieving safer motoring through motor sport, which tests tyres, brakes and other equipment. Sponsorship maintains cultural organisations such as theatres and orchestras, providing educational opportunities through bursaries and fellowships. It advances the interests of sports, possibly saving village, county and Test cricket through the support given by John Haig, Gillette, the Prudential, Britannic, Refuge and Cornhill.

3. Reasons for sponsoring

There are many reasons for sponsoring, but generally there is a PR element, if not the main purpose, which aids understanding and goodwill. The chief reasons for spending business money on sponsorship are as follows:

(a) To augment advertising campaigns through the publicising of company and product names which will often get wide coverage by the media. Show jumping, cricket, football, golf, swimming and tennis, and aircraft, balloon, cycle, horse, motor, motor-cycle, power boat and yacht racing, all have their supporters. They include Sanyo, Prudential, Coca-cola, the *Daily Mail*, Unigate, Raleigh, Whitbread, Elf, and the *Financial Times*.

(b) To assist the marketing policy, as when the sponsor gives financial support to something that interests potential customers and the company or product is associated with an interest such as youth, health, leisure or beauty. Coca-Cola has associated itself with youthful pursuits, Lloyds Bank and the Midland Bank with music, Evian with netball.

(c) To show a sense of social responsibility, as when companies have sponsored university awards, medical research, libraries, theatres, festivals and orchestras.

The principal PR values of sponsorship are in creating awareness of a company or its products – a familiarisation process resulting from repetitive media coverage; showing a company's social responsibility and so creating respect and goodwill; positioning a product with the right publics; and providing a means of giving hospitality to business friends and clients. As was found with Cornhill's support for Test Cricket it proved a way of reaching a new market segment – those who did not buy household insurance through brokers – which advertising could not have done.

TYPES OF SPONSORSHIP

4. The spheres of sponsorship

These may be considered under the following headings:

(a) *Sports.* We have already listed many sports which benefit from business backing. More sponsorship money is devoted to sport than to anything else, no doubt because many sponsors are interested in the mass consumer market which can be reached through sport which attracts media – especially TV – coverage. In particular, Japanese firms have sponsored much of British sport, finding this an excellent way of familiarising the market with Japanese names. Suntory even sponsored a British golf tournament which golf addicts in Japan would see on their TV.

Sports events provide manufacturers with opportunities to test and modify products under exceptional circumstances of hard usage. For example, the modern motor car owes much to the need for tyres, brakes and components which will withstand the stresses of modern driving.

There are certain moral issues concerning some sports sponsorships. Athletes have objected to wearing sports clothing bearing the name of the brewer who is sponsoring the event, and the anti-smoking lobby has been vociferous in condemning the sponsorship of healthy leisure pursuits by cigarette firms.

(b) *Cultural events and interests.* The Midland Bank, for example, has supported opera at Covent Garden. Embassy have sponsored orchestral recordings.

(c) *Publications.* Maps, diaries, guide books, year books and technical works come under this heading. Often they are sold as legitimate commercial publications like the Rothmans sports annuals, Michelin guides, Texaco road maps and, of course, the *Guinness Book of Records*.

(d) *Exhibitions.* Public and trade exhibitions are often sponsored by a magazine or newspaper (e.g. *Daily Mail* Ideal Home Exhibition), or trade associations and other interested bodies (*see* Chapter 15).

(e) *Education.* Fellowships, bursaries, scholarships and other educational awards may be made.

(f) *Causes and charities.* A typical sponsorship here is the making of a documentary about the work of the charity, the financial aid being acknowledged in the credits. Eli Lilley have made videos on diabetes featuring personalities such as Harry Secombe and Elaine Stritch. Manufacturers may supply equipment to colleges or hospitals or some cost may be underwritten.

(g) *Professional awards*. These are often made to journalists, photographers and architects in contests organised by the sponsoring companies. Canon run a contest for press photographers, in association with *UK Press Gazette*. Glenfiddich sponsor awards for food and drink writers. The *Financial Times* makes awards to architects.

(h) *Local events*. It is possible to develop community relations by participating in local events such as carnivals, flower shows and gymkhanas, perhaps supporting an exhibition class with a trophy or cash prize. A number of insurance companies contribute poster blanks, bearing their names, which can be overprinted with the announcement of the event. Rentokil have supported a local cycling team.

PRACTICAL ASPECTS OF SPONSORSHIP

5. Special considerations

Before giving financial support the sponsor should:

(a) Be certain of the objectives

(b) Choose an area of sponsorship which best satisfies those objectives

(c) Be aware of the total costs involved which may not be confined to the award itself. For instance, maintaining a motor car team is very costly. Guests may have to be entertained.

The sponsorship may of course provide the sponsor with opportunities for coincidental advertising and PR activities. Advertisements could mention the sponsored event. Television commercials could include action shots taken during the event. A PR activity could include news releases about the award and the results, naming award winners, or the publication of a book about the event. Documentary videos can also be made with great prospects for PR usage, as described in Chapter 10. Sponsorships make news for staff newspapers, and can help to enhance management–employee relations. The PR implications are endless, even when the sponsorship is basically commercial.

One of the most successful sponsorships ever held in Britain was the Canon Football League which ran for three years and involved 92 football clubs, gained 6 days a week media coverage, and was in the news continuously for many months of the year. Continuity of media coverage is a major accomplishment to be sought after. Many sponsorships are of too short a duration to have sufficient impact relative to the cost. Another sponsorship which gained extensive media coverage was the Cornhill Test Match cricket sponsorship, while the Ever Ready Derby is talked about for months and is a major TV event.

6. Cost

A final reminder is necessary about costs. One of the most expensive forms of sponsorship is financing a racing car and a team of drivers, while an inexpensive one could be supplying the product as a prize at local flower shows or as a supply on an expedition. An inexpensive sponsorship, however, must be reckoned against the likely reward. English cricket has survived largely through generous business support, but Cornhill Insurance have achieved considerably improved public awareness through their support for Test cricket. Yardley, for a time, sponsored motor racing which helped them to change their image from makers of ladies' cosmetics to that of makers of men's toiletries. Sponsorship can be very costly, but it can be highly successful. In many cases, it can have great PR value in winning good customer relations, enhancing public goodwill, or in the establishment of a corporate or product image. Goodwill can be achieved through support for or association with a good cause or public enjoyment. It can help with the establishment of export markets.

Some years ago, Japanese products were very unpopular in Indonesia and Japanese cars were burnt in the streets of Jakarta. A programme of sponsorship and support of charities helped to create a better trading climate and today the majority of the cars in Indonesia are Japanese. Japanese sponsors have been active in Britain, too.

Canon's three-year sponsorship of the Football League made Canon number one in Britain, with a Canon machine in almost every British office.

7. Further examples of sponsorship

(a) *Lloyds Bank.* This British bank is very active in sponsorship and employs a specialist sponsorship manager. It was commended for its sponsorship on BBC 2 of the Young Musician of the Year contest which consisted of a series of well publicised weekly programmes.

Lloyds Bank has also sponsored Fashion Awards which became renamed the Lloyds Bank Fashion Awards and recognised excellence from the UK's leading designers. Lloyds also sponsor the Clothes Show Live Exhibition which attracts 200,000 consumers and retailers. The Lloyds Bank Fashion Challenge, a design contest for 11 to 18 years old, is another sponsorship.

All three fashion events were televised, and the cost was about £2m over three years. The bank chose this 'greenfield' area because sports sponsorship had become overcrowded. The fashion sponsorships were aimed at the broad span of consumers ranging from the youth market to the upmarket woman.

(b) *Mercury Communications*. The UK's largest visual arts sponsorship was that mounted in 1991 by Mercury Communications (BT's competitor) in a link up with *The Independent*, BBC Radio 1 and the Royal Academy. Mercury spent £500,000 and *The Independent* £100,000 to sponsor the Royal Academy's Pop Art exhibition in a deal co-ordinated by sponsorship agency Spero Communications. Radio 1 held a roadshow in the academy's forecourt in Piccadilly, and Radio 1 also featured on a Mercury phonecard. Four other cards featured contemporary artists.

The arts sponsorship complemented Mercury's sponsorship of the Prince's Trust's 15th anniversary, Mercury making donations to the charity from the sales of the phonecards.

(c) *International Distillers & Vintners*. In early 1991 ITV companies offered sponsorship of a number of programmes which were in production. The response was timid, and the first sponsor to be announced was IDV on behalf of Croft Port, the chosen six episode series being Thames Television's *Rumpole of the Bailey* which stars Leo McKern who bears a remarkable resemblance to John Mortimer, author of the Rumpole books and the TV series. For an expenditure of £300,000 IDV got fifteen seconds at the beginning of the programme, 10 seconds at the end and 10 seconds in each of the two commercial breaks, but it was not permitted to deliver a direct sales message. So the viewers enjoyed the programme courtesy of Croft Port. It remains to be seen whether this sort of sponsorship becomes popular when there is no recession, and whether it will be of advertising, marketing or PR value. Its advertising value is clearly weak, but it is a sign of the times that TV production is so expensive that patronage is sought!

(d) *Barter television*. Yet another innovation which arrived in Europe from the USA in 1991 was barter TV whereby a company will itself make a TV soap opera or game show and will supply it free of charge to TV companies provided the sponsor is given all the advertising spots before, during and after transmission.

One intriguing deal was between Worldvision and the Russian TV company Gostelradio to broadcast *Beverley Hills 90210*, *Dallas* and *The Flintstones* free of charge in exchange for the right to sell 48 minutes of advertising time across the week. At the same time Procter and Gamble have sponsored the *US Week* programmes which have a potential audience of 200 million viewers.

8. Sources of information

(a) *The Hollis Press and Public Relations Annual* contains a classified 50 page selection on sponsored activities, sponsors and sponsoring consultancies.

(b) *PR Week* carries a weekly classified section on organisations seeking sponsors.

(c) *The Scottish Sports Council* publishes a monthly newsletter, *Leads*, on sports sponsorship in Scotland.

(d) *Sponsoring Insights* is published every two months and is a noticeboard for forthcoming opportunities and trends in the sponsorship industry. Annual subscription. Hobsons Publishing plc, Bateman Street, Cambridge, Cambs CB2 1LZ.

(e) *Sponsorship News* is a monthly journal providing an update of sponsorship news in sport, the arts, conversation, charities and the media. Annual subscription. Charterhouse Business Publications, PO Box 66, Wokingham, Berks RG11 4RQ.

(f) *Charity Forum News*, 54 Church Street, Tisbury, Salisbury, Wiltshire SP3 6NH.

(g) *The Directory of Social Change*, Radius Works, Back Lane, London NW3 1HL.

(h) *Hollis Sponsorship & Donations Yearbook*, Contact House, Sunbury-on-Thames, Middlesex TW16 5HG.

(i) *Sponsorship Yearbook*, Hobson's Publishing plc, Bateman Street, Cambridge CB2 1LZ.

(j) Arts Council of Great Britain, 14 Great Peter Street, London SW1P 3NQ.

(k) Association for Business Sponsorship of the Arts, Nutmeg House, 60 Gainsford Street, London SE1 2NY.
    European Committee for Business Arts & Culture, Nutmeg House 60 Gainsford Street, London SE1 2NY.

(l) Institute of Sports Sponsorship, Francis House, Francis Street, London SW1P 1DE.

(m) The Sponsorship Advisory Service, The Sports Council, 16 Upper Woburn Place, London WC1H 0QP.

(n) The Sponsorship Advisory Service for Scotland, Caledonian House, South Gyle, Edinburgh EH12 9DQ.

(o) The Sponsorship Association, 16 Partridge Close, Chesham, Buckinghamshire HP5 3LH.

(p) European Sponsorship Consultants Association, 16 Partridge Close, Chesham, Buckinghamshire HP5 3LH.

(q) Business in the Community, 8 Stratton Street, London W1X 5FD.

(r) The Council for Industry and Higher Education, 100 Park Village East, London NW1 3SR.

(s) National Council for Voluntary Organisations, 26 Bedford Square, London WC1B 3HU.

(t) Scottish Council for Voluntary Organisations, 18/19 Claremont Crescent, Edinburgh EH7 4QD.

Progress test 18

1. Why is it essential that a sponsor should be a respected organisation?

2. What are the main reasons for sponsoring?

3. Describe five of the most common areas of sponsorship.

4. Which is the most popular and heavily financed form of sponsorship?

5. What are the three considerations a prospective sponsor should satisfy before entering into a sponsorship agreement?

6. What particular PR objectives are most likely to result from sponsorship?

7. How have the BBC and ITV come to accept the sponsorship of programmes?

8. What is barter TV?

9. Where would you find information on sponsorship?

19

EXPORT PUBLIC RELATIONS

GENERAL CONSIDERATIONS

1. International PR

The first rule of international marketing, whether one is exporting goods from a home base or creating a multinational or transnational organisation, is that every country is a separate market. There is no such thing as a world market, unless one has one of those rare universal products, such as Coca-Cola. The experience more often is that products have to be designed or adapted, packaged, named or distributed, differently for different countries. So-called 'global marketing' can be a mirage.

The same applies to PR. One can rarely blanket the world with the same story. Something that would amuse West Africans might insult Gulf States Arabs. In South East Asian countries, for instance, one cannot afford to offend the large Chinese population. Americans and Canadians have different values and outlooks, so do Indians and Pakistanis. It is therefore imperative to study the market characteristics before undertaking PR directed at overseas countries. It could be foolish to think only in terms of European, North American, South American, Asiatic or African markets. We should not be misled by the concept of the Single European Market. Each country will retain its cultural, political and religious characteristics which in turn will be represented by national media. (However, cross-border media is discussed later in 4.) The advice of nationals on the spot may be rewarding. Chapter 21 explains the very different media situations in developing countries and differences elsewhere will be discussed at the end of this chapter.

EXPORT PR METHOD AND ACHIEVEMENTS

2. UK-based PR

Many of the problems of communicating with overseas markets can be solved by using services which exist in the UK. A selection of these is to be found in the following list of ways of conducting export PR.

(a) *Central Office of Information.* The COI not only handles publicity in the UK for government departments and ministries, but also organises overseas publicity on behalf of Britain. This includes the distribution of news stories, pictures and articles about British industrial and commercial successes or developments which, in effect, are good news about Britain. There is a special film and video department which distributes documentaries to overseas television stations and catalogues them so that they may be borrowed through British embassies and high commissions. Radio tapes are also recorded and distributed. Television and radio programmes are often made about British exhibitions, highlighting new British products.

(b) *BBC External Services.* Stories about British inventions and successes or outstanding export stories are sought by the BBC External Services in Bush House, Aldwych, for broadcasting in over 30 languages. There is the World Service in English and special programmes such as *Science in Action, Business and Industry* and *New Ideas,* which also use such stories.

(c) *British Overseas Trade Board.* The BOTB organises joint ventures, an annual All British Exhibition, British pavilions at international trade fairs, and store promotions. It supports participants in these events by organising PR on their behalf, producing trade fair bulletins, and sponsoring editorial supplements in overseas trade journals.

(d) *EIBIS International.* This is a commercial firm which distributes expertly translated 250–750 word news stories and 760–2,500 word articles to the overseas press, and is familiar with the editorial needs of 26,000 overseas journals divided into 325 categories. Great care is taken to achieve accurate translations – vital in international PR. Feedback is obtained in three ways: by return of an acceptance card, by press cuttings and by reader enquiries.

(e) *Two-Ten Communications.* Two-Ten has access to over 3,500 news media in 138 countries, including 450 financial publications and 330 institutions in the world's commercial capitals. News releases are distributed simultaneously by satellite transmission world-wide, and can reach foreign editors in minutes. Reliable translation services are offered with linguists working in their mother tongue.

(f) *PR Consultancies.* A number of British consultancies have international branches or associates and can undertake overseas PR coverage and activities. Overseas consultancies are listed in the *Hollis Press and Public Relations Annual* and also in *Hollis Europe.*

3. Possible achievements

Just as PR can prepare the way for an advertising campaign, educate distributors and establish an image in the home market, so can it perform a similar valuable function in overseas markets, where the need for knowledge and understanding is even greater. This is sometimes overlooked, with detrimental results, by some of our biggest exporters. Below are some examples of export PR:

(a) The consumer market can be familiarised with the company and its products.

(b) Importers, buying agents and distributors can be educated about the company and its products.

(c) Opinion leaders, including government officials and politicians, can be similarly educated.

(d) Conversely, a survey of the media based on study of publications, or cuttings obtained through a press cutting agency, can provide intelligence on the market situation.

Such a programme can greatly strengthen the efforts of overseas marketing and sales departments, establishing an image, making acceptability of the organisation much easier and producing enquiries about the products or interest in the setting up of agencies, subsidiaries or leasing arrangements.

OVERSEAS MEDIA

4. Existing media

An overseas PR campaign requires careful study and understanding of the media which may be different from those in the UK. Newspapers may be regional rather than national, the trade and technical press may be regional, too, while there may be very few specialist publications.

In some parts of the world, such as the Middle East, Africa and South East Asia, press media (especially trade and technical) may be rare or non-existent. However, mailings of releases can be made direct to government departments, contractors, industrial firms, banks, hospitals, educational establishments and other prospects. Exporters may have their own lists of customers, agents and buyers or the services of EIBIS or Two-Ten may be used.

Although all member states in the Single European Market will retain their national media, there are certain forms of publishing and broadcasting which are cross-frontier and continental. Publishing houses such as Bahr publish different language versions of women's magazines with massive total circulations, while satellite and cable television carry programmes over much of Europe.

In the absence of suitable media it is possible to create one's own media, the two most effective – which can be produced with relevant language versions – being detailed below.

5. The external house journal

An exporter or international company can produce a private magazine and in many parts of the world where journals are scarce it will be welcomed as a contribution to the country's literature, itself a good piece of PR. One journal can serve all countries where English is spoken, but editions in French, Spanish, Portuguese, Japanese, etc. will be necessary for other parts of the world. It is also worth remembering that while people, as in North Europe, may speak English, they may not read the language very easily. Therefore, if the marketing effort is being directed to countries where English is not the first language, it would be more effective to publish in the national language. This will mean more trouble and expense, but that is what effective PR is all about. An *external* is quite different from an *internal* house journal. It should aim to help readers understand company policy and the merits and uses of the company's products. But the contents should be informative, interesting and authoritative and in no way resemble advertising, otherwise the journal will lack credibility.

When producing a journal in different languages it is necessary to design the pages to accept the different lengths of translated copy. The same article in English, French and German will require different type areas, while an Arabic version will read from back page to front page. Care must also be taken over vocabularies and the ability to translate certain words. Bhasa Malay, for example, and the similar language in Indonesia have very limited vocabularies.

6. The documentary video

If care is taken to produce a video that is comprehensible and meaningful for overseas audiences, even to the extent of dubbing in a North American sound track if it is aimed at that market, it can be employed in the following ways:

(a) Used on visits by top executives to overseas countries

(b) Loaned to overseas subsidiaries or agents for showing to local prospects

(c) Distributed through the Acquisitions Department of the COI

(d) Shown on stands or booths at international trade fairs

(e) Placed on the circuits of commercial mobile video units

(f) Made available to overseas television stations.

One way or another, such a video can be made to work very hard and could be an excellent investment if it can reach and teach the right people. Ten to fifteen minutes is probably the best length and if audiences are unsophisticated the subject matter should be presented very simply and with some repetition. It should not resemble a television commercial.

191

7. Overseas mailing lists

Several directories exist which indicate the nature of the world's media, giving titles and addresses for mailing list purposes together with the languages in which the journals are printed. Do not be misled if a journal is said to be printed in English when the majority of the country's publications are printed in the national language or in those of ethnic groups. The English language paper may be mostly read by visitors and expatriates and reach only a minority of nationals. In Arab countries, English-language newspapers will be read by the large non-Arab populations. Overseas media are discussed more fully in Chapters 8 and 21 which supplement this chapter.

The following are very useful sources:

(a) *Benn's Media Directory, Vol 2. Overseas Media*. First established in 1846 as the *Newspaper Press Directory*, *Benn's* is today published in UK and overseas volumes. It is a comprehensive guide to every kind of publication, giving readership and geographical profiles and circulation figures. Overseas press representatives in the UK are also given.

(b) *Willings Press Guide*. Although mainly concerned with the UK, this old-established directory also lists overseas media alphabetically for Europe, the Gulf States and the USA.

(c) *PR-Planner-Europe*. This volume gives classified and tabulated information about the editorial requirements of the European trade, technical and business press.

(d) *PIMS*. Specialising in the reproduction and distribution of news releases, PIMS also offer North American and European services.

(e) *Two-Ten* have a European media directory.

TRANSLATIONS

8. Quality

The quality of translations is always a problem. The UK reader may be familiar with the curious errors in Japanese instruction manuals and Dutch horticultural catalogues.There are excellent translation services, but they are expensive because trouble is taken to check the work with nationals in the countries concerned. It is usually useless to rely only on a translator resident in the UK who may not be up to date on current idiom and jargon. The best way to obtain a reliable translation is to send the version to a national resident in his or her country and ask for it to be translated back into English. This new English version can be compared with the original to see if any errors have occurred.

9. Commissioning

When commissioning translations, it is always wise to attach definitions of technical words or jargon. Unless the translator has perfect understanding of the English words it is possible for too-literal translations to turn out to be nonsense. There may be no exact counterpart in the other language. Sometimes a word has to remain in English, although it should be noted that the French are pedantic about the use of foreign words. Public relations itself is sometimes untranslatable. It may help to supply both an English and a foreign language version of a release or article when it is being sent to editors.

Progress test 19

1. What is the first rule of international marketing which can be applied to export PR?

2. How can the British Government services help the exporter to execute an overseas PR programme?

3. What commercial PR services are available to the exporter?

4. What can overseas PR achieve for an international marketer?

5. How can information be discovered about overseas market situations?

6. What kind of PR media can be created?

7. What directories exist from which overseas media mailing lists can be compiled?

8. How can reliable translations be prepared?

20

MARKETING RESEARCH

DEFINITION

1. Use of the term

Market research is defined by the Market Research Society as 'a branch of social science which uses scientific methods to collect information about markets for goods and services'.

Marketing research covers all the research techniques used to investigate opinions, attitudes, preferences and motives. Advertising research covers studies of circulations, readerships, audiences, advertisement pre-testing (copy testing) and recall, the value of advertisement positions and other tests. Sometimes this broad collection of techniques is simply called marketing research, that is a wider span of studies than market research. However, the terms tend to be used rather loosely. Government studies are usually called social surveys and sociological ones are called behavioural studies. Yet, the same techniques are used, although there are many varieties of application. Basically, a given number of selected people are questioned and the results are analysed and interpreted.

MARKETING RESEARCH FOR THE PR PRACTITIONER

While the cost of research in relation to PR expenditure may sometimes be disproportionate and prohibitive, this is not always the case and increasingly research is applied both to appreciate the situation and to measure results. As pointed out in Chapter 12, evaluation can be by experience or observation and not require scientific research, while desk research can include the interpretation of the volume, readership or audience, tone and quality of media coverage which can be monitored.

Marketing research of the following kinds may be useful to the PR practitioner.

2. Using published survey findings

For various purposes, beginning with the Census of Population, surveys may have been made by official, institutional or commercial organisations. The findings may have been published and made available to interested parties.

It is not always necessary to initiate fresh research if the information already exists. The purpose of the original research should be understood because this will colour the questions and answers. The original purpose may not coincide exactly with that of the PR practitioner, so discretion may have to be applied when reading the results of past studies. But many government statistics can be valuable if interpreted intelligently. For example, the number of car licence holders does not reveal how many people own their own cars, only how many vehicles are on the road. The brief, the summary and the questionnaire of a published survey will show the purpose and relevance of the study. This secondary research is known as 'desk research'.

3. Commissioned surveys

For marketing and advertising purposes the PR practitioner's firm may have commissioned surveys and the results could be helpful when determining the current image and planning a PR programme.

4. Advertising media research

Advertising media research (*see* 8:**13**) such as JICNARS (press), BARB (TV), RAJAR (radio) and JICPAS (posters) are important when measuring readership and audiences, in assessing the value of coverage. ABC figures will provide audited net sales of publications, as distinct from the estimated readership figures based on research. Other advertising research, such as recall tests, for example, which question people about advertisements, or reading and noting tests, which measure the percentage of men and women who recall each part of a published advertisement, may also be helpful.

5. Commissioning original or primary research

As a means of appreciating the situation (using image studies or opinion/ attitude surveys), and of monitoring the progress and success of a PR campaign, original research can be commissioned. Taking a hypothetical case: prior to a PR programme, it is found that only 20 per cent of the people have a clear image of the organisation. The objective is to achieve a 40 per cent understanding. Opinion surveys at, say, six and twelve months can record the extent to which the campaign has succeeded or failed.

6. Terminology

Marketing research has its own special language or jargon. Some of the terms have lay meanings and the student should be careful to understand the precise research meanings of the following terms:

(a) *Population or universe.* In marketing research both words mean the total number of people relevant to a particular survey, e.g. all dentists or university students, depending on the subject of the study. It does not mean all the people living in a town or country, the everyday or even the social science meaning in the sense of a population census.

(b) *Respondent or interviewee.* A person questioned in a survey.

(c) *Sample.* Not to be confused with a 'free sample', a research sample means that proportion of the population or universe which is to be questioned. It is rather like the tea or wine taster's sample – a little is enough to judge the whole.

(d) *Quota sample.* A number of people to be questioned who are selected by quotas (numbers or percentages), usually in proportion to their representation in the census population. A very elementary division into quotas might be: 50 per cent men, 50 per cent women or ten per cent single women and 90 per cent married women. The interviewer would be responsible for finding the various quotas set out in the instructions.

(e) *Random sample.* Sometimes called an *interval* or *probability sample* (these terms being more accurately descriptive), this kind of sample is not chosen 'at random' as the term misleadingly suggests. It is necessary to have a list of people from which names and addresses are picked at regular intervals, for instance every tenth or hundredth name. The size of the sample can be calculated by means of a formula to an agreed degree of accuracy. Thus, a representative cross-section of the particular population is listed. Interviewers then have to call on the named respondents, usually making at least three attempts before using a given substitute. This method is obviously more expensive than a quota sample, but the probability is that every member of the *population* will have an opportunity of being interviewed and so it can be more accurate than a quota sample.

(f) *Characteristics.* These are peculiarities or distinctions which are known to exist in the *population*. A *random sample* will pick up all these characteristics, e.g. cigarette smokers, pipe smokers, cigar smokers and non-smokers.

(g) *Sampling frame.* This is a specification of the kinds of people, and their *characteristics,* who will form the *sample* of respondents.

(h) *Stratified random sample.* To avoid the cost of interviewing people everywhere in the country, the total *population* can be sampled so that people are interviewed in a number of locations only, usually polling districts as defined for election purposes. In other words a sample is taken from polling districts. For example, one national sample uses 1,000 polling districts throughout the country.

(i) *Random walk.* In developing countries, lists of names and addresses may not exist. The random method is adapted to one of calling at houses at determined intervals, for instance every tenth house. This does mean that such surveys have to be confined to urban areas.

196

(j) *Structured interview*. An interview that is conducted with a prepared questionnaire.

(k) *Depth interview*. One with no prepared questionnaire, the interviewer asking open-ended questions, the *respondent* answering at length and the interviewer noting down a summary of the answer. Sometimes called a qualitative survey. This is often used in developing countries where lists are unavailable, and it is difficult to identify quota samples. *See* **8(k)** below.

(l) *Questionnaire*. This is a prepared list of questions (with instructions to the interviewer) which consists of various types of question, the answers to which the interviewer fills in as dictated if it is a person-to-person survey. The introductory questions are usually personal ones, establishing the type of *respondent* being dealt with. Dichotomous questions seek 'yes' or 'no' answers. Multichoice questions consist of lists of items from which the respondent makes a choice. A semantic differential requires the respondent to give ratings from say 'Bad' to 'Excellent', for which points are awarded, such as $-3, -2, -1, 1, 2, 3$. Open-ended questions invite the respondent to comment fully and freely. These four types of question are illustrated in Figure 20.1.

The questionnaire has to be composed very carefully to produce clear understanding and true answers. It is best designed by a professional market researcher. Control questions may be inserted to check either the accuracy of an earlier answer or to check the honesty of the interviewer – the first repeating the question in a different way, the second asking a question requiring known information which will reveal if the question has been genuinely asked.

(m) *Recall*. In certain surveys, ability to recall or remember an item is measured. It may be recall of an advertisement or, more particularly, its content and components. Recall devices may be used, as when cards are shown to respondents, e.g. titles of newspapers, respondents being asked when they last read a copy.

(n) *Social grades*. For many years people were classified into socio-economic groups, these being based on income. In some parts of the world – such as the developing world – socio-economic groups are still used in marketing research because they are still relevant where the majority of people are in the very low income groups, subsistence farmers having virtually no income. At the other extreme the well-to-do are also the better educated who share similar cultural interests. But since 1970, socio-economic groups have been replaced in the UK by social grades based on occupation, not income. This takes into account the fact that some manual workers may earn more than professionals yet not rank in the same grades in respect of job character and seniority, possessions, purchases and activities. Thus, the C[1] white shirt or white blouse office worker may well

(a) Do you drive a car?   YES ☐   NO ☐

If YES, do you own a car?   YES ☐   NO ☐

(b) Which of the following makes of car do you normally drive?

Rover ☐	Mazda ☐	Alfa-Romeo ☐
Talbot ☐	Honda ☐	Audi ☐
Vauxhall ☐	Daewoo ☐	Volkswagen ☐
Ford ☐	Renault ☐	Volvo ☐
Nissan ☐	Citroen ☐	Saab ☐
Toyota ☐	Fiat ☐	Any other ☐

(c) How would you rate the reliability of the car you normally drive?

Very bad   Bad   Poor   Fairly good   Good   Very good
☐   ☐   ☐   ☐   ☐   ☐

(d) State briefly why you would or would not buy the same make of car again

_____

_____

_____

_____

Fig 20.1   Mock questionnaire structured to demonstrate (a) dichotomous, (b) multichoice, (c) semantic differential, and (d) open-ended questions

live next door to the C^2 blue collar mechanic. One may read the *Daily Express* and the other may read the *Daily Mirror* irrespective of earnings. The social gradings, based on *Social Grading on the National Readership Survey*, are as in the table below.

From the figures below it will be seen that added together, the C^1s, C^2s and Ds total 74 per cent, in other words the mass market, those who read the popular press, watch television and listen to commercial radio, in Britain. It should be noted that Grade A does not represent the 'upper class' in the sense of a minority of millionaires, but includes top business people, professionals, academics, civil servants and so on. The social grading system is more realistic than the old socio-economic groupings, especially in view of high earnings by unqualified or unskilled people, and also the rate of inflation in recent years which has made it misleading to attach salary or wage figures to particular groups.

A	Upper middle class: top business people, professionals, etc.	About 3 per cent of total
B	Middle class: executives	About 13 per cent of total
C¹	Lower middle class: white collar workers	About 22 per cent of total
C²	Skilled working class: 'blue collar' workers	About 32 per cent of total
D	Semi-skilled and unskilled working class	About 20 per cent of total
E	Those at lowest subsistence level: pensioners, dependants on national assistance	About 9 per cent of total

TYPES OF RESEARCH AND TECHNIQUES

7. Four kinds of research

Marketing research can be divided into four areas:

(a) *Desk research*, which is the study of existing statistics and survey reports.

(b) *Field research*, which is conducted by interviewing people 'in the field', as when interviewers contact respondents.

(c) *Ad hoc research*, meaning one-off surveys, complete in one project.

(d) *Continuous research*, meaning surveys which are carried out regularly, e.g. monthly, thus recording changes or trends.

8. Research techniques

There are many different ways in which marketing research can be undertaken. One method is not necessarily better or worse than another. The choice may depend on the kind of information that is required, how much time can be given to the project, how accessible the respondents are, or how much money is available and the degrees of accuracy that can be afforded. It may be found desirable to carry out more than one form of research at the same time. Some of the available techniques are given below.

(a) *Opinion, attitude or shift surveys*. Usually seeking 'yes', 'no', 'don't know' answers, often continuous or, at least, repeated at regular intervals, these surveys seek to discover what people know, think or believe and to measure the changes or shifts in awareness, opinions or beliefs.

(b) *Consumer panel*. A panel is a recruited group of respondents who serve more or less permanently to answer questions or to test products. A panel may meet, or be sent questionnaires known as diaries, or be visited regularly. Consumer panel research usually reveals what sort of people buy what sort of goods, in what quantities, how often and where.

(c) *Motivation research*. Pioneered by Dr Ernst Dichter, motivation research seeks, by means of techniques similar to those used in clinical and intelligence testing, to reveal hidden motives, instead of stated opinions or preference. The expression 'hidden persuaders' refers to motivational research techniques, and has nothing to do with public relations.

(d) *Discussion group*. This is a much modified and less expensive form of motivation research, with members of a recruited group spontaneously answering questions set by a leader. A weakness may be that the group may be too small to be representative of the population, unless its members share a common interest. There is also the risk of bias on the part of the leader.

(e) *Telephone questionnaire*. Surveys of distant or scattered respondents can be conducted by pre-arranged telephone interview. This can be useful in industrial research. This method has also been used for quick polls of topics such as voting intentions in a general election. It does depend on the people having telephones and being willing to answer questions in this way.

(f) *Postal questionnaire*. The questionnaire is posted to respondents and return of the completed forms will depend on the extent to which respondents are motivated or will co-operate, perhaps because they are committed to the subject. This is obviously less expensive than using paid interviewers, but could be worthless or biased if too few people or only those deeply concerned responded. The method is used for studies such as professional salary surveys.

(g) *Coupon survey*. This is a questionnaire published in the press, but it has the obvious weakness that only those very interested will bother to submit answers.

(h) *Pantry check*. A sample of 'housewives' – probably a recruited sample – is visited by researchers who note the brands found in the cupboard, refrigerator, freezer, bathroom cabinet and so on.

(i) *Dustbin check*. Another observational test, usually on a panel basis; researchers note the brands purchased as disclosed by discarded containers, plastic sacks being provided for collection purposes.

(j) *Dealer, retail or shop audit*. A form of continuous research made famous by the AC Nielsen Company, whereby the stocks and invoices of a recruited panel of dealers are checked at regular intervals. The figures are taken of goods bought and remaining in stock to reveal sales and stock movement. Thus it is possible to report how various brands are moving out of shops, making comparisons between rival brands and, in the aggregate, showing the market share of each brand. Over a length of time, it can be seen how the popularity of brands improves or wanes and these movements can be interpreted against the effects of advertising, sales promotions and other influences. Panels are usually based on commercial television areas which can be an aid to test marketing when regional TV advertising is used.

(k) *Qualitative research.* Rather like depth interviewing, this is a form of research which has succeeded in overcoming some of the difficulties which hampered research in developing countries where facilities are different from those in industrial countries. The technique is to conduct tape-recorded interviews which may last up to three hours. Obviously, the sample will be small but if representative of both typical customers and ethnic groups, it can produce valuable information. Qualitative surveys about beers and insecticides have been conducted in Nigeria. *See* **6(k)** above.

(l) *Image study.* The object of an image study is to compare the strengths and weaknesses of a number of similar companies, of which the sponsor is one although not identified as such to respondents. Any number of companies can be compared, although for the sake of simplicity only three are shown in the graphical result in Figure 20.2. From such a graph a sponsor can see how his or her company compares, topic by topic, with rival companies. This can reveal areas in which the company is weak and needs to make changes. If the study is repeated when changes have had time to come into effect it will be seen if the company now compares more favourably with its rivals. This sort of research can be a revelation to management as the outside current image could be very different from the internal mirror image.

To conduct an image study, especially for an industrial company supplying, say, chemicals or components, the sample could be small and the survey could be conducted by telephone by pre-arranged appointment.

+	Good service	Good delivery	Good design	Expensive	Reliable	Modern	Good research
C A B							
	Company A — · — ·		Company B ———		Company C - - - - -		
−	Poor service	Poor delivery	Poor design	In-expensive	Unreliable	Old-fashioned	Poor research

Fig 20.2   Graphical representation of an image study

9. Which techniques for PR?

Marketing research is a big subject, but a fascinating one which applies to most of the subjects in both the LCCI and CAM exams. This short introduction provides a broad picture. The techniques most likely to apply to PR are desk research, opinion or awareness polls and especially image studies. These can greatly assist in the planning of cost-effective tangible PR programmes, and in assessing results.

Progress test 20

1. How does the Market Research Society define market research?

2. Is there any difference between market research and marketing research?

3. In what ways can marketing research help the PR practitioner?

4. How do JICNARS and ABC figures differ?

5. What is the universe?

6. How does a random sample differ from a quota sample?

7. Where is the random walk method usually carried out? Why is this method used?

8. What are dichotomous questions?

9. What is desk research? Has it any drawbacks?

10. What is the value of continuous research?

11. How does an opinion survey differ from motivation research?

12. What is meant by an unrepresentative sample?

13. When is a telephone questionnaire likely to be more practical than face to face interviewing?

14. What is the purpose of consumer panels, pantry checks and dustbin checks?

15. What information is provided by dealer audit research?

16. For what are Dr Ernst Dichter and AC Nielsen known in the world of marketing research?

17. What is an image study?

18. What forms of research are most applicable to the planning and assessing of PR programmes?

21

PUBLIC RELATIONS IN DEVELOPING COUNTRIES

INTRODUCTION

Public relations is a subject of great interest in the developing world because there is urgent need to spread knowledge and create understanding of countless subjects in both the public and private sectors. This PR activity must not be confused with propaganda, even if the difference is sometimes slight. In certain countries PR is called public enlightenment, which may or may not imply propagandist overtones.

PROBLEMS OF PR IN DEVELOPING COUNTRIES

1. Communication

Communication is often difficult because of a lack of Western-style media, great distances between cities and remote rural communities, illiteracy, numerous ethnic groups, languages and dialects, together with tribal and religious taboos.

2. Marketing

There are also two marketing dilemmas: half the population is likely to be under 15 years of age and many rural people may be subsistence farmers who sell little of their produce. As a result, a very large number of people – at least half – will probably be outside the cash economy: they will have no buying power.

3. Publics

The élitists, middle-and-upper class, educated and literate who read newspapers and own a television set may be between 10 and 20 per cent of the population. In India this can mean several million people. When populations are huge, a considerable number of people will have attitudes and expectations similar to those in the West, but even so 80 per cent will not, and women, in particular, may generally suffer an inferior position.

4. Mass communication

In Nigeria the biggest circulation daily newspaper reaches no more than London's *The Times*, which has one of the smallest circulations among British nationals. In format, the Nigerian *Daily Times* may resemble the *Daily Mirror* on which it was modelled rather than *The Times* in spite of its élitist readership, while the Nigerian *The Punch* resembles the *Sun*. A media survey in Kenya counted even those who 'listen to newspapers', indicating that a literate member of the family or village community would read the newspaper to others. The same survey referred to the thousands of people who watched mobile cinema shows, but one can ask how many understood what they were watching. In Nigeria mass communication research has pointed out that, although there are radio programmes in regional languages, they cannot possibly reach everyone in a land of 62 languages. A media survey in Zambia showed that listeners preferred music, were disinterested in national or international news and often listened to pop music broadcast from other countries.

In contrast, the vast country of Indonesia which has a population of 180 million scattered throughout 30,000 islands, covering an area as large as the USA, has a satellite system so that television programmes are transmitted by 96 stations in three time zones. Portable receivers using 12-volt car batteries overcome the lack of electricity in many areas.

5. Advertising dilemmas

The standards of advertising in the developing world élitist media can be very confusing. British and Irish visitors will view a Nigerian Guinness television commercial in horror, watching the beer being slopped into a glass instead of being decanted gently, while in Indonesia they may be surprised to hear Guinness being described by waiters as 'black beer'. Meanwhile, a Ghanaian will be equally horrified to see that the characters in a television commercial for an imported product are wearing Nigerian national costume. Similarly, one wonders why the characters in the commercials in Nairobi cinemas are all Europeans, when the audience is almost entirely African or Indian. The problem is frequently that those who advertise even to the educated, literate, well-to-do minority either have little knowledge of the product or have no understanding of the audience. Such advertising, whether offensive or misleading, is bad PR for the companies concerned.

6. Educating the market

In the developing world the PR situation is totally different from that in the the West and yet it is a situation in which PR can thrive because nowhere else are its techniques of greater value. Education – the essential characteristic of PR – is a primary aspect of development. Many of these countries are ambitiously trying to climb into the twentieth century in a situation not unlike Britain before the Education Act of 1870.

The PR task is to educate the market and here credibility is paramount. Moreover, it must be realised that while the urban population may understand the product and use it well, many products will be wholesaled in very small lots and retailed on open-air stalls in hundreds of village markets, in small stores or by roadside vendors, to people of limited understanding. The labelling of goods becomes very important and a vital PR aspect of marketing. It is not enough to print the label and instructions in the local language since the majority of people will not be able to read. Cartoon-type instructions are necessary, although rare. A problem with imported products can be references to weights and measures, which are incomprehensible to people who do not weigh anything nor use rulers or tape measures. This has been a problem with products such as powdered baby milk, many buyers having no means of measuring or sterilisation.

TWO SPECIAL COMMUNICATION TASKS

Unlike PR in the Western World, PR in developing countries has two principal communication tasks:

7. In the public sector

Government departments, state governments, local authorities and official agencies are responsible for informing the people about their policies and programmes. Often, they are endeavouring to build an infrastructure and a range of social services which have been established during the past hundred or more years in the West. For instance, universal primary education was introduced into Nigeria only as recently as 1977, more than a hundred years after the famous British Education Act of 1870. However, this advance should not obscure the fact that Nigeria has for many years had some dozen universities, many technical colleges and secondary schools, plus private schools which were preceded by the missionary schools. Thousands of Nigerians have also been educated abroad and there is an élite of Nigerians trained in universities of the West.

As we shall see when we consider public sector PR in greater detail later in this chapter, this is where the bulk of PR activity may lie. The civil servant PR practitioner is likely to be more common and in greater demand than the industrial and commercial PR practitioner. In addition to government PR at all levels, the PR practitioner will also be found in the armed forces, the police, health, education and other public services. He or she will also be found in the big para-statal corporations which control more or less nationalised industries in countries such as Indonesia, Tanzania and Zambia.

8. In the private sector

Here PR will be of a very mixed kind. Much of it may be initiated by expatriate and multinational companies. Generally, manufacturers, importers and suppliers have an immense task in informing a growing market about new products – familiar, perhaps, in the West for a long time – and in telling people how to use these products most beneficially. This is not easy for the market is childlike in its innocence and ignorance, let alone its illiteracy, language barriers and poverty.

Foreigners rarely understand the communication problems. They sit in London, New York or Geneva, and plan marketing schemes as if they were selling to a mass market in an industrial society. Tragedies have occurred over the high-pressure selling of powdered baby milk to rural mothers who could not read the labels and had no means of either refrigeration or sterilisation. An indication of the poverty problem is that cigarettes are bought by the single stick rather than the packet, transistor radios go into disuse because of the prohibitive cost of batteries, and even the literate cannot always afford the price of a newspaper. At the other extreme, a Lagos middle-class woman may scorn Avon cosmetics as being cheap, and a prosperous business person will live in a tumble-down shack with a Mercedes parked at the door.

A curious but very real difficulty in the private sector is that consumers may have little faith in products produced in their own country. The imported product will be considered to be superior. This sad lack of self-confidence in home-produced goods is not peculiar to developing countries: the myth of Swiss watch-making superiority made the British unwilling to accept that British watches were as good if not better than Swiss ones. It took the Japanese to destroy the Swiss myth, when the Swiss failed to recognise the superiority of the quartz timepiece.

A PR task may well be to foster pride in home production. If the Russian peasant can make Fiat cars why cannot the Zambian? An interesting sign of progress is the success Nigerian paint makers have had in promoting the idea of home decoration, including touching up weather-damaged exterior paintwork. Malaysia has gone to great lengths, e.g. with public exhibitions, to promote home-produced products, and is proud of its Proton car (based on Japanese expertise) which is even exported to Britain.

OPPORTUNITIES FOR PR

The following are some suggestions for PR on behalf of products and services.

9. Foods

Because urbanisation has disturbed farm economies as more people are working in towns, there is great scope for dietary and cookery instruction. This also applies to cooking and kitchen equipment.

10. Motoring

The world's motor manufacturers have descended on every developing country and, while road building has assisted the motorist, he or she has received little other help. How does the motorist care for his or her car? There are no motoring magazines as in the West, unless these are imported. Nowhere is it more necessary to be able to service one's own vehicle. Motoring organisations like the AA and RAC are normally non-existent, breakdown services can be hundreds of miles apart, roadside telephones do not exist, driving and safety standards are appalling, e.g. broken-down vehicles are left stranded at night without warning lights; and spare parts are scarce or black-marketed. In these inevitably hazardous circumstances, the writing of very simple manuals with a wealth of pictures and diagrams is essential PR. Yet in Nigeria the reason why the domestic airline is over-booked is that motorists dare not risk long road journeys in a country where cities are from 200 to 1,000 miles apart and a breakdown cannot be contemplated.

11. Energy

The pace at which electrical and electronic equipment, e.g. TV sets, air-conditioning, fans, cookers, cleaners, sewing machines, hi-fi, is entering the developing world is usually unmatched by the ability of the electricity authority to supply light and power. Often, the authority is blamed for power cuts it is unable to avoid. The PR need is to educate consumers regarding the conservation of energy.

12. Banking

While banks are commonplace in towns, the concept of banking – both depositing and borrowing – is seldom familiar to rural dwellers. Yet it could be advantageous to small farmers and traders if the market was educated. In some developing countries there are mobile banks, but suspicion of banking (and insurance) is something that PR techniques could overcome. The PR transfer process (*see* 5:4) has a positive application here.

13. Analysis of special circumstances

The above examples help to indicate the special circumstances that exist in developing countries. They also apply to many other products such as pharmaceuticals, fertilisers, insecticides and agricultural machinery. These circumstances are compounded of four things:

(a) The unequal pace of development, country by country, according to educational standards, climate, terrain and the economic situation.

(b) Anxiety to adopt Western standards, ideas and aspirations, which may not necessarily be as desirable or superior as may be supposed. In fact, they may be wrongly imposed by foreign importers. There could be a clash of life styles.

(c) Misunderstanding of the market by foreign suppliers, for instance intermediate technology may be more sensible in a country which has a surplus of labour and does not really require labour-saving equipment.

(d) The importation of goods with no back-up service of spares or no trained repair services complete with spares. When many mechanical, electrical or electronic products – which are costly – break down they can only be scrapped. In countries with exchange control problems, retailers of electrical products are often reluctant to tie up currency in spare parts. This creates ill-feeling towards suppliers and manufacturers. It is bad public relations.

MEDIA IN THE DEVELOPING WORLD

14. Differences from Western media

In the developing world the media of communication may differ radically from those in the West in a number of ways:

(a) There are unlikely to be mass media in the same sense that most people read newspapers and watch television, but radio is likely to be widespread.

(b) The media may have to go to the people, travelling to distant villages. In Zambia people on remote lake islands have to be visited by motor-boats of the government information service.

(c) Media regarded as popular or mass in the West are regarded as élitist or minority media in developing countries.

(d) Some media such as magazines, trade and technical journals and young people's journals may be completely absent or there may be very few titles.

(e) Most media will be divided into editions or programmes which serve different language groups. This will make circulations and audiences proportionately smaller than when one language is spoken. In South East Asia television commercials are often subtitled in Chinese. However, in some countries, the situation is not unlike one we could imagine if a London newspaper had county editions because a different language was spoken in each county.

(f) Traditional or folk media may have to be used, not forgetting use of the 'innovator theory' method of first convincing someone in authority, such as the king, oba, emir, sheikh or headman, who will then pass on his recommendation through palace messengers, town criers or gongmen to produce adopters of the idea. Other traditional media may include puppet shows (which have no language problems) and village theatre. Market gossip is another folk medium. These are known as oramedia.

(g) Because people will be unfamiliar with urban, let alone Western, ideas, messages need to take account of the limits of experience of readers, listeners and viewers. Forms of communication imported from abroad (such as films or videos) must not be sophisticated in ways which would be desirable and acceptable in the West. *See* **30** below for a more detailed discussion on cultural differences.

15. The press

The press reflects increasing literacy and prosperity because purchase of a newspaper is a voluntary act. The chief handicap to circulation in spite of literacy can be shortage of newsprint, e.g. in Ghana and Zambia, due to economic circumstances, or the unemployment and lack of purchasing power of even well-educated people, as in India. The contrast can be seen by comparing the eager newsvendors on the streets of Nairobi with the passive ones who squat on the pavements of Lusaka, attitudes to earning money notwithstanding.

In Nigeria, there has been a steady growth of the press since the Civil War, in spite of a military government for several years and state financial interests in several publishers. We have seen the phenomenal growth of *The Punch* which changed from a Sunday to a daily and has chased the *Daily Times* for supremacy. While the *Daily Times* tries to be a national in a country where distances and travelling problems hamper this, there are regional dailies based on the main cities such as the *Daily Star* in Enugu. A business and consumer magazine press is growing and there are three weekly financial papers. But even so, for a country of 100 million people (a quarter of the black population of Africa), with centuries of history, 500 years' association with Europe and a fair standard of education (at least in the coastal South and East, but improving elsewhere), newspapers and circulations under 400,000 perhaps provide a clue to the media problem. If the press is as meagre as it is in Africa's largest, most densely-populated and richest, black African state, it may be expected to be inferior elsewhere in the far less prosperous countries of black Africa.

16. Radio

Two forms of radio are popular in developing lands, the transistor and 'box' or rediffusion, which may be found in both homes and public places. Nowadays, clockwork-powered radios are gaining a foothold (*see* 8:3). To reach farmers, Zambia Radio has subsidised sets or organised listening groups. Ghana has expanded transmissions throughout the country. If broadcasts on the one wavelength are made in a number of languages, it means that speakers of any one language have only a portion of the day when they can listen to their own programmes, so, while radio can reach people who cannot read, vernacular programmes have their limitations. To this must be added the consideration that rural listeners have parochial interests, and care little about affairs in distant cities. A great many listeners prefer the background companionship of music, and will turn to any station if it satisfies them.

17. Television

This used to be the most élitist medium because it was available only to those who could afford to buy a receiver, but rental services are now available in some countries. There is still one serious limitation: there must be an electricity supply and this means that there can be no television service in the bush or in remote villages. In Zambia, there is an expression 'along the line of rail', and TV is limited to towns served by the railway in the copper belt towns, although Zambia is a very big country.

A very interesting innovation in many parts of the developing world has been community viewing in halls where people go in order to watch programmes. In countries where it is not the custom for women to go out-of-doors at night, the audience is entirely male. Employers also provide community viewing and Chinese tin miners, for instance, enjoy this in Malaysia. In Indonesia, the portable TV set powered by a 12-volt car battery is popular, but viewers are very selective because of the cost of re-charging batteries. Africans are renowned talkers, so the TV studio interview is enjoyed and the static nature of African TV is acceptable. This helps to compensate for the scarcity of equipment for live outside broadcasts.

18. Cinema

There are two kinds of cinema in developing countries: static (indoor or drive-in) and mobile. The latter is carried on a Land Rover which tours villages, the screen being mounted on the roof and the audience assembling in the open. Here the audience will be mixed with perhaps a predominance of women and children. Sunset can be very early in the evening, equivalent to winter in Britain, so it becomes dark enough to give good viewing outside. In some countries, mobile cinemas will be part of the state information service, as in Malaysia and Zambia, or are commercial enterprises, as in Kenya, with commercial and documentary films. Not all static cinemas show commercials, while those in the modern cinemas of Nairobi are very Westernised, advertising toiletries and airlines, for instance. Cinema-going can be very expensive. Nowadays, mobile video shows often replace projected films.

19. House journals

Perhaps because of the scarcity of consumer magazines, house journals are popular in most developing countries. However, an employee communications problem can exist in companies where a large proportion of the workforce is illiterate. The pictorial wall newspaper may be one form of employee communication which can overcome illiteracy. The external house journal is also one of the ways in which the importer can educate the market.

20. Documentary films and videos

The usually prohibitive cost of film-making prevents this being a much-used medium but video is less expensive and is becoming popular, provided VCRs are available for play-back. The problem with imported films or videos is that they may be too long, too Westernised, and too full of unfamiliar and irrelevant scenes and situations. Snow and sea scenes could be meaningless to viewers in equatorial or land-locked countries, and *limits of experience* occur (*see* **30**).

21. Exhibitions

These delight the gregarious people of the developing world. Exhibitions possess the fun of the fair or the market-place. They are places where friends can be met and people can talk, and they provide opportunities for family outings. Exhibitions, like the cinema, can be static (usually out-of-doors) or mobile, i.e. road shows with a combination of demonstrations, film or video shows, music and dancing.

22. Traditional or folk media

These oramedia have been described already in **14(f)**. The idea of dealing with the influential community leader is not restricted to developing countries, nor is it a new idea. It has been used since the nineteenth century by farm machinery manufacturers who have found an imaginative and enterprising farmer willing to take up a new machine and then permit his neighbours to come on his land to see a demonstration. Mid-Western American farmers came to adopt McCormick's combine-harvester in this way. The adopter (or innovator) theory works well in countries where villagers will accept the word of the community leader, while suspecting that of strangers from distant parts. Oramedia also extends to music and dance, not forgetting the drum.

PR TECHNIQUES

23. The public sector

We return to this area of PR (*see* **7**) with respect for the efforts that are being made to use PR techniques really effectively. Possibly need is the spur, but in some countries public sector PR can be superior to that of private sector

PR. This is probably because so much consumer communication is dominated by expatriate interests which do not always take sufficient account of the tremendous differences between marketing in North America or Europe and in developing countries. Judging by the many malpractices, such as selling high tar cigarettes or medicines banned in the West or pretending that poor food products such as cocoa possess a fictitious amount of nutritional value, it is also obvious that the developing world is exploited by multinationals which have no interest in honest communication. Unfortunately there are companies in African and Asiatic countries which are adept at 'passing off' inferior products in packages resembling those of reputable ones, which would be illegal in the West. However, some well-known international companies do make PR efforts by sponsoring sports, making educational grants and supporting worthy causes.

24. A typical PR problem

The value of PR techniques can be seen in the holding of censuses of population. The idea of taking censuses has been familiar in Britain and the USA since the early nineteenth century, but it is a novel and tricky concept in most developing countries. Census-taking is vitally important, because without such statistics it would be impossible to plan for the future. Some of the problems are posed below to emphasise both the need for and the value of PR:

(a) Demographic statistics are usually absent or scanty and misleading. For this reason it is very difficult to conduct marketing research in developing countries.

(b) The absence or unreliability of statistics makes it difficult for governments to plan the infrastructure, e.g. roads, telephones, electricity, gas, water, sewage, housing, schools, hospitals and so forth. For example, when Nigeria introduced universal primary education, the authorities underestimated enrolments by more than one million children.

(c) Similarly, it is difficult to conduct reliable social or sociological surveys (as well as market research surveys) if population figures, distribution and characteristics are unknown.

(d) The method of enumeration must be carefully planned. In colonial days attempts were made at head counts by paying enumerators on the basis of the number of households questioned, but this led to abuse. Nowadays, people such as university students are used as enumerators, but an initial task is the PR one of teaching them to understand the importance and implications of census taking. Otherwise they will be no more efficient than the moneymaking head counters of old. Moreover, student enumerators may be resented by older people.

(e) False returns can result from reasons which are understandably bound up in local attitudes and aspirations, religious and tribal beliefs and customs.

If states are to share in some bounty, e.g. oil proceeds in Nigeria, on the basis of population, human nature will tend to exaggerate the figures. There are ethnic groups which regard the counting of children as tantamount to a death sentence, Muslims who will not permit interviews with their womenfolk, and men whose pride insists that they admit to having fictitious children. Others may fear that the enumerators are seeking information for taxation purposes, never trusting anyone from the government. If, in Britain, there are protests from immigrants over disclosure of place of birth in a census, this is a very minor matter compared with those mentioned above.

These reactions are just plain evidence of the negative PR situation: hostility, prejudice, apathy and ignorance. A Nigerian census was abandoned because the results were clearly inaccurate, give or take 20 million! But several years ago in Singapore great efforts were made, such as in the press, to familiarise people with the reasons for census-taking and the way in which the census would be conducted. People were even asked to lock up their dogs!

The above problems make it unsatisfactory to rely on short-term advertising to announce a census taking. This is an instance of the need for well-planned long-term PR to establish a situation in which it is possible for the public announcements to be accepted and acted upon sympathetically.

APPLYING THE SIX-POINT PLANNING MODEL

In Chapter 5 a six-point PR planning model was introduced and this will now be applied to some possible public sector PR programmes which might be conducted in a developing country.

25. Road safety programme

(a) *Situation.* Too many accidents; insufficient road signs; drivers cannot read or understand signs; people walk in the road; dangerous overtaking, especially on corners; drunken driving; too many passengers carried, including whole families on motorcycles; headlights not switched on by motorcyclists in day-time; vehicles parked at night without lights, especially if they have broken down; poor roads, often pot-holed; lack of road drainage, causing flooding and consequently accidents through brake failure; insufficient traffic signals and pedestrian crossings; failure of pedestrians to use crossings; need for foot-bridges; poor driving instruction.

(b) *Objectives.* To educate all road-users, drivers and pedestrians and owners of public transport and commercial vehicles. To encourage local authorities to improve road safety provisions.

213

(c) *Publics*. Private and commercial drivers; fleet owners; traffic police; driving instructors; car sellers; motor-car insurers; pedestrians and schoolchildren; local authority highway officials and councillors.

(d) *Media*. Radio – various language programmes; television; cinema vans; documentary film; posters; the press; leaflets; stickers; through chiefs, teachers; public rallies – open-air meetings.

(e) *Budget*. PR staff; printing posters, leaflets, stickers; making film and copies; rent of poster hoardings; transport to regions; hospitality at press receptions.

(f) *Results*. Feedback from traffic police, insurers, hospitals, etc. regarding accidents and driving behaviour; interpretation of resulting statistics.

26. Resettlement of the handicapped programme

(a) *Situation*. The handicapped include the blind, deaf, dumb, crippled and mentally retarded.

(b) *Objectives*. To help the handicapped and the relatives to know that, thanks to modern aids, they need not be left out of society; the government will help them to become self-reliant. Aid consists of government-sponsored centres to teach skills, e.g. woodwork, weaving, shoe-making, watch-repairing, and bag-making.

(c) *Publics*. The handicapped, their relations, community leaders, doctors, teachers.

(d) *Media*. A radio play with two characters, one negative and one positive and open-minded: the sceptic goes to the centre, stays only two weeks, leaves for the city, becomes a beggar; the other man takes a two-year course at the centre, sets up a shoe-making business, marries, has two children and is accepted by the community. Five years after the day when they both entered the centre, the shoe-maker goes to the city market in his wheelchair and sees a dirty cripple begging: the beggar does not recognise his now prosperous friend whose cordial greeting he rebuffs, but the shoe-maker puts coins in his dish, says begging does not pay, and advises him to go to the training centre where he will also get free board.

The play is to be given two broadcasts in English and each local language. The broadcasts will be publicised in advance. Local communities will be asked to set up listening groups. Each group will appoint a secretary to take down points for group discussion and queries to be sent to the radio station. The points raised will be dealt with in a subsequent question-and-answer radio programme. There will be follow-up announcements from time to time on the radio.

(e) *Budget*. Cost of PR very small: radio station pays playwright, actors; PRO's time in briefing playwright, liaison with radio producer; collecting statistics from training centre.

(f) *Results.* The number of new applicants for training, the number who complete a full course and the number who benefit by gaining employment or setting up businesses, will be recorded and assessed.

27. Dangers of self-medication

(a) *Situation.* Risk of dealing with 'quack' doctors or buying wrong medicines from chemists; exploitation of the sick by pharmaceutical companies; problems of overdoses and wrong diagnosis; use of expired drugs which have been kept in the home too long.

(b) *Objectives.* Ministry of Health to advise against treatment by quacks; to make known dangers of more serious illness, untimely death or spread of infections and epidemics, and need for proper diagnosis, treatment, cure and prevention of epidemics.

(c) *Publics.* Government officials, teachers, doctors, nurses, community leaders and the population as a whole.

(d) *Media.* Production of a small diary-like health guidebook in English and local languages, to be sold at low price capable of recovering cost, news releases to all newspapers, radio, television stations, announcing the booklet; arrange radio and/or TV interviews with Minister of Health; buy TV time to display health aid booklets and pose vocal questions repeated in words on the screen: Do you think you have malaria? How do you know it is malaria? Could it be jaundice or yellow fever? This to be followed by the price and where the booklet can be bought. Time would also be bought on radio to promote sales of the booklet; small posters would be supplied to distributors; complimentary copies would be sent to government officials, libraries, schools, doctors, hospitals and community councils; sales of the booklet would be organised through bookshops, newsvendors, market stalls, post offices, community centres and local government offices.

(e) *Budget.* The booklet would be self-liquidating, the price covering costs including free copies. Major costs would be PR working hours, news releases, TV and radio time and small posters for point-of-sale.

(f) *Results.* The results would be measured in two ways: sale of booklets; survey of hospitals, doctors for opinion on illnesses due to self-medication, before, during and after campaign; also, check on increase in patients seeking advice and treatment instead of attempting to treat themselves.

28. Adult literacy

(a) *Situation.* Three-quarters of adult population illiterate; contributing factors: agricultural background and other manual occupations; mothers marry very young; culture and philosophy of life – people may have good comprehension and communication skills although unable to read or write and therefore be satisfied, with illiteracy seen as no handicap.

(b) *Objectives*. To encourage illiterates to embrace adult education during period of campaign when classes are being set up and organisers are being sought.

(c) *Publics*. Illiterates in villages and townships; religious leaders, teachers, employers and also school children who could carry messages to their parents.

(d) *Media*. Specially made short videos demonstrating advantages of literacy in modern life – ability to read instructions on packaged goods; read road and street signs; read and write letters; read newspapers – and so enjoy a fuller life. These videos to be taken by mobile cinema to the villages, or shown in community halls in townships; also offer them as TV programme material. Debates and discussions on radio to be sought in local languages; talks to local groups; posters to announce video shows and talks; news releases about the literacy programme; opinion leaders and community leaders to be approached direct – chiefs, politicians, religious leaders, teachers who could act as innovators of adult education classes.

(e) *Budget*. Working hours of PR personnel; press reception at inception of literacy programme, another to announce opening of classes and another later when the scheme has taken off and progress can be reported; making of videos and copies; hire of vehicles and VCRs; cost of keeping workers and vehicles on the road; fees of speakers and their expenses; printing of posters.

(f) *Results*. Judged by number of classes opened; number of people enrolled; fall-out rate; number who complete the course; percentage fall in illiteracy rate.

29. Acknowledgement

The census, road safety, resettlement of the handicapped, dangers of self-medication and adult literacy examples are based on schemes actually planned and presented by students during courses run by the author (FJ) in Accra, Enugu, Kabwe, Kano, Lagos, Lusaka and Nairobi. Working in groups, they applied the six-point PR planning model to typical local topics of their own choosing. For the overseas student they show what can be done in circumstances very different from those of London or New York, while for the Western student they should provide an insight into the fascinating problems of solutions and communications in the developing world.

COMMUNICATION PROBLEMS IN THE DEVELOPING WORLD

30. Culture differences

Not least of these problems is that understanding is conditioned by experiences which must be:

(a) different from Western experience

(b) related to life as it is lived in the country concerned.

It is well to remember that anyone living an unsophisticated life will never see anything grow bigger than normal, nor – unless they have been mutilated – will people be seen other than as whole figures. Here we have problems of *limits of experience*, and *limits of scale*. The consequences of this are unfamiliarity with message presentation, e.g. a larger-than-life picture in an advertisement or on a package, or a head and shoulders portrait or a head on a coin, can be meaningless, bewildering or unbelievable: they never see giant mosquitoes or legless, armless or beheaded people.

There is also the question of *sound versus visual symbols* as J.C. Carothers, writer on psychiatry, has explained, saying:

> 'The non-literate rural population lives largely in a world of sound, in contrast to Western Europeans who live largely in a world of vision. Sounds are in a sense dynamic things, or at least are always indicators of dynamic things – of movement, events, activities, for while man is largely unprotected from the hazards of life in the bush or veld, he must be forever on the alert ... Sounds lose much of their significance in Western Europe, where man often develops, and must develop, in general, "seeing is believing"; for rural Africans reality seems to reside far more in what is heard and what is said.'

Different kinds of *literacy* occur in unsophisticated societies. Literacy in developed countries tends to be limited to ability to read and write, and in developing countries there are adult literacy programmes to teach adults how to read and write. There is also the problem of lost literacy because children have left school, gone to work on the land and had no call for reading and writing. But in developing countries there are also remarkable feats of *visual* and *oral* literacy. People carry mental pictures. Whereas in developed countries it is difficult to find accurate witnesses, this is not so among people one might otherwise consider illiterate. Similarly, there is oral literacy like that of the 'postman' in Ghana who carries elaborate messages in his head about weddings and land purchases between townspeople and villagers.

People in unsophisticated societies are less familiar with pictures than those in industrialised societies. So, they *read* pictures by identifying known objects until collectively the picture reveals its total meaning. They do not see the picture as a whole, *gestalt* fashion. Moreover, if the subjects in the pictures are shown flat on, that is without depth, they can be difficult to

217

understand because in real life things are three-dimensional. For example, a ball is spherical, not flat like a plate.

Visual perception time can therefore play an important part in such circumstances, and if a film or video presents too many different scenes or actions too quickly there will be insufficient visual perception time in which to absorb and comprehend them. Thus a film, video or slide show needs to be paced steadily, and repetition will enhance understanding.

The span of consciousness applies in any society but more so where reading is not common and among those whose vocabularies are small. This tends to follow Dr Rudolph Flesch's model of suitable sentence lengths for different categories of reader. How long will people continue to read – or watch a film or video – before becoming tired and bored? The length of the span of consciousness depends on how frequently we read or watch. To some extent it is the difference between the readership of a popular newspaper and a more serious one – except that in many developing countries where only certain people can read newspapers, those newspapers tend to resemble the popular ones in Western countries.

These cultural differences are no criticism of the people concerned, but the above points highlight how people of very different cultures can communicate effectively. Millions of people are involved, and there are some 120 developing, less developed and under-developed countries.

31. Family planning PR

Family planning campaigns are instances of the good and bad use of PR in developing countries. In Kenya, over-complicated films have been shown; in Tanzania the point has been made that all such campaigns should be directed at men, not at women attending clinics; in Zambia men have been sceptical because the country does not have a large population. Examples of good communication in family planning campaigns have been the East African leaflets in Swahili with a cartoon picture showing how the spacing of children can be likened to sowing farm seed carefully and so producing strong plants. In India, Indonesia and other parts of South East Asia, the cartoon posters on the theme of two children, not three, resulting in happy, well-cared-for families, have been meaningful to all sections of the community.

EXTERNAL PR FOR DEVELOPING NATIONS

Developing countries are also involved in external PR on behalf of the country itself and need to make known such assets as an international airline, a shipping line, tourism, culture and exports which may range from coffee to copper. Such countries are seldom wealthy and their funds for such international PR are small by comparison with those of the British,

Americans, West Germans or Japanese. Two important points can be made as outlined below.

32. Media limitations

The media of external PR will be the internationally accepted media, the traditional Western media which (as the examples in **15–21** show) are not so readily available or even so suitable at home. This means that the external PR techniques have to compete with countries long established in the business of international communication. It began with the Vikings, Phoenicians, Romans, Portuguese and many others who went beyond their own shores. This is a challenge to PR practitioners in the developing countries who must use modern techniques and the same high standards of creativity and production.

33. Recognition

Developing countries are also the victims of their own enterprise. As parts of empires they had some recognition, but as independent states with mostly new names the task is prodigious. India was the subcontinent; now it is India, Pakistan and Bangladesh. Ghana, Zambia, Malawi, Guyana, Tanzania, Namibia, Botswana, Sri-Lanka and Tuvalu are relatively new concepts. An atlas printed ten years ago may have the wrong names for several countries. People round the world have difficulty in knowing where developing countries are. This is complicated enough when people in Britain tend to regard Africa as a country rather than a continent made up of 50 different countries, and do not know the difference between Southern and South Africa!

The Pacific Rim countries represent an economic growth area in contrast to the West and its recession in the 1990s. Indonesia, for example, is discovering the value of PR in expanding its non-oil economy.

34. Establishing a PR image

The task of establishing an image, a correct impression, given these problems is a formidable one and it must not be destroyed by confusing *propaganda* with *public relations*. Information circulated abroad must stick to the facts, not try to present a rosy picture. At the same time, this is a challenge to Western media which prefer disaster stories to ones about endeavour and success. The PR practitioner who seeks understanding of a developing country must not be too sensitive about being ignored by the popular media, and of finding that when notice *is* taken by the small circulation *The Times*, *Guardian* or *The Independent* of Britain it is of earthquakes, floods, famine, revolution, civil war, corruption and assassination. The PR practitioner also has to compete with the fact that most people in their own countries, including his or her own, are isolationists who do not hanker after world news.

Progress test 21

1. What is meant by élitist media?

2. Explain the expression 'listening to newspapers'.

3. Give some reasons for the small circulations of newspapers in the developing world.

4. How can language problems be overcome when communicating in a multi-ethnic society?

5. What are the strengths and weaknesses of radio?

6. What are the principal reasons why television is not as widespread in the developing world as in the West?

7. How has television been brought to a wider audience in the developing world?

8. What is meant by static and mobile cinema?

9. What are traditional or folk media, and what are their special values?

10. How can limits of experience affect credibility and hinder communications?

11. What is meant by visual and oral literacy?

12. How does visual perception time affect understanding of a film or video?

13. Explain how the span of consciousness concerns reading matter or a film or video.

14. Why is it particularly difficult for an independent Third World state to establish an image internationally?

15. Why is it necessary to distinguish between public relations and propaganda?

22

SPECIAL USES OF PR

In this chapter we shall look at some of the areas where PR has been particularly beneficial to organisations in recent years. The chapter will demonstrate the versatility of PR, and show how it satisfies the needs of leaders of industry, commerce and in other fields. A criticism often made by PR practitioners is that management rarely understands and appreciates PR. There are scores of MBA courses throughout the world but few, the first being that of Cranfield School of Management in England, where PR is seriously studied as a whole year subject. However, the topics discussed in this chapter are mostly ones for which management has discovered a need for PR and that is where management does learn to understand and appreciate PR.

The special uses of PR discussed in this chapter are:

Crisis management
Desk-top publishing
Corporate identity
Parliamentary liaison
Financial PR.

1. Crisis management

So many crises have been endured in the last decade or so that management has recognised the desperate need to be organised to handle calamities, especially regarding media relations. A well-earned reputation can vanish in seconds, and with satellite TV and services like those of Cable News Network (CNN) a tragedy can be brought into millions of homes worldwide. We have seen this with national disasters, industrial accidents and wars.

Many of these disasters have been the result of human beings being unable to cope with the demands or faults of high technology, as in the cases of the British Midlands air crash on the M1 and that of the Austrian Lauda Air airliner over Thailand. But not every crisis is of major proportions, and the variety of calamities is enormous so that no organisation can afford to take an 'it couldn't happen to me' attitude. Crises can occur over strikes, fires, accidents, takeover bids, new legislation, scandals, deaths and resignations, the effects of recession and countless other causes. No organisation is risk free.

It is therefore essential that any organisation should set up a permanent *crisis management team*. Its make up will differ from one organisation to another according to whether it has a single location or many locations and the nature of its business. A typical crisis management team might comprise the managing director, public relations manager, works manager, safety officer and personnel officer. The team needs to be small so that there is easy communication between them. The members of the team should have deputies in case of absence. At all times they should be easy to locate by the central switchboard, and contactable by radio, pager or mobile telephone. In an emergency it may not be possible for all the members of the team to assemble but at least it should be possible for immediate contact to be established so that concerted action can be agreed. Thanks to recent technology, tele-conferencing is now easy and popular. In most crisis situations, urgency is a supreme consideration. The initiative has to be taken by management, not by media. The organisation should call the media and not the other way round.

The first task of the crisis management team is to identify and decide what to do should any of these emergencies occur. There are two kinds of possible crisis, the *likely* and the *unlikely*. The likely hazards are those associated with the particular organisation, but the unlikely – and no less important ones – are those which are least expected. Thus, a hotel might risk a fire or food poisoning among its guests, but could not anticipate an earthquake or a war or a revolutionary situation. The two lists of possible crises need to be as long as imagination will permit, but there may be no limit to the possibilities and this list can be reviewed and expanded. No possibility, however remote, should be omitted.

From time to time there should be rehearsals, and members of the crisis management team should be trained in how to handle media interviews and press conferences. They must learn how to control these situations, and not be intimidated by the demands of story-hunting journalists. Nothing should be said 'off the record'. Similarly, telephonists and others who are likely to receive the attentions of the media should know how to deal with them. They should all understand that so far as the media are concerned, bad news is good news and that journalists are capable of behaving like vultures unless the provision of information is controlled. Moreover, it would be advisable to vet what is published or broadcast and to correct any errors. All this should follow a drill which should be set out in a crisis manual and supplied to whoever may have to deal with the media.

Two kinds of crisis, neither of which may be the fault of the organisation, are worth special consideration. The first is the contamination of products at retail stores, and the second is the need to recall a product because it has been found to be faulty.

Deliberate contamination of edibles such as chocolate bars and baby foods has been committed by blackmailers and by activist groups. Only a few items have to be tampered with, or hoaxers may merely claim to have done so, and two organisations are faced with a crisis – the retailer and the manufacturer – both of whose reputations are at risk. The retailer will clear shelves and the manufacturer will suffer great financial loss. The need is to resolve the problem quickly and get the product back on the shelves. There is a double crisis of confidence. The whole episode may occupy only a few days.

Country Satin Cream Liqueur
PRODUCT RECALL

A small number of bottles of Country Satin Cream Liqueur have been found to contain fragments of glass.

The bottles concerned can be identified by the words **"PRODUCE OF HOLLAND"** appearing immediately above the bar code on the small back label. Bottles not bearing the words **"Produce of Holland"** are unaffected.

The safety of our customers is our first concern and therefore we are withdrawing all of the **"Produce of Holland"** bottles.

Customers who have one of these bottles should pour away the contents and post the bottle top together with their name and address to: Country Satin,
P.O. Box 55,
Bristol BS99 7JE,
for a replacement voucher.

Retailers should remove all stock bearing the words **"Produce of Holland"** from the shelves and those we have not contacted direct can phone the Country Satin Helpline for further guidance.

VPW, the UK importer of Country Satin, apologises to customers for any inconvenience caused. If any of our customers are concerned in any way please contact us on the following number where one of our advisers will be pleased to help.

COUNTRY SATIN HELPLINE
0171-388 3898

Fig 22.1   A typical product recall advertisement

In the case of 'poisoned' Mars bars when the Animal Liberation Front wrongly believed that the company engaged in animal experiments, there were 10 million Mars bars on display in British shops. The contaminated bars were allegedly marked so that consumers could spot them. The ALF were seeking publicity, and this had to be avoided. Mars refused to withdraw stocks, but every bar was checked in the shops. It proved to be a hoax, but the management crisis team kept the media advised. The police were unable to do anything. Confidence was restored and only a small drop in sales occurred for about three months. Mars were lucky that retailers had not decided to remove the product, but the problem here was that if the company had withdrawn stocks it would have seemed to be an admission of responsibility, so they concentrated on the evidence that no bar had been tampered with.

Occasionally a fault may be detected in a product. It may be that an imported component is malfunctioning, or that there has been a design error, or some weakness emerges only after a product has been in use for some time. One example was a famous beer that was given an unpleasant taste because of the introduction of a wrong ingredient. In another case a computer error led to mercury – a deadly substance – being introduced into cattle feed. In most cases it is foolish to try to cover up and far better publicity to recall the product. The problem may be trying to locate the product, as happened with a coffee pot whose handles fell off. Such products may be bought as gifts, or be tucked away in cupboards anywhere in the country. When a number of customers complain about a dangerous fault it is folly to ignore them, as one motor-car maker did until finally forced by public protest to withdraw the model for inspection and in some cases modification. In practice, a company will be respected for its honesty in publicly admitting a fault and offering to rectify it or supply a refund or replacement.

The usual procedure is to insert warning advertisements in the appropriate press (*see* Figure 22.1), to notify retailers (and even supply display material advising customers to return the product), and to issue news releases to the media.

2. Desk-top publishing

The printed house journal, the world's oldest form of organised PR having survived for some 160 years at least, appeared to be challenged by the advent of the video house journal which clearly has similar advantages to TV over the press. However, video lacks the permanence and portability of print which can be retained and read almost anywhere at any time, and by a wide readership including families of employees, or by shareholders, or by pensioners.

Computers are already being applied to many aspects of commercial printing. It is not surprising that these techniques should be applied to the production of house journals, and by in-house print units producing company print. As in commercial publishing, it has called for different skills and operatives. Craftsmen of hot metal print production have given way to programmers and keyboard operators; in-house journal editing has made the journalist inadequate.

Now house journals can be produced with an Apple Macintosh (*see* Figure 22.2), Compaq or other computer using Adobe PageMaker or Quark Express software. But the DTP editor is not just a keyboard operator who composes and corrects copy on screen. Now this editor has to be a designer and typographer capable of producing final pages which can be sent on disk straight to the printer. No longer can the house journal editor rely on others in-house or in the studio or at the printers to convert copy into print. The editor alone has to do it, eliminating layout artist, typographer and typesetter.

The whole job can, of course, be given to a consultancy like Dewe Rogerson with its Screenplay service which has the specialist staff to produce entire house journals on disks ready for printing.

There are other differences. Felt-tip marker layouts are no longer required, nor is it necessary to cast off copy and specify type sizes. This is done on screen, including the selection of typefaces and point sizes. Headlines are expanded or condensed to fit the space available. Text is justified, enlarged

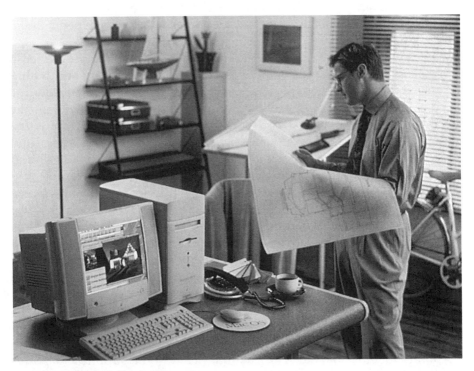

Fig 22.2   Apple home office

or reduced in size, set bold or italic and leaded, by using keyboard or mouse.

DTP systems are very useful, but may need dedicated operators and more of an editor's time than conventional pen, paper and typescript methods. Unless the system is used frequently and fully, and the editor devotes sufficient time to the job, it could be an expensive plaything. That is where a consultancy like Dewe Rogerson, with its Screenplay department staffed by 16 experts with the latest equipment, can be both more economical and more proficient than a less-dedicated in-house DTP operation. Dewe Rogerson prefer to call DTP electronics system publishing.

3. Corporate identity

The creation of the corporate identity scheme is often a PR responsibility because it applies to all aspects of an organisation and is a significant part of the total communication. Thus, it becomes associated not only with marketing and advertising but with employee, shareholder, dealer, consumer, financial and other relations.

Corporate identity, as was explained in Chapter 1, is one of the very oldest forms of communication, its aim being to distinguish and establish visual recognition by means of physical, visible identification. This is done by means of logotype, typography, colour, livery, clothing and so on. One of the best examples of the overall application of a corporate identity scheme is an airline. In fact, transportation in general provides some of the best examples.

To achieve an effective and distinctive corporate identity is neither easy nor cheap since many ideas have to be considered before something original and acceptable is conceived. It is then a costly process to put the scheme into practice. This could involve all print and advertising, the decoration of all vehicles and premises, and clothing of staff, plus the design of items such as tableware, serviettes, drip-mats and coasters, and give-aways. Print includes not only sales literature, but business cards and office stationery. Nevertheless, it can be necessary to create not only distinctiveness but uniformity. It would be silly if, for instance, every branch of a store or a bank had a different facia or different divisions, and branches or subsidiaries had different letterheadings or business cards. A recent example has been the creation of the British Post Office parcel service with its specially designed Parcel Force vans, no doubt in competition with the courier firms such as Parceline and Federal Express. The boldly decorated Parcel Force vans and lorries are very visible on the streets of Britain.

Colours have standard numbers, typefaces have names, logos have particular designs, and no buyer should deviate from what is set out in the corporate identity manual. This manual may also be supplied in poster form, and some companies have made an explanatory video.

A corporate identity may be found necessary when there are mergers, amalgamations or takeovers, and a new identity is required, or where there is need to respond to changes in an organisation. It is not easy to change a corporate identity, although in recent years this has happened with British Airways, Japan Airlines and Malaysia Airlines, BP, British Telecom and Prudential Insurance. The Dutch airline KLM used to have the three initials in italics, but the sloping letters were said to make the passengers feel air-sick, so the logo was revised with vertical roman letters. Zambia Airways used to have its name in condensed letters which implied cramped seating, and the lettering was spaced out more generously.

One of the advantages of a familiar identity scheme is that it has a strong repetitive effect which is both good advertising and good PR.

Some 30 years ago British Gas used the cheerful Mr Therm character (which is still remembered) and its 'flame' successor has failed to equal the popularity of the little figure, even though linked to slogans such as *The flame that obeys you*. Slogans, incidentally, are not usually part of a corporate identity scheme because slogans may be changed. Even though BMW have used the slogan *the ultimate driving machine* for a long time they dropped it when promoting their new '3' series in 1991.

Mr Cube, based on a sugar cube, was used by Tate & Lyle in its anti-nationalisation campaign during a Labour government. A more recent campaign used a well-known television chef, Gary Rhodes, and the slogan *Smile, it's Tate & Lyle*. Johnnie Walker, a striding top-hatted figure, and the rubbery Michelin Man have endured for decades. Animals have also featured in corporate identity schemes, especially as trade marks and brand

Fig 22.3   Coke: corporate identity and international branding *par excellence*. Clearly identifiable, typographically, even when printed right to left for the Hebrew-speaking market

names and the lion has been included in many. Others are the Lloyds Bank black horse, the black and white Scottish terriers of Black and White whisky, the old English sheepdog of ICI's Dulux paints, the Garuda bird of Indonesian Airlines, the kite of Malaysia airlines, and the mouflon mountain sheep of Cyprus Airways.

One British firm which specialises in the creation of corporate identity schemes is Sampson Tyrrell Enterprise. They offer a visual management system which realises the commercial value of a client's visual assets. They go as far as to declare that 'the last thing we do is design'. According to an article by Leslie Roberts in *Business Strategy International*, 'This process entails the consultancy learning the culture and business environment of the client.'

The first stage of visual management is *analysis*: that is, evaluation and planning. Sampson Tyrrell Enterprise need to know what and where the company's visual assets are, how they work, how the client's markets perceive them and – especially – how they influence their customer's ultimate decisions.

Next comes *creativity*: new ways to attain the objectives are created. Once a clear strategy has been defined and agreed, the creative work begins. Analysis measures and defines problems; creative work proposes the solutions. Ideas are put forward in visual form to challenge the imagination, which are refined in discussion with the client. Results are then tested in the market. Whatever works becomes a visual asset.

Finally comes *exploitation*. Only now do Sampson Tyrrell Enterprise follow them through in the market-place. The client's visual assets have to work in the market-place, in many media, at different sizes and levels of visibility. All kinds of people use them, for a hundred different purposes. Visual management looks for opportunities to exploit the client's visual assets in the market-place.

The following three cases studies explain the Sampson Tyrrell Enterprise method.

3A. Shell – managing change

The problem

In the 1980s a number of Shell's fuel retailing competitors introduced a new generation of retail forecourt designs. They were more customer-orientated and more visible. The consistency of their presentation was building powerful global brands. Shell could not afford to be left behind.

By December 1992 Shell had developed a totally new forecourt design that was intended to address the problem, for the first time, on a global basis. But it was a new idea for retail managers across Shell to be asked to be consistent in the application of such detailed visual identity standards. Apart from a few core elements, each national company had historically been free to present itself to its customers as it chose.

It went against this tradition of local autonomy to impose rigorous identity rules from the centre. But faced with a weakening competitive position, global standards had to be established. Sampson Tyrrell Enterprise was invited to devise a way forward.

The solution

Sampson Tyrrell Enterprise began work on a design standards manual that would allow 100 Shell operating companies around the world to implement the agreed retail visual identity throughout their individual networks.

But the task was far more than merely creating a manual. Early on the commitment of the eight largest retailing companies was secured, while test sites provided research that endorsed the new design: it showed that customers felt more welcome and perceived the new forecourt design as warm and friendly.

Now the task was to communicate the *benefits* of the new design to all key managers and the reasons for opting for a global approach. Sampson Tyrrell Enterprise produced internal communications material for Shell that, through the use of powerful photography, graphics and minimal text, broke the mould of traditional Shell internal communications and heralded the change to come.

The next step was to issue *draft* copies of the design standards manual to retail managers. Positioned as a consultative document but produced to a very high standard, this draft incorporated all the feedback on local market issues from the test sites. The clear message was that the expressed needs of the operating companies were being sought, recognised and would be met.

Managers were given three months to review the draft specifications and to discuss them with colleagues and suppliers. They were encouraged to ask questions, examine options and start to plan the changes in their own markets.

Meanwhile Sampson Tyrrell Enterprise worked with Shell to create a presentation for managers that convincingly put the case for strong, universal branding and the role that the retail format could play in creating this.

Finally, the set of definitive manuals was produced, extending way beyond the look and overall appearance of the site; they included engineering and production specifications and a full array of design management support materials. The scope included a new livery for Shell tankers, the convenience store sub-brand 'Select' and the Rainbow carwash

Fig 22.4   Creating a single, consistent global brand

service. Brand consistency became possible not only laterally across national boundaries, but vertically across every aspect of Shell's retail operations.

The benefits

The step-by-step approach devised between Sampson Tyrrell Enterprise and its client allowed the operating companies time to develop a commitment to the new retail identity without feeling it had been imposed upon them.

Consequently, the implementation of the programme met far less resistance in an organisation where central control had always been greatly resisted. The *practicality* of design ensured by incorporating the results from the test sites also minimised objections; while the useability and detail of the manuals has ensured that the new designs are implemented to the highest possible standards.

Shell's global retail format, embraced by its own people, is now helping to ensure that the Shell brand competes as powerfully as any in the global fuel retailing market.

3B. Tarmac – signalling change

The problem

In the early 1990s the construction and building materials group Tarmac went through dramatic development – driven by the group chief executive, Neville Simms – in response to the company's changing markets world-wide.

The group had grown from its quarry and road surfacing origins into the associated areas of design and build, specialist engineering and facilities management, but research showed that Tarmac was still perceived as a roads and materials business.

Although Tarmac had become a better managed, more competitive and stronger organisation, perception lagged behind reality. Throughout the process of change, the company's corporate identity had not been touched and consequently reflected the values of the 'old' company. Tomorrow's Tarmac was now in danger of being constrained by yesterday's identity.

In addition to this, the existing Tarmac brand was fragmented, ragged and inconsistent. It distracted and detracted from what the individual parts of the Group were trying to achieve in their individual markets; many of these Group companies were recent acquisitions who shared little commonality with the Tarmac brand.

Fig 22.5   The old Tarmac identity

This combination meant that Tarmac's identity failed to reflect the strength of an organisation with 24,000 employees, £1 billion of net assets, operating in building and construction-related industries across 24 countries with a turnover of £2.5 billion. An organisation with considerable heritage, pride, technical skills, experience and expertise, Tarmac's corporate identity sold the company short.

The solution

Sampson Tyrrell Enterprise was appointed to define the elements of the new Tarmac brand and create and communicate a new corporate identity for the Group, including all its operating companies world-wide. At the heart of the programme was the development of an effective, integrated identity management system. This would communicate what the new identity would mean to all Tarmac's stakeholders.

Sampson Tyrrell Enterprise's first task was to evaluate Tarmac's existing identity, to work with it, around it and build upon it, but not to change for change's sake. Taking action to strengthen the corporate brand was a priority, creating a new look just for the sake of it was not.

To do this, Sampson Tyrrell Enterprise interviewed Tarmac's senior executives, nearly 200 customers and key advisors. At the same time a comprehensive visual audit of the existing identity was carried out. From the results of this research, a single corporate aim was agreed upon and adopted across the entire group.

> 'We in Tarmac aim to be an innovative, world class provider of high quality products and services which add value to our customers in the built environment.'

While evolutions of the existing 7Ts logo were explored, it soon became clear that this symbol was closely associated with the traditional construction activities of the Group, rather than the innovative, customer-driven values of the new broader-based business. All the evolutions of the 7Ts logo also failed to emphasise sufficiently one group with one vision.

It was agreed that a new symbol was required, one that would represent a single, dynamic, world-class group; one which would promote rather than restrict its growth in the key markets of North America, Europe and the Far East.

Tarmac

Fig 22.6   The new identity

231

Alternative designs were explored; once the final marque was agreed, the new identity was rolled out across everything from site signage and cement mixers to hard hats and computer screen-savers.

Throughout the consultation process, Tarmac had been keeping its staff informed of progress. For four months prior to the launch of the new identity and in the months following, key teams were briefed on the rationale behind the identity and, importantly, how to manage it. A launch toolkit devised by Sampson Tyrrell Enterprise – but delivered by line managers – comprised visual aids, a video, presenter scripts, and anticipated answers to questions. In addition, a leaflet sent directly to all employees sought their support and a special edition of the staff newsletter ensured that everyone felt a part of the change process.

The benefits

The introduction of a new symbol served as a focus to draw together all Group companies under one vision, a common set of values and a clearly expressed sense of purpose. Nevertheless, the system was designed to be sufficiently flexible so that acquired companies benefiting from strong recognition of their own existing name could retain their name, while clearly being seen to be part of the Tarmac Group.

The brightening of the company's corporate colours of green and yellow conveyed the dynamism and single-mindedness of the business, while also increasing visibility and distinctiveness in a competitive marketplace.

The launch of the new identity was coupled with the re-launching of a re-vitalised Target 2000, Tarmac's internal programme to motivate employees and align behaviour with the Group's professed values. This provided Neville Simms with a platform on which to present the new identity as the outward manifestation of a period of internal change. On the one hand the launch served to regenerate staff morale while, on the other, Tarmac could be confident that the new look represented more than merely cosmetic change.

Finally, new procurement practices were established. While the quality of applications was improved, significant economies of scale, improvements in purchasing power and a reduction in waste were effected, through reviewing and recommending single source suppliers. Savings of 20 tonnes of paper per annum were made in one division alone.

Fig 22.7   New-liveried Tarmac subsidiary

As the Chief Executive put it, 'our new corporate identity is proving to be a strong catalyst in adding value to the Tarmac brand.'

3C. Bulgari – crafting change

The problem

As one of the world's most exclusive jewellery brands, Bulgari understood its brand better than most. Its positioning was intuitive while its identity had barely changed since the company was founded over 100 years ago. Bulgari had traded very successfully on its values of quality and exclusivity for all that time.

Nevertheless, Bulgari was keen to exploit the full potential of its prestigious name as 'the Italian jeweller' and by expanding sales of its non-jewellery lines in the fragrance and accessories markets. The name stood for old world quality but its new markets also demanded a contemporary look that would make it accessible to younger generations. But style in letterforms had moved on since the Bulgari namestyle was first designed and, while still conveying exclusivity, it had begun to date.

In addition, a practical issue had arisen: the outline rendering of the namestyle did not work well, for example, on bottles of *eau de parfum*. To solve this problem, for some applications Bulgari's own designers would 'fill in' the letters, resulting in inconsistent use of the namestyle. Clarification was needed to restore consistency.

Bulgari recognised the benefits that could accrue from addressing these issues now.

The solution

Sampson Tyrrell Enterprise in this instance was invited to concentrate on applying simply its design craftsmanship to meet a specific brief: to create a more contemporary feel to the namestyle but so discretely that few customers would notice the difference, and without losing any of its distinctiveness. And to design a system for application that would lend itself as much to printing on glass as it would to being embossed in gold.

The consultancy began by collecting together the marques of the world's leading jewellery and *haute couture* brands. Many had symbols but many, like Bulgari, used their namestyle as their principal identifier. Bulgari's point of difference was the elongated appearance of its name; Sampson Tyrrell Enterprise found that by opening up the space between the letters slightly, this point of difference could be maximised, while at the same time increasing its sense of luxury and elegance.

Next, each individual letter was evaluated for its form, distinctiveness and relationship to the other letters. All the letters were slightly re-crafted but in particular the G and R were re-visited in minute detail to take on a more generous and contemporary feel.

Finally, the question of the two versions of the old namestyle was simply addressed: the decision was taken to drop the outline rendition – or 'dropped shadow' version – altogether. By rendering it in solid black form only, the rules for application were greatly simplified.

BVLGARI

Fig 22.8   Old namestyle

BVLGARI

Fig 22.9   New namestyle

Once Sampson Tyrrell Enterprise's typographic specialists had finished their work, the new namestyle was documented in a manual, which showed in practical terms how the new namestyle should be applied and how it should be used in conjunction with the names of different parts of Bulgari's business.

Sampson Tyrrell Enterprise at the same time re-designed Bulgari's stationery so that its overall look reflected the simplicity and elegance of the namestyle. It also advised its client on the colours that should be used, for example, in packaging so as to ensure that the customer's experience of the Bulgari brand was unique and special in every way.

The benefits

The new namestyle has been applied gradually across all Bulgari's products such that, in accordance with the brief, few customers will have noticed the difference. However, its revitalised elegance is helping to ensure that Bulgari remains one of the most coveted names in the world's most exclusive shopping streets, appealing equally to long-standing customers and a younger generation of discretely acquisitive style-setters.

While losing none of its finesse, the brand has reasserted itself and speaks quiet confidence whether on jewellery, watches or scarves. Bulgari's own designers appreciate the simplicity of the one namestyle that works for them wherever they need to apply it. And while not attributing success solely to the new namestyle, the Bulgari family are happy too – as sales continue to climb and new markets present challenges for new products the world over.

4. Parliamentary liaison

First, let us clarify what this means. It covers relations between organisations, perhaps using specialist consultants, with government, Members of both Houses of Parliament and Civil Service officials at ministries and departments. This includes, in Europe, the national and European Parliament, and the Commission in Brussels. A lobby consists of a special interest group such as old age pensioners, doctors, farmers, motorists or teachers. *Lobbying* means presenting a case to politicians and civil servants. A *lobbyist* should not be confused with a *lobby correspondent* who is a political journalist entitled to interview ministers and MPs in the lobby of the House, and to receive in confidence advance copies of White Papers and other government documents. Nor should parliamentary liaison be confused with PR activities conducted by the government on its own behalf.

Parliamentary liaison usually consists of two kinds: keeping politicians and civil servants aware of an organisation's interests, and keeping organisations aware of parliamentary activities and procedures such as the committee stages of Bills which may lead to new legislation, and the activities of Select Committees and Royal Commissions to which it may be valuable for organisations to give evidence.

In the USA 'lobbies' are powerful institutions for liaison with elected representatives, and the biggest lobby is said to be the 'gun lobby' which – as a result of America's frontier history – protects the right of citizens to carry guns. In Britain, successful lobbying led to the introduction of lead-free petrol, abolition of the National Dock Labour Scheme, watering down of proposed changes in the brewing industry regarding ownership of public houses, public lending rights for authors who now receive a small payment on loans of their books, and the modification of rulings about airline routes.

Two attitudes may be taken to lobbying. It may be claimed that only those with enough money can effectively lobby and influence government policy and legislation. In contrast, it can also be said that it is easier for a government to rule and legislate if it can have discussions with a representative body.

Corruption is unlikely in Britain where MPs must declare their interests when asking questions or expressing views in Parliament, and any MP who has financial interests in PR is obliged to declare them in a register kept for this purpose. A number of MPs are paid fees to advise clients on parliamentary procedures, but not to take political action on behalf of clients.

5. Financial PR

The PR consultancy specialising in financial and corporate PR has long been established in financial centres like London and New York. They have been concerned with a range of PR services, from private companies 'going public' and being quoted on stock exchanges, to those associated with the year-round financial communications of public corporations.

During the 1980s this suddenly became a growth area for a number of reasons which emphasised the importance of PR as the means of creating understanding and confidence.

A spate of takeover bids of gigantic proportions called for PR services on behalf of 'target' and 'predator' companies – that is those who were the victims and those who sought to take them over. Associated with this were certain 'insider dealing' scandals, and the PRCA issued recommendations on how PR consultancies should conduct their services professionally. The Takeover Panel of the London Stock Exchange condemned the knocking (i.e. derogatory) copy in some of the advertisements issued by the parties involved in takeover bids. These financial battles were often bitter, and PR consultancies had to be careful to conduct themselves within codes of practice and Stock Exchange rules.

During the same period, and continuing still, we have seen the phenomenon of privatisation in Britain and elsewhere. Governments have sold off nationalised industries or their financial stakes in certain industries. This was a favourite tactic of political leaders such as Mrs Thatcher. It has sought to break down nationalised industries (although many like the Post Office, BBC, ITC, British Rail and so on were actually created by the Conservatives); to raise money instead of borrowing it for government expenditure; to encourage the greater efficiency of privately owned companies; and to create a greater share-owning public (although millions of shares were sold to make a quick profit).

Privatisation called for considerable PR efforts not only to educate the money market about an industry being sold off but also to educate the new breed of small shareholder in what share-buying and share-owning were all about. As a result, millions of people who had never been share-owners, bought shares in British Telecom, British Gas, British Petroleum, British Airways, British Airports and water and electricity undertakings. Employees were also made special share offers.

On 27 October 1986 came the 'Big Bang' when the London Stock exchange was deregulated so that it was no longer necessary to buy shares through jobbers, and fixed commissions were ended. Instead, market makers took over from jobbers and brokers, working from computer workstations in dealing rooms instead of on the trading floor of the Stock Exchange. The effect has been to spread share trading to new kinds of dealers ranging from individuals to banks and building societies. The latter became free to conduct many other forms of business (such as property selling or real estate) as a result of the Building Societies Act 1986 which came into effect in early 1987.

In the midst of all this was a growth in the number of unit trusts, which provide a share in a large number of investments made by the unit trust managers. Some of these specialise in different parts of the world such as Europe, the Far East and the USA, as well as the UK.

All these developments called for an increased use of PR, both by in-house PROs and by specialist PR consultants.

It also led to the Stock Exchange introducing its own computerised financial news service, a feature of which has been a ban on embargoed news stories in order to avoid the possible leakage of sensitive financial information.

Financial PR has thus become a very important growth area. It calls for a special knowledge of the financial world, how it works, and the new regulatory controls set up by the Stock Exchange, plus the implications of international dealings among the major stock exchanges of the world enjoying satellite facilities. Today, it is not just a matter of knowing what is going on in London, for New York, Frankfurt, Paris, Amsterdam, Zurich, Hong Kong, Tokyo, Sydney and the other major stock exchanges are linked by satellite. Similarly, financial newspapers and magazines have international editions, again serviced by satellite transmission.

Progress test 22

1. Why is a crisis management team necessary?

2. What is meant by 'likely' and 'unlikely' crises?

3. Describe what happened regarding 'poisoned' Mars bars.

4. What is meant by 'product recall'?

5. In what way has desk-top publishing taken over from conventional methods of editing house journals?

6. What are the main elements of a corporate identity scheme?

7. Name some of the trade characters which have appeared in corporate identity schemes.

8. Explain the Sampson Tyrrell visual management method of creating a corporate identity scheme.

9. Distinguish between lobbying and lobby correspondents.

10. What are target and predator companies?

11. What was the Big Bang, and what effect did it have?

12. Why does the London Stock Exchange ban embargoes?

23

NEW DEVELOPMENTS AND TRENDS

In this final chapter we shall look at some of the topics and developments which now concern PR. They include the 'grey revolution', the Single European Market, the emergent economies and growth area of the Pacific rim countries, the research into mission statements by Ashridge Strategic Management Centre, the video news release and media coverage research.

It shows the all-embracing span of PR which has spread far beyond mere press relations, even if we still have the remarkable paradox that few PR practitioners can write a publishable news release.

1. The 'grey revolution'

This is the phenomenon of an ageing population, with an increasing number of people either becoming redundant or retiring early. Advertising people like Tim Ashton (art director of Howell Henry Chaldicott Levy who produced a controversial Fuji film commercial showing an old couple kissing) recognise that by the year 2000 there will be 12.5 million British people in the 50–69 age group but only 10.75 million 15–29 year olds. Advertising has to be targeted differently now.

Linda Grant, in an article in the *Independent on Sunday* (30 June 1991) on the effect of the grey revolution on advertising closed with the following words:

'In 15 years time, the great demographic bulge of the baby boom generation will be in and beyond middle-age. The youth market will be a tiny proportion of the buying public ... The crumblies and the wrinklies ... may begin to exercise their own economic revolution in Adland.'

It is already happening. Middle-aged and elderly characters are featured in TV commercials such as those for insurance companies. The TV listings magazine *TV Plus* was promoted by a TV commercial featuring a middle-aged actress. Another actress, Maureen Lipman, was made up as middle-aged character 'Beattie' in a popular British Telecom advertisement series. Middle-aged men are now seen mowing lawns in TV commercials. This situation has come about because the yuppie market has almost vanished with the recession which began in 1990. It is older people who are booking holidays abroad, buying VCRs, videos and CDs, cars and microwave ovens. The car market is a good example, with many retired people surrendering their company cars and buying their own.

Here, then, is a vast and growing public on which PR needs to concentrate – older people who are not necessarily poor and who may well be wealthier than those young people disadvantaged by either high mortgages or unemployment and little income. It calls for a new approach to media. What newspapers and magazines do they read? What broadcast programmes do they watch or listen to? They used to be the forgotten people in advertising: not so any more, and the same applies to PR.

2. PR and the Single European Market

Good communication is essential to successful trading in a continental market where language poses a serious problem. This not only concerns translation of news releases, picture captions, feature articles, external house journals, educational literature and scripts for videos, but the continental approach to many elements of the marketing mix. A new partnership between PR and marketing is essential.

One important area is in the labelling of products and the writing of instructions on packages and in instruction leaflets and manuals. This is second nature to companies which have always served international markets. But many products which normally have only a home market now not only need to compete with imports from across the Channel and North Sea. They need to sell wherever possible in Europe. Information in English only does not suffice.

One useful device is the fix-a-form label which, when fixed to the outside of, say, a bottle or a jar, can be unfolded concertina-fashion. Multi-lingual instructions can be printed on the panels of the label.

The media situation in Europe is different from that in Britain. Partly because of the size of countries, or the political origins of countries which were formerly several states or kingdoms like Italy and Germany, there are few national newspapers but many regional or local dailies. And the smaller the country the fewer the number of magazines, especially trade, technical and professional ones. The make up and nature or existence of press media can be studied by examining the sources given in Chapter 9.

It is also necessary to comply with the various EU directives which affect the advertising of some products such as cigarettes, fast cars and green products. Even if some of these directives are restricted in Britain, they are still likely to apply in Europe. Already there are national and EU controls affecting sales promotion offers, direct mail and the use of computerised data. It may be that, because of certain promotional restrictions, there is scope for better PR tactics.

However, EU directives could work the other way. EU regulations affecting classes of advertising such as tobacco, pharmaceuticals and cars, limiting eco-labelling claims, and restricting the use of database information for selling subscriptions, never experienced in the UK, could have a detrimental effect on press relations. This is because there could be fewer publications, or circulation figures could be reduced. The scope for press relations work could be far less than hitherto in the UK. Greater reliance may also have to be placed on created PR media, such as external house journals, videos, private exhibitions, sponsorship, conferences and seminars.

3. Pacific rim developments

While recession hit Western economies, especially the British in the 1990s, growth areas and emergent economies occurred in Asiatic countries such as Indonesia, Korea, Malaysia, Taiwan and Thailand. Indonesia threw off its dependence on oil exports and expanded the export of non-oil products including manufactures. Malaysia, having created the home-built Proton car with the aid of Mitsubishi, actually exported the car to Britain. The Japanese invested in manufacturing plants in other Asiatic countries, especially Korea and Thailand. This prosperity among ASEAN and Far Eastern countries has led to an awakening regarding PR, particularly in Indonesia where courses and conferences have been mounted to explain the use of PR and to train Indonesians in PR techniques.

Japan is a big player in these markets. There was a time when Japan depended on its long-term philosophy of marketing (compared with the American anxiety to maximise early profits), but today the Japanese are taking a great interest in PR techniques. Japan is also involved in the Chinese market, and the Chinese themselves with their trend towards a market economy are taking a great interest in PR to the extent of translating and publishing PR books of British and American origin.

Meanwhile, Singapore is strategically placed as one of the dragon or newly industrialised countries (NICs), and it is a sophisticated centre of commerce, industry, printing and education. Its vast international airport provides a crossroad for numerous airlines.

Thus the Pacific Rim or Pacific Basin countries provide a trading zone which vies with those of Europe and North America. These are lands rich in culture, and China was the original source of paper-making and printing. Their innate ability to communicate makes their appreciation of PR all the stronger.

4. Mission statements

These are not new, but they were given fresh emphasis by the research conducted by the Ashridge Strategic Management Centre, which began in 1987 and was published by *The Economist* in 1990. The report, *Do You Need a Mission Statement?*, was written by Andrew Campbell and Sally Yeung. The point of a mission statement is to define where a company is going and what it stands for. Surprisingly, many chief executives do not really know. It has become a form of PR to establish a mission statement, especially regarding major changes such as the European market, the increasing influence of the EU, topics such as the effect of Asiatic development (see 3 above) on imports and competitive world trade.

The Ashridge report presented the concept of a 'sense of mission', and that companies should not be trying to write mission statements so much as create a sense of mission among employees. In many respects it is the staff who need to be imbued with a sense of mission.

Mission is largely to do with the behaviour standards and values of an organisation, the company culture, which can differ enormously from one company to another. It is very much a PR concept and part of management–employee relations.

The report quotes the mission statement by the TI Group. The company was completely restructured round the mission. The annual report declared 'TI's strategic thrust is to become an international engineering group concentrating on specialised engineering business, operating in selected niches on a global basis. Key businesses must be able to command positions of sustainable technological and market share leadership.'

Mission, the researchers conceded, is about culture and about strategy. This now takes us beyond internal PR to external PR because any objectively planned PR programme is more likely to succeed if it reflects an organisation's defined mission at all levels. A mission statement 'can help to clarify detailed issues, serve as a symbol of the common cause shared by the people in the company, and it can help individuals who get 'led astray' by events to pull themselves back to the original mission.'

But the authors also warn that 'mission statements frequently do more harm than good because they imply a sense of direction, clarity of thinking and unity that rarely exist. More often they describe values and behaviour standards that are unrealistic and certainly not part of the employees' normal behaviour.' It can create cynicism.

Now here is a PR problem and it begs this question: who should write a mission statement? An outsider such as a PR consultant who may not be intimately aware of what is realistic, or an in-house PRO who is more familiar with realities? Or is the consultant more likely to be impartial and the in-house PRO biased? A mission statement must be workable, whoever writes it.

In understanding mission, the authors narrow it down to two approaches, that of business strategy, and that of behaviour. The first owes much to the thinking of Ted Levett of Harvard who believed that companies defined their business too narrowly, and should ask what business they were really in. On the other hand a company such as IBM concentrated on a cultural view of mission (and it is true that its people are very dedicated), while Marks and Spencer applied both forms of mission.

The Ashridge Mission Model is illustrated in Figure 23.1.

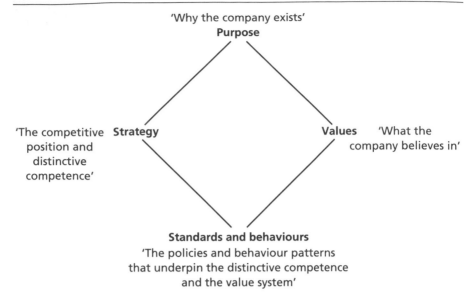

'Why the company exists'
Purpose

Strategy — 'The competitive position and distinctive competence'

Values — 'What the company believes in'

Standards and behaviours
'The policies and behaviour patterns
that underpin the distinctive competence
and the value system'

Fig 23.1   The Ashridge mission model

The authors believe that a sense of mission occurs when there is a match between the values of an organisation and those of an individual. They emphasise the importance of values. The model states that organisation values need to be compatible with employee values. Values must be embedded in behaviour standards, while the model also demands that strategy and values reinforce one another. This is a brief commentary on the Executive summary of the full report, but it should be sufficient to recommend the Ashridge case for producing a mission statement that is practical.

5. The video news release

Again this is not a new concept, but it is a comparatively recent development in the UK where specialist firms are now producing VNRs for clients. To demonstrate the technique, there is the work of Bulletin International's Bulletin Television News Service, 5–8 Hardwick Street, London EC1R 4RB. They are very successful in gaining TV coverage for their clients.

The advantage of a VNR is that it provides TV producers with the means of using visual material to which they might not otherwise have access, or are not prepared to cover with a camera crew. Bulletin produces VNRs and then contact TV news editors or programme producers to whom the VNR is offered. There is no speculative distribution as there might be with ordinary releases.

Some typical uses of Bulletin VNRs have been for the national launch of Royal Mail Parcel Force, a National Freephone information service for Help the Aged, the Kenco RAC London to Brighton Veteran Car Run and the opening of Digital Equipment Corporation's new Scottish manufacturing facility. The following is the case study of the Digital VNR.

Story
Digital Equipment Corporation officially opens the most advanced computer chip manufacturing facility in the world.

Client
Digital Equipment Corporation.

Background
Digital had invested £85 million building the most advanced computer chip manufacturing facility in the world at South Queensferry in Scotland. Production began in June 1990 and at that time Bulletin produced a VNR project aimed at UK broadcasters that achieved nine separate broadcasts totalling 13 minutes of coverage. For the official opening Digital required broadcasters to be targeted internationally.

Client needs
To achieve the maximum amount of television coverage for the official opening in the UK and internationally in France, Germany, Italy, Switzerland and the United States.

Bulletin action
A background VNR was made illustrating the operation of the plant. Bulletin contacted broadcasters internationally to 'sell in' the story idea and supply the background tape. On the day of the official opening, Bulletin covered the event in Scotland and distributed the pictures by satellite.

Results achieved
The video news release project achieved a total of 17 broadcasts ranging from Scottish, Swiss and German TV to American and pan-European outlets. The total coverage achieved by the June and September projects was 26 separate broadcasts totalling over 30 minutes.

6. Media coverage research

Although PR practitioners have long since discarded the evaluation of media coverage on an advertisement rate card basis, are not content with totting up column centimetres, adopt rating charts for appearances in different grades of journal, and study the quality and tone of coverage, this does not necessarily go far enough. Media Measurement Ltd of Stony Stratford, Milton Keynes have produced a computerised system of assessing the effectiveness of press coverage. 'Effectiveness' does have a double meaning, and it is necessary to understand that the Media Measurement system *analyses* press cuttings and provides clients with a Press Relations Performance Review. That clearly goes a long way beyond an elementary appraisal of press cuttings received. The second kind of effectiveness can only be assessed by the organisation which sought media coverage. What effect did it have on readers? Did it produce enquiries, or increase understanding, overcome hostility, prejudice, apathy or ignorance, or in other ways contribute to achieving the objectives of the PR programme? If there is an objective, planned PR programme then news releases will not be sent out willy-nilly, but will be one of the techniques adopted to achieve the desired PR result.

Consequently, the excellent Media Measurement system is a sophisticated way of assessing the *quality* and *tone* of press coverage.

The Press Relations Performance Review is a computer-based form of analysis which uses a client's key words and phrases, press cuttings and a database of British publications. The data is processed and a report is supplied.

The principal, secondary and other notable key words make possible close examination of the effectiveness of the coverage in achieving impact, interest, persuasiveness, quality and tone, opportunities for response generation and so on, including both text and pictures. With the information supplied in monthly tables and charts, a press relations campaign can be evaluated and this can assist future costing and planning. It can indicate how much press coverage is possible or needed, lead times necessary to achieve coverage, and target journalists both good and bad.

7. The green issue

When an organisation introduces a production system, designs a product or adopts a form of packaging which reduces pollution and helps to protect the environment, this is very much to the credit of the organisation. A number of products, for instance, have refillable containers, which means that the original one does not have to add to the mounting pile of plastic refuse. The PR practitioner is entitled to seek credit for such socially-conscious achievements.

But there have been cases of 'green-washing' whereby companies have climbed on the green band-wagon and made spurious claims about the environmental friendliness of their products. The advertising world calls it 'green-washing' and the Advertising Standards Authority has warned against improper claims. Some marketing people, being sceptical of PR, have even adopted the idea that false green claims are a form of PR!

But the European Union is beginning to make real demands on manufacturers to protect the environment. One German law requires that all containers be returned by consumers to the manufacturers, and a consortium of manufacturers is supplying consumers with bins for this purpose.

Fig. 23.2 Scene to screen: the digital camera is the PRO's direct route to high-resolution photo reproduction. Pictures can be edited on screen, added to image databases and Internet pages. This is the Epson PhotoPC 500.

Making products environmentally friendly can increase prices, but it is significant that many people today are prepared to pay for quality and pollution-free products. With government support, lead-free petrol is actually cheaper than leaded.

This is a sensitive area in which the PRO has a responsible role to play. This includes educating markets about environmentally friendly products, and advising managements against making imprudent claims. This will help to gain recognition of efforts being made by their companies to protect the world in which we live.

Progress test 23

1. What effect has the 'grey revolution' had on the choice of publics for a PR programme?

2. How will EU directives affect the Single European Market?

3. What part of the world is showing new interest in PR, and why is this?

4. What is a mission statement?

5. Describe how a video news release is best distributed.

6. How can media coverage research help in the planning of a press relations activity?

Appendix 1

EXAMINATION TECHNIQUE

Revision

1. Introduction

All students have their own methods of revising and you will certainly have yours. It is likely, however, that you will benefit by spending a few minutes reading this short guide to revision.

Your revision should have three main aims:

1. Complete understanding of the subject
2. Retention and recall of the subject
3. And ability to explain and apply the subject.

Understanding is the key to both the learning and use of a subject. Thus it is understanding which is crucial to examination success and your revision should be designed above all to reinforce understanding. This understanding should be related to the questions in the past examination papers printed in Appendix 3. How well do you understand the questions? If you do not you should revise these subjects in the text.

Plan for positive revision:
1. Consult this book frequently
2. Revise one chapter at a time
3. Re-read each chapter
4. Make revision notes
5. Keep them simple
6. Test your knowledge of each topic
7. Construct topic charts
8. Keep diagrams simple
9. List key principles
10. Answer the progress tests
11. Plan answers to specimen exam questions
12. Answer fully if necessary
13. Read the notes on answering exam questions

Fig A1.1 Pre-exam revision programme

2. Revision programme

Tedium in revision is caused mainly by reading the same original notes over and over again. This is also unproductive. It is far better to adopt a positive revision programme, one which uses your time profitably and enables you to teach yourself. This book is the perfect basis for such a programme.

The examination

3. Examination technique

(a) Read the examination instructions carefully, and obey them. For example, number your answers correctly: do not number them in the order in which you answer them. Also number each page.

(b) Read through the whole paper and tick the questions you think that you can answer. Be careful not to assume that a past question you have answered is the

---

1. Read the instructions carefully
2. Note the marking system
3. Allocate your time accordingly
4. Allow half an hour for each question
5. Read the whole exam paper
6. Read the questions carefully
7. Tick the ones you can answer
8. Answer all compulsory questions
9. Be careful not to misread questions
10. Follow the instructions within each question
11. Answer every part of a question
12. Number the answers correctly
13. Outline a rough answer
14. Cross out rough work tidily
15. Develop answers fully and relevantly
16. Do not introduce irrelevant material
17. Present answers neatly
18. Use short paragraphs
19. Use subheads and section-numbering
20. Use a black ink pen
21. Do not use coloured pens
22. Use a ruler for neat charts
23. Number each page of your paper
24. Allow time for checking accuracy, spelling and punctuation

---

Fig A1.2   Examination technique

same as the one which looks similar in the new paper. Marks are often lost because candidates misread questions. Make sure that you answer every part of a question. In LCCI exams each part is numbered and the marks awarded are stated. This is not always the case in CAM questions.

(c) Scribble a rough outline of your answer, but cross it out so that it is not confused with your actual answer. You can do this in the answer book. Planning is essential.

(d) Marks are given for imagination and intelligent application of knowledge. Essay-type questions need full development, and should occupy about 1½ pages. However, long tedious essays are seldom required, and in many cases – such as discussion questions – you will help the examiner by using subheadings and numbering sections, especially when a question has more than one part. A list of notes will earn few if any marks. In contrast, if you are asked to briefly explain terms, a concise sentence is sufficient in each case.

(e) In a three-hour examination, allow half-an-hour for each answer, then get on with the next one. This allows time to read the paper and re-read your answers. Leave a space at the end of each answer so that you can add if you have the time. This method prevents you from spending too much time on one answer and then finding you lack time to answer the final question.

(f) Present your answers as neatly as possible so that they are easy for the examiner to read and mark. Do not cross out untidily. Use short paragraphs.

(g) Remember, the examiner does not fail candidates: they fail themselves, usually by misreading questions, presenting knowledge irrelevant to questions, failing to follow instructions, but mostly because their answers are too short.

Revision should be done a chapter at a time. Try adopting the following sequence:

(a) *Re-read* the chapter thoroughly.

(b) Make revision notes. These can consist of no more than the headings in the text with a very brief note about important principles. Take each note in turn and try to recall and explain the subject matter. If you can, proceed to the next; if you cannot, look in this book. By doing this, you will revise, test your knowledge and spend your time profitably by concentrating your revision on those aspects of the subject with which you are least familiar. In addition, you will have an excellent last-minute revision aid.

(c) Construct a chart for each topic using the headings in this book. Many people respond well to dramatic explanations and summaries which provide an extremely quick and efficient means of revision. You need to think how best to construct them and in doing so you teach yourself and better understand the subject.

Two tips: do not try to include too much on each diagram, and do not try to economise on paper. The impact and usefulness of a diagram depends very much on its visual simplicity. The same applies to revision notes.

(d) Prepare concise explanations of key principles that you are likely to need so that during the examination you do not have to think about how to explain something which you probably know well but cannot easily put into words there and then.

(e) Answer the progress tests again. You should find a significant improvement in the number of questions that you can answer immediately. This exercise will primarily test your ability to recall and explain facts.

(f) Plan answers to the specimen examination questions in this book and any others set by the relevant examining body. Planning answers is often a more useful exercise than actually writing the answer out in full. In planning you have in effect answered the question and writing it out is a largely mechanical exercise. If, however, you feel that you need the practice in essay writing, answer some fully.

Read the notes on answering questions before planning any answers.

(g) Try to make it easy to read and mark your answers. Do not use coloured pens. Write your answers in a black ink pen: feint blue is not easy to read. Remember to take a ruler so that you can draw charts neatly.

4. CAM and LCCI examinations

There is often a difference in style between CAM and LCCI examination questions. CAM questions do not always number parts but simply link them together in one sentence. LCCI questions are usually more clearly divided into parts, and the marks awarded for each part are stated. For instance, you may be asked to explain ten terms with two marks for each answer. Do not be put off because you do not know all ten terms. Five good answers will gain ten marks.

Watch out for compulsory questions, which occur in most LCCI and CAM papers. Your paper may be disqualified if you omit to answer the compulsory question.

Appendix 2

SYLLABUS OF THE CAM CERTIFICATE PUBLIC RELATIONS EXAMINATION

Aim

To provide candidates with an awareness of the role of public relations in relation to the many different publics with which an organisation is concerned. Also to provide an understanding of all means of communication by which those publics can be reached. Finally, a knowledge of the organisational and professional context in which people working full-time in public relations operate.

Objectives

On completion of this module candidates should have a broad understanding in the context of the EU of the:

- nature of public relations, its history and background and its relationship with other departments of an organisation
- organisation and operations of public relations
- legal and self-regulatory constraints under which public relations operates
- various techniques and skills involved and media employed in public relations
- use of telecommunications and the skills involved in modern office practice
- variations in different countries, particularly in the EU.

1. Background
- History
- Definitions
- Ethics
- Trade and professional bodies (e.g. IPR, PRCA, IPRA, CERP)

2. Public relations as a management function
- Where PR fits into management structures
- Departmental and in-house organisation and structures
- The in-house and consultancy options
- The corporate, counselling, marketing, financial and employee roles
- The function of public relations, two-way information and communication
- Setting and managing a budget

3. Public relations as an external source
- Consultancies, specialist and freelance
- Client relationships and management tools
- Consultancy structures, management and operations

4. The role of public relations within an organisation
- Commercial organisations and public sector
- Non-commercial organisations including national, cross-border and local government, charities, groups and professional associations
- Their roles, responsibilities and position within the organisation

5. Definition of publics – internal, local (national), regional (pan-European)
Consideration of the various internal and external publics with which an organisation's public relations programme may be concerned, such as (but not exclusively)

- Customers and potential customers
- Employees
- Media
- Investors and financial community
- Local community, educational establishments and bodies
- Suppliers
- Opinion formers
- Government

6. Public relations techniques and their use
- Description, characteristics, advantages/disadvantages of different techniques
- Editorial media (printed and broadcast)
- Requirements for all types of editorial media
- Public relations material – what is required, how it is used
- Writing and distribution of material for the media – news, features and promotions
- Editorial responsibilities and constraints, embargoes, political balance, freedom of the media
- Free media
- Events, promotions and functions (such as conferences, facility visits, exhibitions)
- Educational activities

7. Media production
- Print, broadcast, electronic
- Research and preparation of scripts and presentation material
- Proof-reading and sub-editing
- Printed work (advertisements, direct mail, literature)
- Annual reports, employee reports, house journals
- Graphics (photography, slides, charts, displays)
- Video/film/audio-visual

8. Public relations planning and programming including crisis/contingency
- Situation analysis
- Research and appraisal
- Objectives and strategy
- Programme planning
- Programme implementation

251

- Evaluation and progress reporting
- Budgets
- Assessment of results

9. Legal and self-regulatory controls
- Codes of Conduct and their rationale (e.g. IPR, PRCA)
- Laws affecting public relations practice including (but not exclusively)
Defamation and slander
Copyright
Financial Services Acts
Companies Acts
Codes and codification (e.g. the role of the OFT)
Employment Acts

Appendix 3

CAM CERTIFICATE EXAMINATION IN PUBLIC RELATIONS

November 1995

Time allowed: THREE HOURS

All candidates are required to answer QUESTION ONE and THREE OTHER QUESTIONS.

ALL questions carry equal marks.

Rough work should be included in the answer book(s) and ruled through, but will **not** be accepted as part of the candidate's answers.

Whenever possible, candidates should include examples from real life situations.

Question One (Mandatory)
Write a news release announcing the launch of a new mobile telephone network. Your release should be set out in the correct format. You should also indicate what other information you might include in the pack that would be given to journalists at the launch of the new network.

Question Two
You work in the in-house public relations department of a generic marketing association whose objective is to promote the purchase and consumption of English apples. The association's main activities take place during 'English Apple Week', held each year at the beginning of September. This year's objective is to encourage young people to become more aware of the nutritional value of apples and encourage them to buy apples instead of convenience snack foods.

The head of your department has asked you to draft a memo outlining the promotional activities that could be organised by the association this year. Write the memo. You should include a budget, outline the planning timetable needed for the one-week promotion and say how you would evaluate its effectiveness.

Question Three
The local council for which you work has a policy of sending young offenders on a combined outward bound and community aid course. The course has proved very effective in preventing young people from re-offending. There has been a report in a local newspaper, followed by a report on local radio, implying that your council's programme is like those of other local authorities, with teenagers being sent on exotic holidays with public money.

A meeting has been called to discuss how the council should respond to this issue. Write an action plan for the meeting, including a timetable, outlining your recommendations as to how the council should respond and how its response could be evaluated.

Question Four

You work in a public relations consultancy in the West Midlands which has many business-to-business clients. Your account director has been asked to speak at a local Chamber of Commerce meeting about editorial coverage in the trade press. Her talk is provisionally entitled: 'Has the UK trade press lost its editorial independence and integrity?' and she has asked you to prepare notes for the talk. She has particularly asked you to cover the topics of colour separations, advertorials and product features.

Prepare the notes.

Question Five

The newly appointed managing director of the manufacturing company for which you work has recently told you that he thinks that public relations is 'just free advertising'. You disagreed at the time, and he asked you to write an article of about five hundred words for the company's in-house magazine explaining why. Write the article, and include examples of your company's and other organisations' successful public relations campaigns to refute this assertion.

Question Six

You work in the public relations department of the largest department store in a town where a new local radio station will shortly be launched. Your head of department has asked you to investigate the promotional opportunities afforded by the new station.

Write an action plan illustrating how you would go about finding out the relevant information. (10 marks)

Outline **three** PR-related promotional ideas, involving the radio station, for your store. Include information about the cost implications of each. (15 marks)

Question Seven

A charity which provides riding holidays for disabled children has asked your public relations consultancy for help with its communications programme. The national director of the charity is particularly concerned about the effect that the National Lottery has had on donations from the public. Write a public relations plan showing how the charity might raise its profile.

Question Eight

The public relations department of the company where you work has recently recruited a graduate trainee who has had no relevant work experience. You have been asked to prepare an induction programme for him.

Draft a plan of activity for his first week. (12 marks)

Draft a memo outlining the legal and voluntary constraints under which he will be working as a public relations practitioner. (13 marks)

June 1996

Time allowed: THREE HOURS

All candidates are required to answer QUESTION ONE and THREE OTHER QUESTIONS.

All questions carry equal marks.

Rough work should be included in the answer book(s) and ruled through, but will **not** be accepted as part of the candidate's answers.

Whenever possible, candidates should include examples from real life situations.

Question One (Mandatory)
You are an account manager with a public relations agency which has won a pitch to undertake the publicity for the local authority's bid to host the next Olympics.

(a) Write a news release announcing the win and explaining the consultancy's brief and function. (15 marks)
(b) Outline the target audiences for the announcement and list the types of media you would use to reach them, giving examples of each type of medium. (10 marks)

Question Two
You work in the in-house public relations department of Browns Ltd, a privately owned company that is considering going public within the next two years to raise some additional share capital. You have been asked to prepare a report for the Board detailing:

(a) the financial publics and media concerned (15 marks)
(b) the communications issues involved (10 marks)

Draft the report, using appropriate subheadings within your answer to highlight important points.

Question Three
You have been asked to give a presentation to a group of first year students studying for a BA in Communication Studies at your local university. The subject you have chosen is: 'Planning and implementing a media relations campaign'. Write outline notes for the presentation, which should set media relations in the wider context of public relations as a whole.

Question Four
You work in the public relations department of a large pharmaceutical company, which has just merged with another of similar size. The manager of your department has asked you to submit a proposal as to how the newly merged firm should review its existing corporate literature and develop new corporate literature for the combined group. Write the proposal in memo form, outlining:

(a) The process you would use for the review (9 marks)
(b) The recommendations you might make following the review (12 marks)
(c) Your timetable for the project (4 marks).

Question Five
You work in the public relations department of a company which provides professional training. It has training centres in several major cities in the UK. The Chief Executive wants to develop a community relations programme, and has asked you to prepare a report on the subject. Draft the report, which should include a definition of community relations, possible criteria and aims for the company's programme, possible benefits to both the company and the community, suitable activities for the programme, evaluation techniques and examples of two recent successful community relations programmes.

Question Six

You work for a government agency which is launching new guidelines for increasing energy efficiency in offices. A free booklet will be available on request, and a subsidised 'energy audit' of individual premises will be offered. You have been asked to handle the media launch. Prepare a plan for the event. You should indicate the categories of journalists who would be invited, giving examples where possible, outline the aims of the event, provide your suggested schedule for the actual launch day (to include venue and speakers), identify possible questions from the media and give details of the contents of the press pack. How will you measure whether the event has been a success?

Question Seven

A charity which provides hospice care has approached your public relations agency about its plans to publicise its centenary next year. A member of the Royal Family is its patron and a number of celebrities are members of a 'Friends committee'. The charity wants to raise awareness of their hospices and encourage legacies and voluntary help. Write notes for a proposal to the charity on how your agency could help to meet its objectives. In addition to the activities involved, you should also outline how the programme would be evaluated, and any budget considerations.

Question Eight

You work in the public relations department of a large clothing manufacturer. You have become aware that an investigative journalist working for a broadsheet national daily newspaper is researching an article about the damaging environmental impact of the clothing industry, and that she is using your company as a case study to illustrate the apparent lack of responsibility in the sector. The article is due to be published in two weeks' time. Write a plan for the board of your company showing how you would manage the situation.

Appendix 4

EXTENDED SYLLABUS OF THE LCCI PUBLIC RELATIONS THIRD LEVEL EXAMINATION

Aim

To assess candidates' knowledge and understanding of the profession of Public Relations, its role within an organisation and the role of the Public Relations consultancy; to define the strategic role of Public Relations' in the management of communications throughout an organisation, including the use of different types of media, production and eventing and the identification of management–employee relations.

Notes

1   It is expected that candidates will have an up-to-date, but not necessarily an in-depth knowledge of modern communications techniques. Although a question might not specifically call for the application of such techniques, candidates will be rewarded for demonstrating how such techniques can help in the efficient operation/management of a communications programme.

2   An appreciation of human relations problems arising from the effects of technological change will be expected.

3   At least one question within the examination paper may require an answer in either report or memorandum format.

4   Question 1 will always be a compulsory question.

The syllabus is designed to be of benefit to:

(a) Candidates who wish to acquire a background of the core activities found in both Public Relations consultancy and in-house departments.

(b) Candidates wishing to obtain the LCCIEB Third Level Group Diplomas in Public Relations in Business Management.

(c) Candidates intending to progress to more advanced administrative and management qualifications, especially in Public Relations, ie. CAM Certificate, CAM Diploma or a BA, MBA in Public Relations.

Syllabus

1. The nature of Public Relations

1.1   Definition of Public Relations as defined by The Institute of Public Relations
1.2   What is meant by Public Relations
1.3   How Public Relations differs from advertising

1.4   The relationship between Public Relations and Marketing

1.5   Public Relations and Sales Promotion

1.6   The difference between Public Relations and propaganda

1.7   The difference between Public Relations and Publicity

1.8   Public Relations as a management function and its position within an organisation

1.9   Public Relations and the commercial environment

1.10 Public Relations in non-commercial organisations

1.11 The use of Public Relations in the financial market, parliamentary enforcement and the uses of controlled Public Relations in a crisis situation

1.12 Public Relations in co-ordinating the corporate image and corporate identity

2. Law and voluntary codes

2.1   Distinguishing between legal and voluntary controls

2.2   Comparison of the effectiveness of legal and voluntary controls

2.3   Identification of the principal statutory controls of Public Relations

2.4   Explanation of the codes of conduct of the IPR, the IPRA, the PRCA and CERP

2.5   The Trade Descriptions Act in relation to Public Relations claims

2.6   The Law of Copyright

2.7   The influence of the Consumer Protection Act

3. Public Relations in developing countries

3.1   The role of Public Relations within the overall communications of developing countries

3.2   Explanation of the role of Public Relations and marketing within developing countries

3.3   The role of Public Relations in educating the many publics within the identified market segments

3.4   Identification of the opportunities for using Public Relations within the limitations of communications

3.5   The media differences between industrial nations and developing nations

3.6   The use of Public Relations techniques within the media constraints

4. Export Public Relations

4.1   Government overseas information services

4.2   UK based information services – COI, BOTB, FO, DTI and EBIS

4.3   Overseas media

4.4   Home media with overseas circulation

4.5   Documentary video uses

4.6   Overseas mailing houses and lists

4.7   Translation services

5. The organisation of Public Relations

5.1   The Public Relations department

5.2   The role and function of a Public Relations department

5.3   The responsibilities of a Public Relations department

5.4   The role and function of the Public Relations manager

5.5   The staffing of the Public Relations department
5.6   The function of a Public Relations consultancy
5.7   The services available for client use
5.8   Methods used in fee structure
5.9   Preparation of an organisational charge for an internal Public Relations department and a consultancy
5.10 Evaluation of the options of Public Relations in-house or through a consultancy

6. The conduct of Public Relations

6.1   Planning a Public Relations programme
6.2   Assessing the situation
6.3   Defining the objectives
6.4   Identification of the publics
6.5   Choice of media and techniques
6.6   The programme time scale
6.7   Cost in terms of man hours and production
6.8   Ability to assess the results by response to editorial attitude and use of releases

7. Media relations

7.1   Understanding the news media
7.2   Researching material for the media
7.3   Writing and presentation of the news release
7.4   Negotiating publication of feature articles and/or special articles and syndicated articles
7.5   Media interviewing techniques for the press, TV and radio
7.6   Organising press conferences, receptions and facility visits
7.7   How to achieve good press relations
7.8   Writing style for news releases, feature articles and syndicated articles
7.9   Aids to be used in press organised functions (7.6)

8. The publics of Public Relations

8.1   The difference between market segmentation and publics
8.2   The difference of target audiences and publics
8.3   Defining the publics of an organisation
8.4   Identifying the 8 major publics of an organisation
8.5   The consequences of not targeting the correct publics

9. The media of Public Relations

9.1   The news media organisation of press, TV and radio
9.2   News gathering through news agencies at home and through international agencies, freelance journalists, contributors, correspondents and stringers
9.3   The media and the principles of good press relations
9.4   What makes a good news story

10. Audio and visual aids

10.1 Production of film/video and costs
10.2 The purpose of the use of visual aids in a Public Relations programme

10.3 Distribution of film/video either for the home or overseas market
10.4 The use of slides/synchronised slide presentations
10.5 The use of photography as a Public Relations technique
10.6 How Public Relations officers work with a photographer
10.7 Communicating with pictures
10.8 Photo caption stories
10.9 Technical considerations

11. Public Relations own media

11.1 House journals – planning and make up
11.2 Non-employee journals, the use and abuse of different types of journals
11.3 Annual reports and accounts
11.4 Annual reports
11.5 Corporate brochures
11.6 Educational literature
11.7 Seminars and Sales/Dealer conferences
11.8 Private exhibitions

12. Exhibitions

12.1 How Public Relations can aid an exhibition with prior media notification, stand design and media facilities
12.2 Public Relations and the exhibition organiser's Public Relations office
12.3 Post exhibition media contact with news items
12.4 Different types of exhibitions including: consumer exhibitions, business-to-business exhibitions, private exhibitions, Expo International exhibitions and travelling exhibitions

13. Sponsorship

13.1 Public Relations uses of sponsorship, as distinguished from those of advertising
13.2 Different types of sponsorship available
13.3 Eventing and use of different ideas and use of personalities
13.4 Use of sponsorship and eventing for the media
13.5 Evaluation of the costs and benefits sponsorship offers the Public Relations officer
13.6 Explanation of the objectives of sponsorship
13.7 Evaluation of how the impact of sponsorship can vary according to how visible its presence is

14. Ancillary services

14.1 Print services. Different types of printing processes and their use
14.2 Typography
14.3 The implications of desk top publishing
14.4 Proof reading and proof marks
14.5 Explanation of the term 'type mark up'

15. Research

15.1 Definition of the social grades and the importance of social grades in research
15.2 Explanation of what is meant by desk research
15.3 Distinguishing between qualitative and quantitative research
15.4 Recommended means by which public opinion can be measured
15.5 Awareness of how ACORN and MOSAIC are relevant to both Marketing and Public Relations
15.6 Definition of the term 'tracking study'

16. Developments and trends

16.1 Awareness of changes in the world of media
16.2 Awareness of the many changes in satellite communications
16.3 Cable television and its growth
16.4 Printing techniques

Reproduced by kind permission of the London Chamber of Commerce and Industry Examinations Board, 6 Graphite Square, London SE11 5EE, from whom a comprehensive package of support materials is available.

Appendix 5

ADDRESSES OF SOCIETIES AND EDUCATIONAL ORGANISATIONS

The Advertising Standards Authority (ASA). Brook House, 2–16 Torrington Place, London WC1E 7HN; 0171 580 5555

The British Association of Industrial Editors. 3 Locks Yard, High Street, Sevenoaks, Kent YN13 1LT; 01732 459331. Membership: Editors of house journals. Entry by examination. *BAIE News.*

The Chartered Institute of Marketing (CIM). Moor Hall, Cookham, Maidenhead, Berkshire SL6 9QH. 01628 427 500.

The Communication, Advertising and Marketing Education Foundation (CAM). Abford House, 15 Wilton Road, London SW1V 1NJ; 0171 828 7506. Certificate and diploma examinations. Vocational examination for those working in British communications industry. Holders of CIM Diploma exempt from Certificate, except PR, if they wish to take CAM Diploma in PR.

Institute of Public Relations. The Old Trading House, 15 Northburgh Street, London EC1V 0PR; 0171 253 5151. Membership by age and experience plus CAM Diploma or its equivalent.

International Association of Business Communicators. One Hallidic Plaza, Suite 600, San Francisco, CA 94102, USA. Membership, Accredited Membership (by exam). *IABC News, Communication World.* Annual Gold Quill awards.

International Public Relations Association. Case Postale 126, CH-1211 Geneva 20, Switzerland. Has members in 70 countries. Membership by election according to international PR experience. *IPRA Newsletter, International Public Relations Review, international* conferences.

Journal *Public Relations.* Annual Sword of Excellence awards.

The London Chamber of Commerce and Industry. Examinations Board, Marlow House, Station Road, Sidcup, Kent DA15 7BJ; 0171 302 0261. Third Level Certificate Examinations in Advertising, Marketing, Public Relations, Selling and Sales Management (with Diplomas for passes in three or four subjects taken at the same time). Diploma in Management Studies if three subjects passed at different times.

The London College of Printing. Elephant & Castle, London SE1; 0171 735 8484.

London Management Training Centre. 166 Upper Richmond Road, London SW15 2SH; 01342 326704.

Public Relations Consultants Association (PRCA). Willow House, Willow Place, London SW1P 1JH; 0171 233 6026. Corporate membership. Overseas Associates. *Public Relations Year Book. What's Happening at the PRCA newsletters. Guidance Papers (training). Briefing papers (legal).*

Appendix 6

GLOSSARY OF PUBLIC RELATIONS TERMS

Account. A PR consultancy client.

Account executive. PR consultancy executive who liaises with clients.

ACORN. Acronym for A Classification of Residential Neighbourhoods. A marketing research database classification technique built around the premise that people in similar neighbourhoods are likely to have similar behavioural, purchasing and lifestyle habits. Used by marketers to understand the behaviour and lifestyle habits of all UK households, and to see how trends in those habits change year on year. Provides a tool for identifying consumers and targeting them in the right areas. *See* MONICA.

Advance. Monthly source of information about forthcoming editorial programmes. Published by Themetree Ltd, Aylesbury.

Adversarial situation. State of conflict which exists between journalists and PR practitioners, due to different reasons for publishing or seeking publication of information.

Advertorials. Advertising on controversial issues, or joint advertising/PR features to promote a product in a journal.

Appreciation of the situation. Assessment of the current situation, using observation, experience or scientific research, in order to identify communication strengths and weaknesses before making recommendations for a PR campaign.

Attitude research. Method of assessing original situation, or changes in attitude as a result of PR activity.

Audience flow. TV audience inherited from a previous programme.

Audiovisual. Sound and visual device such as synchronised slide presentation with audio cassette, compact disc interactive (CDI), or video cassette. Usually portable.

Awareness survey. Similar to attitude survey and opinion poll, method of researching familiarity with subject, including increased awareness as a result of PR activity.

Benn's Media Directory. First published 1846. Two-volume world media guide, listing editorial details of some 12,000 UK publications and more than 23,000 overseas, plus other media information.

Big Bang. Deregulation of London Stock Exchange on 27 October 1986, ending division between jobbers and brokers. Resulted in tight rules on insider trading (*see*), and banning of sensitive embargoed financial news releases. *See* Company News Service.

Bleed. Print carried to edge of page, and achieved by printed area being larger than final page so that it can be trimmed or bled off.

Book face. Typeface used for text of editorial, books. Usually a serif (*see*) face since easier to read in the mass than sans serif (*see*) type. Examples: Times, Plantin, Palatino.

Book style. Traditional and most legible way of typing and setting text matter. First paragraph not indented. Succeeding paragraphs indented, until a sub-heading occurs when procedure repeated.

Broadsheet. Large page newspaper format, like the London *Times*, printed across the breadth of the web of newsprint. The other format is tabloid (*see*) like the *Daily Mirror*.

Business press. Newspapers and magazines read mostly by businessmen, e.g. *Financial Times*, *The Economist* and *Investor's Chronicle* but also serious newspapers with considerable business sections such as *The Times*, *Daily Telegraph*, *The Independent*, *Sunday Times*, etc. *See* Quality Press.

By-line. Name of journalist credited with a newspaper report, and printed below headline.

Capital letters. Known as 'caps;, should be used sparingly in editorial material and restricted to names of organisations, people's names, geographical place names, registered names, but only for a very few top people's names and not business or job titles. Whole words or brand names should not be spelt entirely in caps.

Caption, photo. All photographs should have a caption fixed to the back, usually with Sellotape. Wording should state what the picture cannot say for itself, and include name, address and telephone number of the sender (not the photographer). Pictures should not be pasted on a sheet of paper or on a news release. Flapped captions liable to become detached.

Ceefax. BBC non-commercial teletext service. *See* Teletext.

Centre Européen des Relations Publiques. CERP. European federation of public relations organisations.

Centrefold spread. Centre spread or middle pages of a journal which can be opened flat if not 'perfect bound', that is wire-stitched (*see*). Usually printed right across both pages, permitting large pictures and headlines. Called 'naturals'.

Character. Single letter, digit or symbol in typesetting.

Circulation. Average audited net sale of a journal, as certified in many countries by an Audit Bureau of Circulations which issues ABC figures at regular intervals.

City editor or business editor. Edits the financial section of a newspaper. In London, offices are in the City and separate from main editorial office. However, in some countries the chief editor or news editor may be called the city editor.

Clip. In TV, short piece of film or videotape shown during a live show.

Clubline. First line of a paragraph at the foot of page, rest of paragraph running on to next column or page. Can be ugly and is best avoided.

CNN. American-based international satellite TV news service Cable News Network, which provides live news of world events including crisis situations and wars.

Cold-set. Drying of print on the machine without heat. Achieved by printing one colour at a time and feeding in sheets again for other colours, or because paper is absorbent, or with wet-on-wet printing of colours. *See* heat-set.

Colour separation. Separation of full-colour pictures into four separate process colours, yellow, magenta, cyan and black, by computer or optical filters, for platemaking.

Column inch/centimetre. Measure of depth of column space as used when measuring press media coverage. However, this volume is only one possible assessment. Tone and quality of coverage also important.

Columnist. Journalist who writes a regular feature with by-line.

Company News Service. Introduced by London Stock Exchange in 1986 (*see* Big Bang) and linked with trading floors in Birmingham, Dublin, Glasgow and Manchester. Receives, prepares and releases information electronically. Stock Exchange booklet *Company News Services* lays down format for news releases and discourages embargoes.

Computer graphics. Post-production technique of drawing designs with a computer for taping and transference to video tapes. *See* also Paintbox. Can be used for making slides.

Condensed. Narrow version of a typeface. Can also be generated by computerised typesetting software.

Contact report. Written by account executive after meeting with a client. Should state decisions taken, with right-hand column giving initials of those responsible for next action. Distributed to all relevant parties on consultancy and client sides. Also known as call report. File of reports called the facts book (*see*).

Controlled circulation. Publication such as trade journal distributed free of charge to a list of recipients selected by publishers. To earn Audit Bureau of Circulation certification, proportion of distribution list must be requested and request cards are inserted in issues. Merits of CC journals is their greater penetration of the market compared with those requiring subscription. CC method often used to launch new magazines, readers, eventually being asked to pay a subscription.

Cool media. Marshal McLuhan's term for participatory media such as films and TV. *See* hot media.

Copy. In printing, all material including pictures for publication. Editorially, the text. In advertising, the wording of an advertisement. Or a single 'copy' of a journal.

Copy date. Deadline when editor, advertisement department or printer requires all material for printing.

Copyright. Copyright, Designs and Patents Act 1988 made different provisions from the former Act. Copyright now endures for 70 years from the date of the author's death, a film is released or a broadcast made. However, whereas photographer possessed copyright of negative only now he owns copyright of print (unless he is a staff photographer), and customer, when ordering photography, should ask photographer to sign form assigning copyright to customer. New element is intellectual property and a creator (e.g. in a film or video) is entitled to be credited. He is also protected against alterations to the work which detract from it.

Corporate advertising. Kind of PR advertising, usually aimed at telling company story and building correct image. Typical example in business journals such as *The Economist*.

Corporate culture. The pattern of shared values and beliefs which shapes behaviour in an organisation. Set out in mission statements.

Corporate identity. Visible and physical representation of an organisation using logo, house colour, typography, clothing, livery, etc.

Corporate image. Mental impression or perceived image of an organisation based on knowledge and experience. Cannot be invented but may be changed. Different people may hold different corporate images, e.g. employees, shareholders, distributors or customers according to their personal knowledge and experience. Consequently impossible to polish a poor image, but PR can build a true image by developing knowledge and understanding.

Correspondent. Journalist who contributes material on specialised topics, e.g. agriculture, education, motoring, politics, shipping, or war. Usually a freelance, but could be editor of a specialised magazine who acts as a special correspondent on his subject to newspapers.

Cover price. Retail price as printed on cover of journal.

Coverage. Extent to which PR material has been used by the media. Not to be calculated on cost of advertising space or airtime. Best evaluation a mix of volume, tone (how the message was conveyed) and quality (where and when the message appeared). *See* Voice.

Credibility factor. Extent to which a PR message is believed.

Crisis PR. Organisation of a small crisis management team which has manual of instructions, and conducts rehearsals, in readiness to deal with any crisis should one occur, especially in handling the media. A result of the spate of crises in recent years in chemical, oil and other vulnerable industries.

Crop. To trim or mask a photograph in order to reproduce only a certain part of the negative. Can be done before ordering final PR prints.

Crosshead. Small heading, set in centre of column, separating two paragraphs.

Cue-card. Card sent with audio tape of radio interview to radio station, giving introductory and closing words.

Current image. Perceived image. How organisation is seen by outsiders. *See* Corporate, Favourable, Multiple image.

Customer relations. PR activity directed at customer such as external house journals, works visits, questionnaires, after-sales services.

Cyan. Standard blue colour in four-colour printing process.

Dealer magazine. External house journal addressed to distributors.

Dealer relations. PR activities directed at distributors such as dealer magazines, works visits, window dressing contests, conferences, invitations to exhibition stands, and training schemes for sales assistants.

De-massification. As originated by Alvin Toffler in his books on futurism, the fractionisation of media, especially TV as has been seen with alternatives to BBC/ITV programmes, e.g. cable, satellite, VCRs, video games etc.

Desk research. Study of existing internal and external records and surveys.

Desk-top publishing. Use of computer hardware such as Apple Macintosh and software such as PageMaker and Quark Express, which enable editor to set, layout and record on disk publications which can be sent or transmitted direct to the printer.

Digital printing. A printing technology which allows printed material to be produced without printing plates, image-setting, film, stripping, halftone screening or scanning. The colour quality is as good as, or better than, high-quality conventional litho printing. The system accepts data in PostScript form, either direct from a disk or via ISDN.

DipCAM. Vocational qualification for British PR practitioners, requiring passing of six subjects at Certificate level and three at Diploma level. Conducted by Communication, Advertising and Marketing Education Foundation. Applicants for full membership of Institute of Public Relations (*see*) required to have DipCam (PR) or its equivalent.

Direct input. Paperless news-room in which journalist keys news into computer, sub-editor subs story on VDU, and page made-up on computer, final copy to mainframe computer for production of copy for plate-making.

Direct to plate. Computerised platemaking system, which images digital page data onto printing plates with no need for intermediate film. This technique offers savings in time, as well as labour and materials, while avoiding the environmental impact of film processing.

Dirty copy, proof. Printing copy with many handwritten corrections or additions, or proof containing many errors. Opposite to clean copy or proof.

Drop capital. First character of a word at the beginning of a paragraph, set larger than the body copy. A style often used in editorials, the first letter occupying a depth of two, three or more lines of copy.

Edit suites. Studios for video post production such as editing, titling, computer graphics.

Edition binding. System of binding in signatures (sets) of 16 or 32 pages sewn together, glued to bookback and then bound into covers.

Egyptian. Slab or square serif typeface, serifs same thickness as rest of character as with Cairo, Karnak, Rockwell typefaces.

EIBIS International. Long established international press service which distributes translated feature articles and news releases to foreign press.

Electronic mail. Delivery of messages, including PR staff information, via personal computers and hard copy printers.

Electronic media. Newscaster, radio, TV, VCR and via the Internet.

Elitist media. In developing countries, media which appeal to better educated or wealthier minority, as distinct from radio and folk media (*see*).

Embargo. Request to editor not to print a story before a stated date and time. Frivolous use invites rejection. Should be a privilege to editor to have material in advance e.g. advance copy of a speech or report. Acceptable when international time differences need to be observed.

Employee newspaper. Internal house journal (*see*), often tabloid (*see*) format, but may be A4 magazine.

Evaluation of results. Assessment of achievements of a PR programme. Tangible PR based on measuring or observing whether targets were met or objectives achieved. If a PR programme sets out to achieve specific results the degree of success or otherwise can be evaluated at the end of the campaign period by means of experience, observation or scientific method (marketing research (*see*)).

Eventing. The systematic organisation and implementation of a programme of PR events in order to influence, educate and inform targeted publics (*see*). Includes press conferences, facility visits, dealer seminars, and participation in exhibitions.

Exclusive. Material appearing in only one publication. Unwise to grant exclusive on news stories or pictures, but signed feature articles (*see*) are exclusives. Syndicated articles (*see*) are not.

Expanded. Broad or extended typeface.

Expenses. Cost of travelling, meals, hospitality, hotel bills and other reimbursements at cost and recoverable from client or employer.

External house journals. Those addressed to external readerships such as distributors, customers, specifiers or shareholders. One of the oldest forms of house journal, more prevalent in USA than in UK. Must avoid looking like sales literature and should resemble commercial publications.

Face. A particular design of printing type of which there are several hundred display and text faces.

Facility visit. A PR visit when journalists are invited or taken to make a visit in order to write a story or prepare a radio or TV programme.

Facsimile machine. Device for sending reproduction of message by telephone line. Two-Ten Communications have a special fax news service, but unless invited to do so it can be unwise to make general distribution of news releases by fax as this involves publisher paying for unsolicited material. Newspapers using contract printers (e.g. *The Independent*) may edit in London and fax pages to printers.

Facts book. Collection of contact reports (*see*). Very useful when compiling end-of-year report on services conducted for client.

Family (typographical). All variations of a typeface such as light, medium, bold, condensed, expanded and italic.

Favourable image. 'An unfortunate but common PR term since an image can only be as perceived. Implication is that an organisation with a bad image can be given a favourable one, but a good image has to be deserved and depends on knowledge and understanding. *See* Corporate, Current, Multiple image.

Feature article. Press item with greater substance than a news report and usually bearing author's name. A PR article should be negotiated with editor, and written to suit editor's instructions.

Fee. Remuneration of a PR consultant, usually based on an hourly or daily rate which represents time, overheads and profit, but exclusive of materials and expenses. Not to be confused with a retainer (*see*) which usually only gives exclusivity.

Financial PR. Specialised field of PR which deals with financial affairs of a public limited company, or one about to go public. Covers annual report and accounts, shareholder relations, City page news, information for investment analysts, take-over bids and privatisation share flotations. Many specialist financial PR consultancies.

Five Ws. Journalist's news story formula. Who is story about, what happened, when did it happen, where did it happen, and why did it happen? But *see* Seven-point formula for news release.

Finish. Quality of a paper surface, e.g. art, supercalendered. A finished paper is polished.

Flatbed. Printing machine with printing image flat on bed of machine and not on curved plates or cylinder as with rotary presses.

Flesch, Rudolf. 1911–1986. Austrian who lived in USA. Set out criteria: 'Use short words – 150 syllables per 100 words; short sentences – no more than 19 words per sentence'. Recommended number of words per sentence for different classes of reader from pulp magazine to scientific treatise. Contained in *Art of Readable Writing* (Harper Bros, New York, 1949).

Flexography. Form of letterpress printing, originally used for printing on delicate materials such as foil, but adapted by Americans for newspaper printing, and introduced by Daily Mail Group in 1988. Rotary web presses use flexible plates and fast-drying solvent or water-based inks. System now specially adapted for newspaper production with improved polymer plates and inks. Reproduction of pictures and colour is superior to offset-litho, and the ink does not come off on the reader's fingers.

FMCGs. Fast moving consumer goods.

Folio. A page or page number.

Folk media. Traditional media or oramedia (*see*) as found in developing countries, particularly in rural areas. According to country can include gongman (palace messenger or town crier), market gossip, drums, music, dance, village theatre, puppet shows, shadow theatre, masks.

Font. *See* fount.

Footprint. Land area reached by satellite broadcast.

Format. The physical style of a print job, e.g. brochure, magazine or newspaper, A3, A4, broadsheet (*see*) or tabloid (*see*). In photosetting and desk-top publishing, repetitive typographical commands stored in a computer.

Fount. Pronounced 'font'. Complete set of characters of one typeface, e.g. letters, figures, signs. Two possible origins. From old French for casting, from *fondre*, to melt or cast. Also said to derive from monastic founts in which alphabets of type were stored when printing was carried out in medieval monasteries.

Four-colour process. Colour printing using primary colours yellow, magenta (beetroot red), cyan (blue) and black. Colours separated by computer or optical filters.

Free magazines. Some 300 British magazines (excluding weekend newspaper magazines) distributed free, door-to-door, in the street, at retail premises or by post. Income derived from advertising.

Free newspapers. More than 800 titles. Most local weeklies delivered door-to-door, providing saturation coverage of urban areas. Useful for domestic-interest PR stories. Many published by existing paid-for newspaper publishers, e.g. *Croydon Advertiser*, *Kentish Times*. Also known as freesheets. Income derived from advertising.

Freelance. Self-employed writer, artist, photographer. Recent development has been the freelance PR practitioner who undertakes *ad hoc* assignments or augments consultancy staff.

Frequency. How often a publication is issued, e.g. daily, weekly, monthly or quarterly.

Front organisation. An apparently independent organisation which actually represents commercial interests. Banned by IPR Code of Professional Conduct under clause 2.3 which reads 'A member shall have a duty to ensure that the actual interest of any organisation with which he or she may be professionally concerned is adequately declared'. A member of the IPR was suspended for promoting a front organisation.

Galley proof. Printer's proof with typesetting set solid, run on without spacing, columns, headlines or sub-headings. Name originated from placing metal type in a long galley tray.

Gatefold. Page in publication which folds out to double page size.

Gathering. Collection and collation of sequence of pages for binding.

Generic terms. Words such as cornflakes, hovercraft, petrol or polythene which describe a product and are not registered trade names and do not require an initial capital letter.

Gestalt psychology. School of psychology associated with Max Wertheimer in 1912 which adopted premises that people perceive things in patterns or entireties, e.g. a complete room and not as separate furnishings. This contrasts with people who are unfamiliar with pictures and have to read a picture item by item.

Ghost writer. Journalist who writes material which is credited to another who has commissioned the work, e.g. 'autobiographies' or PR articles by company leaders.

Glossy. Magazine printed on high-class paper, e.g. art paper. Almost extinct today. Not to be confused with popular magazines printed on better quality paper than newsprint. Also, glossy inks as used in offset-litho (*see*) printing.

Gothic. Black-letter typeface resembling Medieval script.

Grapevine. Information based on rumour. Can be provoked by lack of information, or exploited as a means of leaking information.

Gutter. Space or margin between pairs of pages, where they may be folded, or white space between columns of type where there is no vertical dividing rule.

Halftone. Applicable to all printing processes except photogravure, a means of making it possible to print tonal pictures (e.g. photographs, paintings) by use of a dot screen. Picture is photographed through a screen which produces a new picture consisting of dots. Coarse screens used for poor paper, fine screens for better quality paper. Screens for litho printing much finer than for letterpress printing, a fact which has made it possible to print more detailed photographs in modern litho-printed newspapers such as *The Independent*.

Halftone screen rulings. Metric in brackets. 50 (20), 55 (22), 60 (24), 65 (26), 75 (30), 80 (32), 85 (34), 100 (40), 120 (48), 133 (54), 150 (60), 175 (70), 200 (80).

Hanging indent. First paragraph set wider than following paragraphs as in opening of some newspaper reports.

Hard-bound. Case-bound or hardback as in book binding.

Hard news. General news about people and events, as distinct from business or product news which may be legitimately used by feature writers. News agencies (*see*) deal mostly in hard news.

Hearst, William Randolph. 1863–1951. American newspaper owner who said 'News is what someone somewhere doesn't want you to print: the rest is advertising'.

Heat-set. Drying print with heat boxes as each colour is printed, four colour printing being continuous on rotary machine. (*See* cold-set.)

Hidden persuaders. Much misunderstood term sometimes mistakenly applied to PR. Actually refers to motivational research for advertising as described in Vance Packard's 1950s book *Hidden Persuaders*.

Hollis Press and Public Relations Annual. Classified annual directory of press and PR contacts in industry, commerce, government and press information sources. PR consultancies and their clients and many allied services listed. Also special section on sponsorships.

Horizontal journal. Publication aimed at broad readership with common interests, e.g. TV listings magazine, compared with vertical journals which appeal to readers with special interests.

Hosting. Somewhat dubious system prevalent in continental Europe whereby sponsor pays for publication of PR articles. Usually applies to small circulation journals with limited income, which may imply that journal has little influence and sponsor is merely subsidising publisher. PR material should be published on its merits.

Hot media. Non-participatory media, such as print and radio according to Canadian academic Marshall McLuhan. *See* Cool media.

House corrections. Typesetting errors marked on first proof before submission to client.

House journal. Also known as house organ or company newspaper. Private journal, either internal for staff or external for outside readers. One of the oldest forms of organised PR. Charles Dickens referred to *The Lowell Offering* in his book *American Notes* (1842). A PR medium to be found in most countries throughout the world.

House style. Part of corporate identity (*see*). Uniform style of design, typography. Usually set out in manual for printing, decorating, advertising agents to follow.

Hyphenless justification. Justification of lines of type without breaking words. Avoids silly word-breaks, but can result in ugly gaps in narrow columns.

Iconic medium. A medium such as film, video or TV in which images resemble reality.

Image. In PR, correct impression of organisation, its policy, people, products or services. In photography, the subject. In printing, printing areas of a litho plate. *See* also Corporate, Current, Favourable, Mirror, Multiple image.

Image study. Form of marketing research (*see*) useful in PR to determine perceived image of organisation, policy, people, products or services, usually by comparing respondent's view of similar subjects over a range of topics. Semantic differential (*see*) method of assessment can be used, and results can be demonstrated with sets of graphs which show varying responses, all organisations being compared with one another, the sponsor being one of them.

Imitation art. Printing paper made from china clay and wood pulp and polished, unlike art paper which has china clay applied to the surface and then polished.

Imposition. Arranging pages of a publication so that 8, 12 or 16 pages may be printed together so that they may be cut or folded for binding.

Imposition table. One on which artwork and typesettings can be laid or pasted down for photography to make litho plate or photogravure sleeve.

Impression. Pressure of inked printing plate on paper to achieve a printed copy. The impression cylinder holds paper against printing plate or, in litho, the blanket cylinder. Complete run or edition of a book, e.g. first impression, second impression.

Imprint. Usually found at foot of last page of a piece of print to identify the printer. Provides legal proof in case of dispute.

Indent. To start a paragraph with a blank space, as with conventional book style (*see*). Aids readability.

Independent Television Commission. Replaced IBA in 1991 under Broadcasting Act 1990. Awards licences to commercial ITV contractors. Administers ITC Code of Advertising Standards and Practice. Publishes ITC Code of Programme Sponsorship. Stations represented by the ITV Association.

Independent local radio. Commercial radio. Originally introduced into Britain by the Sound Broadcasting Act 1972, but now controlled by the Radio Authority under the Broadcasting Act 1990. Stations represented by the Association of Independent Radio Contractors.

Independent Radio News. IRN. News service for commercial independent local radio stations.

Independent Television News. Owned partly by ITV contractors. Provides news such as *News At Ten* to ITV stations.

Induction material. Material for new recruits to an organisation, such as videocassettes, slide presentations and company literature.

Industrial film. Documentary film or video.

In-flight magazines. Magazines published by airlines and distributed in-flight to passengers, being placed in fixtures on backs of seats. More than 100 in-flight magazines, many produced for airlines by specialist firms.

Informal leaders. Leaders of special interest groups, or village leaders in developing countries. May act as innovator. *See* innovator theory.

In-house. Work handled within an organisation as 'in-house PR department'.

Innovator theory. Or dispersion theory. An innovator tries and recommends. Early adopters take up the idea, followed by late majority who copy. Finally there are the more reluctant, conservative-minded laggards who eventually become adopters. Useful in PR where a new idea or product depends on this process, and widely applicable in both developed and developing countries.

Used by McCormick in Mid-West of USA in mid-19th century farm trials of machinery, but also in modern times to promote family planning in developing countries.

Insider trader. Person who misuses sensitive financial information for his own benefit.

Institute of Public Relations. British professional body for PR practitioners. Members elected on basis of experience and CAM Diploma or equivalent. Has Code of Professional Conduct. Publishes journal *Public Relations*. Holds annual Sword of Excellence awards competition.

Intaglio. Printing from a recessed image as with copper engraving or photogravure (*see*).

Interleaves. Sheets of paper, often flimsy, inserted between pages to provide protection, or to prevent set-off from wet printed sheets.

International Association of Business Communicators. Based in San Francisco but with overseas chapters in many countries including UK. Holds accreditation exams and awards ABC. Publishes *Communication World* monthly.

International Public Relations Association. Has senior practitioner members in some 70 countries. Holds World Congress every three years. Publishes Gold papers on topics such as 'A Model for Public Relations Education for Professional Practice' and 'Public Relations Education. Recommendations and Standards'. Publishes members' newsletter and journal *International Public Relations Review*.

ISDN. Integrated Systems Digital Network. A digital telephone exchange line which enables the user to send and receive large volumes of information in a variety of forms. These include voice, data, images and video. ISDN works on a dial-up basis via the public network, but with the speed and clarity of private networks. Since ISDN is a public network service, the user pays only for what is used. Connection can be made, worldwide, to any other ISDN user. Being digital, ISDN allows fast call set-up, then takes only a fraction of the normal time to send information. This can result in substantial cost savings.

Issue advertising. Or advocacy advertising which presents an organisation's point of view on current issues such as the environment or government policy. *See* op-ed.

Italic. Right-hand sloping type.

Job press. Platen (*see*) printing press used for small jobs such as business cards.

Job sheet. Sheet bearing job number, client code and job title on which PR consultant records orders and expenditures in order to bill client for work done. Similar to that used by printer to record all details and progress of a print job. Means of controlling work and charging out.

Klischograph hard-dot gravure. Improved form of photogravure (*see*) printing in which there are surface areas of various sizes according to depth of tone instead of recessed surface of sleeve (*see*).

Laminate. To stick a transparent plastic film on printed surface to create a glossy protective finish as with record sleeves, book jackets, picture postcards, or wall charts.

Landscape. Horizontal orientation of page, picture or print, wider than it is high. *See* Portrait.

Letterpress. Versatile printing process, formerly used for most newspaper printing. Relief method, printing surface being raised like a rubber stamp but consisting of metal type and plates, these being inked and paper being pressed on them to receive impression. Platen (*see*) flat-bed and rotary presses. Largely replaced by lithography (*see*) or flexography (*see*) but still used for a variety of classes of work.

Lineage. Some European journals try to charge sponsors of PR stories 'by the line'. *See* also hosting.

Literacy. Ability to read and write is common form of literacy, but in developing countries there is also oral literacy or ability to remember and recite messages, and visual literacy consisting of mental pictures.

Literal. Composing error for which printer is responsible.

Lithography. Planographic printing process, originally from a slab of porous stone, but now from metal plates. Principle is based on the fact that grease and water will not mix. The image area on the plate is greasy and the plate is dampened so that ink adheres only to the image. Flat-bed and rotary presses. Offset-litho (*see*) has an intervening blanket cylinder which receives the impression from the plate and transfers it to the paper. Advantages of speed, high-pigment inks, fine screens and better quality paper.

Livery. House styling and identification of all forms of transportation, e.g. tankers, lorries, vans, aircraft as part of corporate identity (*see*) scheme.

Lobby correspondent. Journalist accredited to mix with Ministers, MPs and party officials to write about political events and to report 'off the record' statements from 'non-attributable sources' which are usually politicians not wishing to be named. Privileged to receive White Papers 24 hours before publication. Not to be confused with Press Gallery reporters who make verbatim reports on speeches made in the House. Lobby correspondents are accredited by the Serjeant at Arms and are allowed access to the parts of the Palace of Westminster not usually open to members of the public.

Lobbyists. Not to be confused with lobby correspondents who are journalists, lobbyists represent pressure groups and will endeavour to inform MPs, Ministers and civil servants of their causes. Various groups such as farmers, nurses, doctors, teachers, old age pensioners and so on have their 'lobbies' or representations to politicians. There are specialist PR consultancies which undertake lobbying on behalf of clients.

Logotype. Visual presentation associated with a certain organisation, and used as a form of identification and as part of a corporate identity (*see*) scheme. May be registered as a trade mark. Abbreviated as 'logo'.

London Chamber of Commerce and Industry. Examinations Board located at Sidcup, Kent. Has run business studies examinations world-wide for more than a century. Has Group Diploma in Public Relations which is acceptable by CAM as an entry requirement.

Low profile. Attempt to avoid publicity. Rather negative and silly PR tactic by companies which are afraid of criticism.

Lower case. Small characters of a typeface. Originally taken by hand compositor from the lower case or drawer of a type cabinet. All characters except capitals which are upper case.

Machine coated. Paper which is given a coated surface on the papermaking machine.

Machine proof. Proof, such as a colour proof, which is checked at the printers.

Magenta. Standard red colour used in four-colour process (*see*).

Make-up. Layout and design of pages of a publication.

Managed news. Managed and sometimes leaked news by politicians. Attempt to control political news.

Margins. In printing, (unless bled off, *see* bleed) usually four to a page, back, head, fore-edge and tail. Best proportions 1, 1½, 2 and 2½ respectively.

Marked proof. One on which printer has made corrections before submitting to client.

Market theory. Based on Ricardo's theory of an international division of labour, that goods should be produced where most economic or efficient to do so, e.g. aircraft in USA. Not to be confused with marketing theory (*see*).

Marketing. As defined by Chartered Institute of Marketing. 'Marketing is the management process responsible for identifying, anticipating and satisfying customers requirements' profitably'. This goes beyond selling what you have to sell, to selling what you believe people will buy, and to make a profit in so doing. This also goes beyond a mere exchange process.

Marketing communications. All the elements and techniques necessary to communicate with the market ranging from business cards, labels and packaging to advertising, public relations and after-sales services.

Marketing concept. Business philosophy as expressed in the CIM definition above, starting with needs of the consumer.

Marketing mix. All the elements contained in the marketing strategy as originated by Neil Borden, but taking in many more elements than the original set, and preferably considered in chronological order of application rather than in the narrow Four Ps concept of product, price, place and promotion. Public relations is not a separate part of the marketing mix, as advertising is, because there is a public relations aspect to most elements of the mix.

Marketing research. Scientific and statistical study of everything concerned with marketing. Some of its techniques can also be applied to PR in appreciating and assessing results.

Mass media. Media such as press, radio, TV and cinema which reach large numbers of people as distinct from some private or created PR media used to reach specific publics (*see*).

Masthead. Distinctive title design of a publication, not unlike a logo.

Matt. Dull, unpolished paper.

Meanline. The x-height of a typeface, that is the height of small letters like a, e, i and o. The greater this height the more legible the text. Some display faces have low x-heights which make them unsuitable as text types.

Media. Plural of medium. Vehicles of communication. The press is a medium, but the press, radio and TV are media.

Media explosion. The development of new media such as cable and satellite TV video, interactive compact discs, teletext and so on.

Mediaspeak. Literary corruption or pollution such as 'at this point in time' instead of 'now'.

Mexican Statement. One of the best definitions of PR resulting from a PR conference in Mexico City in 1978. Public relations practice is the art and social science of analysing trends, predicting their consequences, counselling organisation leaders and implementing planned programmes of action which will serve both the organisation's and the public interest.

mf. More follows, as in bottom right-hand corner of a news release when there is a continuation.

MF. Machine or mill finished. Paper calendered (polished) on papermaking machine.

MG. Machine or mill glazed. Paper with glossy finish on one side.

Microfiche. Method of storing publications and other records photographically on sheets of film, which can be viewed on optical viewing equipment.

Mirror image. How an organisation sees itself which could be contrary to that held by outsiders. *See* Current, Corporate, Multiple image.

Modern face. Typefaces with upright thicknesses to sides of letters like O. Late 18th century.

MONICA. A marketing research database tool which predicts the likely age group of consumers on the basis of their first names. *See* ACORN.

Monitor. To record radio and TV programming. Conducted by specialist firms such as Tellex Monitors, and CMR Media Watch in the USA.

Mono press. Publications printed in black and white only.

Monochrome. Single colour, usually black.

Morgue. In newspaper offices, ready written obituaries of VIPs.

Multi-image presentation. Combined audio tape/35 mm slide presentation.

Multiple image. Problem that different representatives of the same organisation give individual images. Hence, attempts at creating uniformity such as staff clothing, for example in banks, building societies and retail stores.

Multiple-screen slide presentation. Theatrical show with large screen made up of multiples of 35 mm slides back-projected by batteries of computerised projectors. Screen can be split into two, four, eight or more smaller pictures simultaneously.

National press. Newspapers and magazines distributed nationally, a phenomenon peculiar to Britain where London is the main press centre. Other countries, because of size, geography or history, tend to have regional rather than national newspapers although magazines may mostly be national. Satellites have, however, increased number of nationals in USA.

Naturals. Centre-fold/spread (*see*).

Neckline. White space below a headline.

Networking. TV programmes and advertisements transmitted by all TV stations, although not necessarily at the same time.

News. Information that is not already known to recipients.

News agency. News gathering and distribution service, usually computerised, such as Press Association (UK domestic news), Reuters (foreign news), UPITN (TV news), Associated Press (American), Tass (Russian), Two-Ten Communications. The latter distributes company news for a fee.

News desk. Part of newspaper office which receives news from various sources such as reporters, wire services, PR practitioners and so on.

News release. News story supplied to the media by a PR source. Should resemble a news report as printed in the press. Subject should be in first few words. Opening paragraph should summarise whole story and should be capable of telling basic story even if nothing else is printed. *See* Seven-point formula.

Newsprint. Poor quality absorbent paper made from mechanical pulp and used for printing newspapers and some magazines.

No comment. Negative statement which should be avoided. Journalists should not be snubbed and are entitled to even a generalised answer.

Number. Single issue of a journal. Occasionally there may be a 'special number' on a particular topic.

Off-the-record. Statement made to journalist unofficially. Best avoided in general PR interviews as stricture may be overlooked, but normal when dealing with non-attributable sources like politicians when journalist will refer to say 'A usually reliable source'. *See* lobby correspondent.

Offset-litho. *See* lithography, web-offset litho.

Old face, old style. Early 17th century type of style with sloping thickness to sides of letters like O. *See* modern face.

On-line computing. Direct telephone line link between journalist and newsroom, or between DTP editor and printer.

On-screen layout. Direct input of layout and other copy into a computer or DTP system, and viewed on computer screen. Can often be viewed on computers or terminals throughout the newspaper or magazine editorial department, PR department or printing organisation.

On-the-run. While printing presses are running. As when full-colour is printed in a continuous run on a web-offset-litho (*see*) machine.

Op-ed. Opposite editorial. Tactic of placing corporate (*see*), issue (*see*) or advocacy advertisement on, say, leader page of a newspaper. Used very effectively by Mobil in USA and described by Herb Schmertz in *Goodbye to the Low Profile*.

Opinion leaders, formers. People who express their opinions about subjects, and may be regarded as authorities. Can be anyone who influences others, from parents to politicians.

Oramedia. Folk media as found in developing countries. Unlike mass media, very personal and addressed to small audiences, being based on local culture and symbolism. Includes rumour, oratory, poetry, music, dance, singing, drum, masks, village theatre, puppet shows, town crier, shadow theatre.

Outside broadcast. OB. Radio or TV programme produced live out-of-doors.

Over matter. Typesetting which exceeds available space.

PageMaker. Software for use with DTP systems such as Apple Macintosh.

Page proof. Proof of page made up as it will be printed. *See* galley proof.

Pagination. List of items to appear page by page.

Paintbox. Quantel's design computer, a video paint system with images created with curves and natural colour mixing. Popular in video and TV production.

Pan-media. Cross-frontier or international media.

Pantone. Colour matching system with numerous numbered colours and shades for selection of printing inks.

Parastatal. As in many developing countries, an enterprise which is an autonomous part state-owned part privately-owned organisation.

Perfect binding. Inexpensive form of binding books and magazines. Backs of leaves are trimmed off and glued to cover. However, can result in pages bursting free.

Photo agency. Supplier of news photos to press or other users. Newspapers receive pictures by computer.

Photogravure. Intaglio printing process. Plate (cylindrical 'sleeve' (*see*)) has image recessed, depth of cells according to depth of tone. Surface of plate broken up by square grid called the resist. Ink volatile so that it dries by evaporation. Doctor blade wipes excess ink from the surface, leaving ink in recessed cells from which it is sucked by the paper. Photographs reproduced with velvety, not sharp effect. Principally used for printing large-run popular magazines on super-calendered paper. Better quality gravure used for printing art prints and postage stamps. Newer hard-dot system called Klischograph (*see*).

pi characters. Typesetting characters or symbols not included in usual alphabet or fount (*see*).

Platen. Small letterpress (*see*) printing machine, used for jobbing work, which works like an oyster, bringing paper and type-bed together under pressure.

Point system. Typographical system of measuring the height of typefaces. Based on Didot's, where 72 points = 1 inch, and 1 point = 0.0138 inch.

Portrait. Upright page or picture. Opposite to landscape (*see*).

PR. Abbreviation of public relations. Expression 'A PR' should be avoided as a PR practitioner cannot be 'A public relations' which is not English.

PR Week. British weekly PR newspaper. First successful PR newspaper.

Press conference. An informal media briefing at which journalists are given a statement.

Press kit or pack. Means of assembling press information for use at a press event. Should be convenient to carry and contain only essential material. Too many are over-elaborate printed cardboard wallets stuffed with irrelevant material, and are soon discarded by journalists who merely want a story.

Press officer. Member of the PR team, usually an ex-journalist, who specialises in press relations.

Press relations. Better described as 'media relations', that part of public relations which is to do with supplying news material to the media, including handling press enquiries.

Press release. *See* news release.

Press office. At an exhibition, the place where journalists are supplied with media and product information.

Progressive proofs. Proofs pulled from each colour plate, showing sequence and build-up of full colour when laid on top of each other.

Propaganda. Biased information used to gain support for an opinion, cause or belief. Not to be confused with public relations.

Public affairs. Mainly an American idea, those aspects of PR which deal with corporate rather than product matters. Considered by some to be an artificial division.

Public relations. As defined by IPR, public relations practice is the planned and sustained effort to establish and maintain goodwill and mutual understanding between an organisation and its publics. *See* also Mexican Statement.

Public Relations. Award-winning journal of the Institute of Public Relations.

Public Relations Consultants Association. Trade body of PR consultants. Corporate membership. Has Charter which is compatible with IPR Code. Represents largest consultancies conducting bulk of consultancy business.

Public Relations Register. Holds videos, information on contributing PR consultancies which may be viewed by potential clients.

Public Relations Yearbook. Annual published by Public Relations Consultants Association (*see*).

Publicity. Good or bad result of something being made public.

Publics. Groups of people with which an organisation communicates, e.g. neighbours, potential employees, employees, suppliers, consumers, opinion leaders, shareholders and others. Many more categories than the target audiences in advertising.

Publisher. Person or firm responsible for printing and distributing publications. The publisher is the person responsible for print orders, and is nowadays also concerned with promotion and profitability.

Puff, puffery. Original name for advertising. Editor's derisory term for news releases which resemble advertisements. News releases should not contain superlatives and self praise.

Pull. Printer's proof pulled up on small proofing machine.

Quality circles. Of Japanese origin, regular meeting of groups of employees with supervisors to brainstorm ideas.

Quality press. The more intellectual daily and Sunday newspapers. *See* Business press.

Quotations marks. These should be restricted to quotes such as reported speech or from printed statements. Product names should not be given quotation marks, nor should quotation marks be used to give emphasis.

Quotations. A news release may be strengthened if it contains a quotation from an important person whose remarks add useful information.

Radio Authority. Government-backed body which replaced IBA in 1991. Controls independent local radio (*see*).

Readership. As conducted by JICNARS, researches those who read as distinct from those who buy newspapers and magazines, thus estimating secondary readership. Consequently readership figure greater than circulation (*see*) figure.

Register. Correct positioning of printed colours on a press during a print run. If the image is blurred during printing, it is 'out of register'.

Retainer. Term often used wrongly to mean fee (*see*) but should refer to an exclusivity fee should professional services be required from time to time.

Road show. National or international show to promote an interest. In UK refers to travelling by highway, but in USA by railroad.

Roman. Upright type as distinct from italics (*see*).

Royal protocol. Rules regarding number of journalists, photographers and cameramen permitted when members of the Royal Family are present. Rota system controlled by Newspaper Publishers Association.

Saddle stitch. Popular form of wire stitched binding from spine to centre spread as used for many magazines.

Sales promotion. Marketing activity whereby a product is given extrinsic value such as a gift or price reduction. Not to be confused with PR.

Sans serif. Typeface without serifs at ends of strokes. Good for bold displays. Bad for text in small type. Less easy to read on shiny paper than on newsprint or matt surface paper.

Semantic differential. Research technique in which the respondent selects a quality, e.g. Bad, Very poor, Poor, Fairly good, Good, Excellent, using numerical ratings, e.g. $-3, -2, -1, 1, 2, 3$.

Serif. Short, thin lines at ends of stems and arms of typeface. Book or text typefaces have serifs. *See* slab serif.

Seven-point formula. The SOLAADS for news releases: 1. Subject, 2. Organisation, 3. Location, 4. Advantages, 5. Applications, 6. Details, 7. Source.

Sheet. Whole size of a piece of paper before cutting or folding.

Sheet fed. Printed with separate sheets of paper, not reels or webs.

Signatures. In printing, sets of pages, usually 16 or 32.

Slab serif. Serif (*see*) of the same thickness as stems and arms of the character, *See* Egyptian.

Sleeve. Cylindrical printing plate used in photogravure (*see*).

Stock. The kind of paper or film to be used.

Strap. Sub-heading appearing above headline.

Stringer. Local freelance correspondent of national media. Could work on a local newspaper.

Stylebook. Manual setting out corporate style, such as colour with number, logo, typeface, stationery design, and vehicle livery.

Syndicated article. Feature article for publication in more than one journal. Best negotiated with editors of non-competing circulation journals rather than despatched like news releases.

Tabloid. Small page newspaper like *The Sun*. Originated in 1884 by chemist Henry Wellcome who combined 'tablet' and 'alkaloid' to identify his product. Wellcome Foundation lost legal battle with newspaper proprietors in 1903. Small format newspapers called tabloids ever since.

Template. Shape used for printing solid panels.

Text. Undisplayed reading matter as in newspaper columns or a book.

Text type. Printing type, usually smaller than 12 point and preferably serifed, used for text or body of printed matter.

Thermography. Method of emulating raised surface of die stamping, and less expensive way of printing letterheadings in this style. Print dusted with resinous powder which, under heat, fuses with ink to give raised, glazed print.

Upper case. Capital letters. *See* lower case.

Upward communication. Communication from staff to management as seen with speak-up schemes, quality circles (*see*), open door policies, works councils, co-partnerships and house journals with candid reader comments.

Vernacular newspapers. In developing countries with many languages, vernacular newspapers, sometimes government sponsored, are a means of reaching ethnic groups.

Vertical journals. Ones read by people of varying status in the same industry or profession.

Videocassette. Largely replaced 16 mm and 35 mm film, important PR medium as house journal, documentary, or for induction and training purposes, and for use at press receptions and on exhibition stands. Advantage of compactness compared with cans of film.

Video news release. Usually offered to TV companies rather than distributed like printed news release. Means of providing topical background information for news and other TV programmes.

Voice. Extent of media coverage.

Web. Large reel of paper.

Web-offset-litho. Rotary lithography printing from a large web of paper, as with most newspaper printing.

Widow. Lonely single word on last line of paragraph which should be removed if possible by shortening sentence.

Willings Press Guide. Annual directory of UK and principal overseas press, with alphabetical listing.

x-height. *See* meanline.

Yapp. Edges of a binding which exceeds pages of a book.

INDEX